CAR CARE
For Car Guys

Ralph Kalal

CarTech®

Edited by: Peter Bodensteiner
Designed by: Monica Bahr

ISBN-13 978-1-932494-55-6

Printed in China

CarTech®

39966 Grand Avenue
North Branch, MN 55056
Telephone (651) 277-1200 • (800) 551-4754 • Fax: (651) 277-1203
www.cartechbooks.com

OVERSEAS DISTRIBUTION BY:

Brooklands Books Ltd.
P.O. Box 146, Cobham, Surrey, KT11 1LG, England
Telephone 01932 865051 • Fax 01932 868803
www.brooklands-books.com

Brooklands Books Aus.
3/37-39 Green Street, Banksmeadow, NSW 2019, Australia
Telephone 2 9695 7055 • Fax 2 9695 7355

CONTENTS

CONTENTS

YOU CAN DO IT

You *can* do it. I can do it, so I know you can do it. Part of the fun of a car is taking care of it. Letting someone else do that is missing out on the reward, satisfaction, and pleasure that comes from taking care of it yourself.

But you might be a bit scared about doing it yourself because you fear you can also screw it up yourself. What if you get in over your head? What about all the things you don't know? What if something goes wrong, or you encounter a problem you didn't expect?

This book is designed to tell you how to work on your car, to show you the proper approach to doing it yourself, and to provide the how-to information that mechanics already know, but you don't.

This book does not provide step-by-step instructions for working on every specific make and model ever built. It is, however, the book that's designed to fill in the knowledge gaps that shop manuals don't cover. It uses readable language, and even explains those technical terms you'll need to know.

For example, the instructions in most shop manuals for changing spark plugs boil down to this: unscrew old spark plug, screw in new spark plug. You already know that. The challenge in replacing spark plugs is usually getting at them, and knowing how tightly the new ones should be installed. This book covers that. Another example: servicing brakes. The typical shop manual tells

you how to remove and replace the worn pads or rotors. But what do you do when the Phillips-head screw holding the rotor in place is rusted solid? How do you prevent your new brake pads from squealing or causing your rotors to "warp?" This book covers all of that, and more. With the help of this book, you *can* do it.

ACKNOWLEDGMENTS

This book was the idea of Peter Bodensteiner, the editor in chief of CarTech Books. I am grateful that he was willing to let me write it. Being entrusted with someone's vision is a special honor.

Peter Bodensteiner is one of those unique and insightful people who can ask you a simple question in ten words or less that results in your spending a month researching and rewriting something that already took a month to write. If only I'd been able to catch him being wrong, just once.

The book is also for my son, Ralph. The best thing about writing this book has been sharing the dream of writing it with my son, another Ralph, who took many of the photographs (including the cover). He was there when I needed him, put up with

me when I panicked, and believed I could do it when I didn't. I also appreciated the help of my stepdaughter, Kimberly Bennett, who was always there when I needed someone to put a foot on the brake pedal, turn the key, and be the "assistant."

There were some commercial organizations that came through to help, too. Taking pictures of stuff you don't own or doesn't fit your car, but is necessary to explain working on someone else's car, could run into real money. Thankfully, Rock Auto was there to save the day.

Rock Auto is an Internet retail parts distributor with a friendly staff, a great website, and really, really good prices. They loaned me a bunch of parts for the photography in this book. In return, all they asked is that I mention their name,

give them a copy of the book, and return the parts. That was more than fair, but I still lust after the new front rotors they loaned for this book. They couldn't have been nicer; they're a family owned company, and they love cars.

Innova makes code readers and scan tools, both for OBD-I and OBD-II products; Innova online at www.iequus.com. They were kind enough to allow me to use their product—I asked them a simple question and they gave me a very good answer.

Mostly, however, I'd like to thank you, the reader. Cars are supposed to be fun. People who enjoy cars are among the finest people on earth. I hope this book contributes to your enjoyment of cars helps and those people who love them.

CHAPTER 1

WHAT YOU NEED

TOOLS, SUPPLIES AND PARTS

To work on your car, you need tools. The proper tool can be the difference between having trouble and no trouble at all. For example, if you're disconnecting a brake line or oil cooler line and you don't have a flare nut wrench, then you might be tempted to use an ordinary open-end wrench. A flare-nut wrench (sometimes called a line wrench) is the proper tool for loosening flare nut fittings, which are usually made of soft metal, often brass. A flare-nut wrench is designed to grip the nut on all six of its sides, so it is less likely to slip than an ordinary open-end wrench.

This is a set of flare-nut wrenches, used for removing brake lines, fuel lines, and some oil lines. This set was made by Snap-On, a manufacturer of very high quality automotive tools.

Faced with this dilemma, there are two choices: either buy the correct flare nut wrench and use it to remove the flare nut or, after the open end wrench slips, use a Vice-Grip wrench to loosen the flare nut (mangling it), then cut the end of the line off, slide on a new flare nut, and then re-flare the line with a flare tool. After going through all that, you'll probably decide to buy a flare nut wrench before tightening the fitting.

Cheap tools are as bad as not having the proper tool. Cheap tools not only create unnecessary problems, they can be dangerous. Quality wrenches and screwdrivers are forged from fine-grained steel designed for tool manufacture, machined to very precise tolerances, and tempered to a high degree of hardness. Cheap tools are made from ordinary steel, imprecisely machined, and poorly tempered. Imprecise machining makes a loose tool, one that will slip and damage the fastener (whether a nut, a bolt, or a screw) when a quality tool would have held and removed it. Poor tempering means that cheap tools are thicker and heavier than quality tools. Compare the ends of two box-end wrenches, one cheap and the other top-line. The walls of the box-ends on the cheap wrench are much thicker because the manufacturer has attempted to compensate for the weaker metal by adding mass. When

clearance around a bolt head is tight, a quality wrench will fit when a cheap one does not.

Moreover, automotive fasteners are made of high strength materials able to survive extreme stress. A cheap tool may be softer than the fastener it is being used to remove. In a contest between a hard fastener and a cheap tool, the tool can break. When it does, you can be seriously hurt. Even if flying bits of metal don't put your eye out, Newton's Second Law says you're going to hurt yourself when all the force you've been applying to the tool is suddenly released. Murphy's Law says the fastener will be ruined, too.

Quality doesn't mean expensive; it just means "not cheap." You can feel quality by the heft and balance of a tool, and see it in the precision of its surfaces. Think about the tools you already own. Which are your favorites? Those are quality tools. You trust them, you enjoy them every time you use them, and they give you confidence in what you're doing (see Sidebar: "Tool Quality").

You do not need a lot of tools to work on your car. You need basic tools, of course. Start with a 3/8-inch- and 1/2-inch-drive set of ratchets and sockets, which should include standard and metric sockets, short and long extensions, several deep well sockets (the tall ones), a universal joint socket, and spark

Tool Quality

Buy quality tools, you say. But, they all look pretty much alike. Who makes quality tools? What's it going to cost?

The big-name tool manufacturers in the United States are Snap-On Incorporated, Danaher Corporation, and The Stanley Works. Snap-On makes tools under that name, which are sold primarily to professional mechanics, cost a small fortune, and are generally regarded as the best. But it also makes the Kobalt line of medium priced tools, sold exclusively at Lowe's, and Bahco, another medium priced brand sold through other retailers. Danaher has manufactured Craftsman hand tools since the early 1990s. Before that, Craftsman was manufactured by Stanley. Danaher also manufactures Matco tools, a slightly lower-priced Snap-On competitor (also sold primarily to professional mechanics), and the K-D, Allen, Armstrong, and Holo-Chrome brands sold through tool dealers and retailers. Stanley, apart from tools bearing that name, manufactures Mac Tools (another Snap-On competitor), and Husky tools sold by Home Depot. S-K tools, sold by tool dealers and retailers including Sears, was owned by Falcon (a European company) until a management buyout in 2005. It is now an independently owned American company, S-K Hand Tools Corp. There are also a number of other American manufacturers who produce excellent tools, including Wright Tool Company, Lisle Corporation, Klein Tools, Inc., and V-8 Tools, Inc., all of which market tools under their company names through tool dealers and retailers. Wright also manufactures the Cougar tool line. Tools made by these manufacturers are quality tools. Tools imported from China are probably cheap tools.

So, what does it all cost? How much you spend on tools is a personal judgment. Most of us start with a set of Craftsman tools and add to it over time. Craftsman tool sets are an excellent value. A basic Craftsman mechanic's wrench set costs about $100. $200 gets you a very comprehensive set. A Craftsman screwdriver set costs between $30 and $50. So, for $130 to $250, you can buy most of the tools you'll need for most car jobs. If you wait until Sears has a Father's Day or Christmas sale, you'll spend even less.

For the person who is working on cars for fun, not for a living, spending money for the highest-end tools may seem hard to justify. There are two circumstances, however, in which it may make sense for the amateur mechanic to buy something more expensive: when it's a tool you use a lot, such as a screwdriver; and, when it's a tool in which absolute precision really matters, such as a flare nut wrench.

There are reasons more expensive tools are worth their price. Compare a Snap-On screwdriver to an ordinary screwdriver; the Snap-On handle is shaped sort of like a squared-off Coke bottle. It gives an excellent grip and doesn't fatigue the

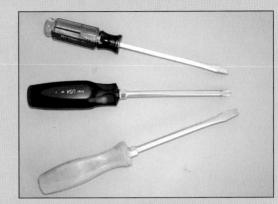

Three screwdrivers, each a different brand: a typical Craftsman screwdriver is at the top, a Snap-On screwdriver at the bottom, and a Craftsman Professional crewdriver in the middle.

hand. A nut with perfectly hexagonal sides is cast into the shaft, so that a wrench can be used help turn the screwdriver. The dimensions of the blade tip are precise and it is hardened by a proprietary process that makes it exceptionally strong. After you've used one, you're spoiled. It just makes the job easier. That's why professional mechanics buy them.

How much more expensive are high-end tools? Using a 1/2-in combination open-end box-end wrench as an example, a new Snap-On is about $32, a mid-priced brand, such as S-K, costs about half that, and a Craftsman is about $8. If you want to buy new, Snap-On, Mac, and Matco all sell directly to the consumer through their websites. Alternatively, used Snap-On and Mac tools usually sell on eBay for about half their new price.

A word about wrenches: there are two types of sockets and box-end wrenches, 12-point and 6-point. Each has an advantage. The 12-point wrenches and sockets are ordinarily easier to use than 6-point; they fit the fastener at more angles and can fit in tighter spaces because their walls are thinner. But a 6-point wrench or socket has one big advantage; it's less likely to slip. Because a 6-point has more contact with the flat sides of a fastener, a 6-point wrench or socket may remove a stubborn fastener or one with rounded corners when a 12-point would slip. There are also differences among open-end wrenches. Several brands, including Kobalt, Bahco, Craftsman, and Wright, are promoting modified-design open-end wrenches. They claim these are less likely to slip than the traditional design. Some of these designs combine features of both box-end and open-end wrenches, so that one side of the wrench jaw contacts the flat side of the fastener while the other side of the jaw grips a corner of the fastener. Others add serrations to portions of the jaws to diminish slip.

plug sockets. Also buy: a set of combination open-end and box-end wrenches (including metric); a screwdriver set (standard and Phillips); needle nose pliers; and Vice-Grips. There are tools, such as TORX screwdrivers (and sockets) and Allen (hex) wrenches, which you may need eventually (or sooner if you work on certain types of cars, particularly European ones). But you can wait to buy these tools until they're needed or, at least, until they're on sale.

Beyond these, there are some other tools that are so useful when working on your car that they are, in essence, basic tools, and there are also specialized tools designed for specific automotive jobs, without which those jobs cannot be accomplished.

You're also going to need supplies and parts. Those are covered in Sidebar: "Supplies," and Sidebar: "Parts" later in this chapter.

The Other Basic Tools

Torque wrench
See Sidebar: The Indispensable Torque Wrench.

This is a "breaker bar." As the name implies, its length gives extra leverage to loosen nuts and bolts. This one is from the Craftsman tool line sold at Sears.

1/2-inch drive breaker bar
A "breaker bar," also called an "extension bar," is a heavy-duty socket wrench about 20 inches long, but it does not have a ratchet. It does what its name implies: it breaks loose stubborn nuts and bolts. The leverage it provides also allows you to apply steady, smooth, and controlled force. That vastly reduces the risk of breaking off a bolt or stripping threads.

Breaker bars are available with 3/8-inch drive, but the purpose of a breaker bar is to apply maximum force. The 1/2-inch drive version is preferable because it is longer and stronger. Cost: under $20.

A very large and long screwdriver—this one is another Craftsman tool—is one of those tools you may not know you need, but once you have it, you'll wonder what you did without it.

Big flat-bladed screwdriver with a shank at least a foot long
You will use it often, though often not as a screwdriver. When you need to lever the alternator up while installing a new belt, this is the tool that does it. When you need to pop loose a wheel cover, just slip the blade under the cover's edge and twist. In all sorts of situations where you need to pry something, but also control the force, this is the tool that'll do it. It costs about $10 and, as a bonus, is also perfect screwdriver for installing license plates.

Fender cover
Technically, it may not be a tool, but it is indispensable. A fender cover protects

A fender cover protects your car against you: scratches from your clothes, dents from the tools you might drop. This is a common type of padded cover, which is designed with pleats that form a trough in which to set tools as you work.

Another type of fender cover is made of a rubber-like material that grips the fender and also grips tools placed on it.

the paint. Because it is padded, it also protects against denting the fender if you drop a wrench. For about $20, you can even get one with the car logo of your choice. Be sure the fender is clean before you put a cover on it. Otherwise, the dirt underneath will sandpaper the paint's finish.

A really good flashlight, so that you can see what you're doing, makes the job much easier. This is a Mag-Lite. When a part falls into some inaccessible area around the engine, fishing it out may be impossible without a magnetic pick-up tool. The flexible shaft allows you to retrieve small parts that you can't even see.

Magnetic parts tray
Made in various sizes, these trays are made of steel with a rubberized magnetic base. In effect, the tray is one big magnet, so it holds steel parts in place. Even if you accidentally knock it over, the parts stay contained. Because the base is magnetized, it sticks to any steel surface of the car. but it won't scratch, because the base is rubberized. Cost: under $10.

Flexible-shaft magnetic pick up tool
You are going to drop something small and irreplaceable ("irreplaceable": adj.; a small part that cannot be purchased except as part of a larger assembly). A magnetic pick up tool with a

flexible shaft allows you to fish for something that has fallen into a hidden place you can neither reach nor see. About $20.

A really good flashlight

A Mag-Lite in the two D-cell size is perfect because it provides a strong adjustable beam, is made from aluminum for durability, and is small enough that it's easy to manipulate

The Indispensable Torque Wrench

Most automotive fasteners function by tension. That is, when two parts are held together by a bolt, the bolt must be tightened to a specific tension, which not only applies force to the bolt but also applies clamping force to the parts it's holding together. If the bolt is under too much tension, it will break. If it's under too little tension, there will be no clamping force on the other parts, the bolt will bear the entire load, and it will break. So, tightening the bolt to the proper tension is essential.

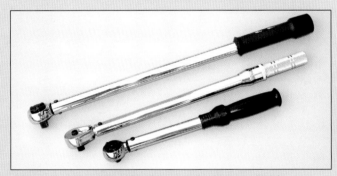

Almost every automotive fastener is designed to be tightened to a specific torque value, which requires a torque wrench. These three are Craftsman: the top two read in ft-lbs and the bottom one reads in in-lbs.

To assure the proper tension, a torque wrench measures the bolt's rotational resistance in foot-pounds (ft-lbs), inch-pounds (in-lbs), or Newton-meters (Nm), the later being the metric version. Converting ft-lbs to in-lbs is simply a matter of dividing by twelve. One ft-lb equals 1.356 Nm, but you shouldn't really need to know this because any quality torque wrench will include both standard and metric scales.

There are three types of torque wrenches: beam, click, and dial. Avoid beam-type torque wrenches. They're cheap at about $15 and better than having no torque wrench, but they're not very accurate. Dial-type torque wrenches are the most accurate, but they're very expensive, at least $200. Quality click-type torque wrenches are reasonably accurate and reasonably priced, starting at about $65. With a click-type torque wrench, you pre-set the desired torque. When that torque is reached, the wrench makes a click that you can both feel and hear. The drawback is that the click can be very subtle at the lower torque values; if you miss it, you'll over tighten the fastener.

When shopping for a torque wrench, there are several things to consider: drive size, the range of torque values to which the wrench may be set, and length. Also, pull out the shop manual for your car, find the chart that gives the torque values for the various fasteners, and check the range of values that you may encounter when working on it. It may turn out that you need two torque wrenches, not one.

A typical click-type torque wrench will be 1/2-inch drive, measure from 20–150 ft-lbs, and be almost 2 feet long. This may be just perfect for you, but it may be a complete waste of your money. It depends on your car. For example, torque values for many engine components on a C5 Corvette are specified in in-lbs and the spark plugs are tightened to only 11 ft-lbs (i.e., 132 in-lbs), but the brake-caliper mounting-bracket bolts (which must be removed to replace the rotors) must be tightened to 166 ft-lbs. This combination of values is outside the typical wrench's range. Buying two torque wrenches, one reading from 25 to 250 in-lbs and one reading from 25 to 250 ft-lbs, is the solution. You may end up wanting a third wrench, one with 3/8-inch drive reading from about 10 to 100 ft-lbs with a handle 15 to 18 inches long that fits into places the bigger one won't (I know I've got my eye on one).

A torque wrench should only be used for final tightening and never to loosen a nut or bolt. To obtain an accurate reading, the socket must be squarely on the nut or bolt head. The torque wrench should then be pulled smoothly and continuously until the specified torque is reached. Using an extension between the torque wrench and the socket will not affect the torque reading, provided that the extension is perfectly in line with the shaft of the bolt (straight, in other words).

When not in use, a click-type torque wrench should always be returned to its lowest setting. A torque wrench is basically a calibrated spring, so it will lose accuracy if that spring stretches out, either from use or exceeding its maximum torque setting. Manufacturers normally recommend recalibration of a torque wrench at least annually. While that may be overkill for most of us, if you have a sense that your torque wrench may not be accurate, send it out to be recalibrated. There are a number of torque wrench calibration services around the country, including: Team Torque in Bismarck, North Dakota, online at teamtorque.com; Mountz, Inc. in San Jose, California, and Foley, Alabama, online at etorque.com; Precision Metrology in Milwaukee, Wisconsin, and South Branch, Florida, online at precisionmetrology.com; and, JLW Instruments, Inc., in Chicago, Illinois, online at jlwinstruments.com/aws-torque.htm.

under a car or under a hood. For about $20, it even includes a spare bulb under the end cap. Spend an extra $15 and you can get the latest Mag-Lite: the LED version.

Hard rubber mallets allow you to strike without causing damage to what is hit. Even when you just need to deliver a light tap to fit a part into place, this is the tool to use.

Rubber mallet

For hitting gently. Spend enough to get a really good one, because it will last longer and work better than a cheap one. The difference is in the hardness of the rubber: a harder one gives you more control over the force, because it flexes less. It is the perfect tool for encouraging a part into place, without damaging it. Cost: under $20.

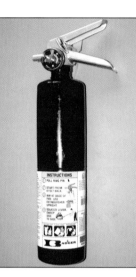

A fire extinguisher is a basic precaution, and it should be effective on all classes of fires likely to occur when working on a car.

Fire extinguisher

Again, the reason should be obvious. The fire extinguisher should be rated "ABC," which means that it can be used on wood and paper fires, gasoline and oil fires, and electrical fires. There will also be numbers in the rating, for example: "3-A: 40-B; 20-C." The numbers refer to the firefighting power of the extinguisher; the higher the number, the greater the power. The extinguisher should bear the "UL" seal of Underwriters Laboratories (most states require it). It should also meet ANSI/UL standard 711, which assures that the extinguisher meets the standards for the ABC rating, and ANSI/UL standard 299, which is a safety standard governing its construction. A fire extinguisher usually comes with a holder, so that it can be wall mounted. A dial on the fire extinguisher tells you when the extinguisher needs to be replaced (most small portable fire extinguishers cannot be recharged). Typical home-size fire extinguishers cost less than $20. Larger extinguishers cost from $50 to $100.

frames. Lenses must be able to take the impact of a steel ball traveling 150 feet per second without damage. Safety glasses should always cover the side of the eye area, not just the front. The average price ranges between $5 and $15. Prescription safety glasses are available from eyewear retailers.

Floor jack

A "floor jack," also called a "service jack," is a heavy-duty jack on wheels with a long handle that is pumped up and down to raise the jack's "cradle" and lift the car. Floor jacks are hydraulic. That is, fluid is pumped into a cylinder and pushes against a piston that, in turn, causes the jack to lift the vehicle. Twisting the handle clockwise and counter-clockwise controls the valve that releases the hydraulic pressure. Rubber seals inside the jack are designed to prevent fluid leakage past the piston, so that the jack holds the lift height until the hydraulic pressure is released. More information is in a sidebar in Chapter 2.

Jack stands

A "jack stand" consists of two parts: a pyramid- shaped base (open at the top) with a ratchet lever, and a toothed neck that fits into the ratchet mechanism in the base and adjusts for height. A jack stand's legs should be connected to each other at the bottom of the jack so that the legs cannot spread under load. They're sold in pairs and you will need four of them to completely lift a vehicle. More information about jack stands and how to buy them is provided in a sidebar in Chapter 2.

Specialized Tools

Some jobs are impossible without specialized tools; others are merely almost impossible. There are two kinds of specialized tools: those designed for a special purpose, such as a steering wheel puller, and "special service tools." Special service tools are unique tools that are required to perform a particular service procedure on one specific make or model of vehicle.

Whenever you hit the proverbial brick wall in a car job, it is a good idea to question whether you've got the proper tool. For example: a number of automobile manufacturers use "quick-connect" fittings on certain hoses and lines, such as the hose to the transmission oil cooler and fuel lines. These often require a special quick-disconnect tool to disconnect them. If so, there is no substitute for that tool.

Safety glasses are the practical alternative to wearing a dashing patch over an eye blinded by flying debris—because you weren't wearing safety glasses.

Safety glasses

The reason should be obvious: we want you to be able to read this book. Safety glasses are *not* the same as glasses with heat-treated or hardened lenses. Safety glasses have lenses and frames that meet 2003 ANSI (American National Standards Institute) standard Z87.1.) Frames are stronger than ordinary glasses

Special Service Tools

Sooner or later, you're going to discover that you need a special service tool to perform a repair on your car. This is not good news because you won't have that tool and there won't be any possible substitute for that tool.

What's a "special service tool?" Every car manufacturer designs unique parts for which no ordinary tool can be used. So, they design a tool to work with the part. In a sense, the design of the tool is what makes that part's design possible. The tool that works with the part is a special service tool.

When the factory shop manual specifies using a special service tool, it usually means that an ordinary tool won't do the job. Occasionally, a special service tool is designed merely to make a particular service procedure easier to perform, in which case it likely can be done with standard tools. But that's the exception. The rule is that the special service tool is the only way to do the job.

For example, General Motors has designed a type of water pump that is installed by turning the entire pump counterclockwise (yes, counterclockwise) within its housing until the pump seats. Installing or removing the pump requires a special service tool that is basically a huge socket with a special tooth pattern to the open end. For a Cadillac Northstar V-8, it's the "J-38816-1A Water Pump Remover and Installer." Without the necessary special service tool, it is physically impossible to remove the water pump.

So, how do you procure the special service tool? Some auto manufacturers sell special service tools directly and you can order them online. Other auto makers leave selling the tools to the company that makes the tools, which, more often than not, is SPX Corporation. SPX manufactures and sells special service tools through its Kent-Moore, Miller Special Tools, and OTC divisions. As this is written, with the exception of OTC, the SPX tool catalogs are not yet available online, though they're working on it. Location information: SPX: 800-336-6687, online at dealerequipment.com; Kent-Moore: 800-345-2233, online at spxkentmoore.com; Miller Tools: 800-801-5420, online at miller.spx.com; OTC: 1-800-345-2233, online at otctools.com or email through the websites.

SPX does, however, have special service tools for a number of import brands available online. These include Hyundai, Isuzu, Jaguar, Land Rover, Lexus, Mitsubishi, Subaru, Toyota, and Volvo. The addresses for these websites all follow the same pattern at brandofcar.spx.com. Aston-Martin and Volvo, however, are exceptions: online at: astonmartintechinfo.com/spx/amd2/index.html and volvocars.spx.com.

Equipment Solutions, a division of Snap-On: 800-426-6260, and online at equipmentsolutions.com, also sells special tools for Lexus and Toyota.

Special service tools for GM products, including Saturn, are sold by SPX Kent-Moore: 800-GM-TOOLS and are not currently available online. Chrysler, Dodge, and Jeep service tools are sold by SPX Miller Special Tools: 800-801-5420, and online at miller.spx.com. Ford, Mercury, and Lincoln "Essential Special Service Tools" are available only by calling Ford: 800-Rotunda, Option #4.)

Acura and Honda special service tools are available by contacting SPX OTC directly. Equipment Solutions also sells special tools for these brands.

Mercedes-Benz sells its special tools directly from its website: startekinfo.com. Audi and Volkswagen special tools are sold by Equipment Solutions.

A number of auto manufacturers sell their special service tools online at their technical information websites, including Aston Martin, BMW, Infiniti, Kia, Mazda, Mini, Mitsubishi, Nissan, and Suzuki. Most of these use the same format for their websites: nameofcar + techinfo.com (e.g., bmwtechinfo.com). Exceptions to the above formula are: Suzuki, at suzukipitstop.com; Infiniti, at nissan-techinfo.com/infiniti; and, Nissan, at nissan-techinfo.com. If Aston Martin's website demands a password, type "Aston Martin tech info" into Google, then go to home once you're in the site. Equipment Solutions also sells special Kia and Mazda tools.

There are also retail tool vendors who sell special service tools online. These include: Baum Tools at baumtools.com (foreign makes); Pelican Parts at pelicanparts.com (Audi, BMW, Mercedes-Benz, Volkswagen, and Volvo); Skywaytools.com (most makes, including Fiat and Yugo); and, Samstag Sales atsamstagsales.com (German tools for German brands). Also, sometimes the tools are so frequently used for particular brands that the tool companies catering to professional mechanics—Snap-on, Mac Tools, and Matco—make their own versions. Other tool companies also manufacture special service tools, even though they're not the authorized tool manufacturer. These include Schley Products, Inc., OTC Tools, and Lisle Corporation. Their tools are commonly available through online parts retailers.

Last, but not necessarily least, there is your local parts store. Well-stocked parts retailers often carry special tools required to perform common repairs on popular vehicle makes. Some, such as AutoZone, will even loan them to you.

Here are some of the specialized tools needed for jobs described in this book, or that you may need to go beyond what's within these covers:

The Factory Shop Manual

The factory shop manual details the service procedures for your car and will also tell you if a special purpose tool is needed. See Sidebar: The Factory Shop Manual.

A digital multimeter is very inexpensive, but will allow you to diagnose a variety of electrical systems in the car, including the battery, the alternator, and many of the sensors used in the electronic engine management system.

Digital multimeter

If you are going to do any electrical diagnosis, you need a digital multimeter (DMM). A DMM has a digital read-out, in contrast to an analog multimeter that uses a moving needle to read results. Though you can spend a lot more, an adequate DMM can be had for less than $100.

Features to look for include: "autoranging," which automatically moves the decimal point to display the result in the most accurate form possible; a wide selection of test leads including probes (needles that can be pushed through a wire's insulation), alligator clips, a "current clamp," also called an "inductive current pick-up," or "probe," or "inductive clamp"(this looks like a plastic clamp and goes around an insulated wire, such as a spark plug wire, and measures amperage without being part of the circuit); and, a port for testing milliamps. If possible, try to find a DMM with an "audible continuity beep." That's a feature that beeps to indicate

adequate current flow in the circuit being tested, so you can hear the meter even when you can't see it. "Data hold" is also useful, so that the meter displays the data even after disconnecting the probes. Also pay attention to the unit's "maximum current rating" and its safety rating. It will be printed by the amps and milliamps jacks on the DMM. You should not exceed that rating when using the DMM. So, a higher amp rating makes the unit usable for more tests and gives you a larger margin of safety. Last, but certainly not least, it should meet the CAT-III standard of the International Electrotechnical Commission's (IEC) and be Underwriter's Laboratory approved. There is more about this and the use of the DMM in Chapter 6.

A code reader or scan tool— this one is a CanOBD2 code reader made by Innova— retrieves the diagnostic trouble codes stored in your car's computer. With it, you can get the same data that professional mechanics use to diagnose engine-related problems.

Code reader or scan tool

From model year 1996 on, your car can provide information about problems it is experiencing via On-Board Diagnostics II (OBD-II). Retrieving that information requires a code reader or scan tool. You can do basic stuff—changing the oil, spark plugs, and brake pads—without one, but, for engine diagnosis on a modern automobile, a code reader or scan tool is essential. A code reader can retrieve diagnostic trouble codes and certain other data. A scan tool can, in addition to those functions, read and store "real time" information about engine

operation. Good-quality code readers and scan tools are available at auto parts stores and on Internet sites such as Amazon.com for about $200. For more information, check the sidebar in Chapter 10.

Flex-drive and swivel drive spark plug sockets

A "flex-drive" socket has a universal joint attached to the end that attaches to the socket ratchet. A "swivel drive" socket is similar, except it uses a ball-type joint that allows the socket to move at almost any angle. There is even a double swivel spark plug socket that has two joints. S-K Tools makes them and they're sold on Amazon.com, by Autobarn (autobarn.net), and SJ Discount Tools (sjdiscounttools.com). One of these can make it possible to remove a spark plug that otherwise could not be turned. A set of both 5/8-inch and 13/16-inch swivel drive sockets cost from $60 to $70, an individual swivel drive socket costs about $30, and flex-drive spark plug sockets cost about from $5 to $10 less.

A spark plug gap tool allows you to verify that the plug is correctly gapped and includes a tool for adjusting the gap if it isn't set properly.

Spark plug gap gauge

Sometimes also called a "feeler gauge," the spark plug gap gauge is designed to measure the distance between the spark plug's center and side electrodes. It consists of a series of wires of specified diameters. Inserting the wire in the gap allows measuring it. There are two kinds: standard, and "high energy." Newer cars often specify a larger spark plug gap than was normally the case a

The Factory Shop Manual

Now that you've bought this book, the best possible advice is that you buy another one, a more expensive one: the factory shop manual for your car.

This is a factory shop manual, an encyclopedia written about your car. This four-volume set covers the proper repair procedures for the 1997 Corvette and totals about 4,400 pages.

There is no substitute for the factory shop manual (also sometimes called a factory service manual). Certainly, you can live without it. But sooner or later, you're going to have a question to which you cannot find the answer.

That answer is in the factory shop manual. It is an encyclopedia written about your car, a compendium of information written by engineers and factory mechanics for dealer mechanics. Why wouldn't you want to have the same advantages they have? Cost is usually about $100, sometimes more, but worth it.

You can order a new copy of the official factory shop manual for cars and trucks made by General Motors (including Hummer and Saab), Ford Motor Company, Acura and Honda, Hyundai, Isuzu, Jaguar, and Mitsubishi, online directly from Helm, Inc. at helminc.com. Acura and Honda manuals can also be ordered online from Honda Service Express (www.techinfo.honda.com). Chrysler, Dodge, and Jeep manuals can be ordered online from Dyment Distribution at techauthority.gltghosting.com. Jaguar manuals also can be ordered online from Jaguar Global Technical Reference at jaguartechinfo.com (registration required). Land Rover manuals can be ordered online, as well at landrovertechinfo.com. GM also offers technical information online at Goodwrench.com. Ford offers online technical information at MotorcraftService.com. Saab maintains the subscription-only Saab Workshop Information System online at saabtechinfo.com.

Toyota and Lexus manuals are sold by the Toyota Distribution Center in California: 800-622-2033. Nissan and Infiniti factory manuals are sold online at nissantechinfo.com and nissantechinfo.com/infiniti. Hyundai manuals can be ordered online through Hyundai Service Technology at hmaservice.com. Isuzu manuals can be ordered from the online Isuzu Source Store at isuzusource.com. Kia manuals are available online through the Kia Global Information System at kiatechinfo.com (registration required). Mazda manuals can be ordered online at Mazda Technical Information at mazdatechinfo.com. Mitsubishi manuals can be ordered online from Mitsubishi Motors Service Information Retrieval at mitsubishitechinfo.com (subscription not required to order materials). Subaru manuals are available online for download from the Subaru Technical Information System at techinfo.subaru.com. Suzuki manuals are available at the Suzuki Pit Stop in either printed or online form at suzukipitstop.com.

Aston Martin manuals are available online at astonmartintechinfo.com. If the website demands a password, type "Aston Martin tech info" into Google, then go to the home page once you're in the site. Audi manuals can be ordered online from the Audi Technical Literature Ordering Center at audi.ddsltd.com. Bentley offers its "ASSIST" technical information service both on CD-ROM and online at bentleytechinfo.com. BMW manuals can also be ordered online at bmwtechinfo.com—(registration and fee required to enter the site, but not to order materials). Mercedes-Benz manuals, some of which are available only on CD ROM, can be ordered by calling 1-800-FOR-MERC (the Mercedes technical website is startekinfo.com). Porsche manuals can be downloaded from Porsche Technical Service Information at techinfo.porsche.com (registration required). Volkswagen manuals can be ordered online at vw.ddsltd.com. Volvo manuals are available only in electronic format, either DVD or through Internet access at volvotechinfo.com. Audi and VW also offer online technical information through their erWin websites at erwin.audi.de and erwin.volkswagen.de.

Many manufacturers' websites also provide access, either free or by subscription, to extensive collections of online service information, including technical bulletins, diagnostic guides, and much more.

You can also find used copies of most factory shop manuals, even for recent models. One online source is eBay; Amazon.com is another. There are also online book dealers who specialize in used factory manuals, including: Roth Auto Books at rothautobooks.com; Lloyd's Automotive Literature at lloydsautolit.com; Factory Auto Manuals, online at factoryautomanuals.com; Faxon Auto Literature at faxonautolit.com; Bishko Automobile Literature At autobooksbishko.com; H.D. Rogers & Sons at hdrogers.com (British and Italian cars); Books4Cars.com; and, AutoRepairManuals.biz.

decade ago. The "high energy" spark plug gauge has larger wires to measure these bigger gaps. Blade-type feeler gauges are also available, but should only be used to measure new spark plugs. Because a used spark plug will have an irregular surface on the side electrode due to deposits, a wire gauge will fit into the valleys in the worn electrode while a blade gauge will rest across the peaks. The wire gauge will give a more accurate reading. Cost: under $3.

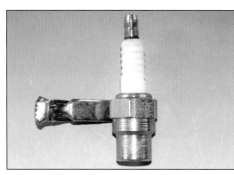

This is a spark plug tester. It can be clipped to a ground on the engine and the other end attached to the spark plug cable to test whether enough current is reaching the spark plug to fire it.

Spark plug tester

This tool, which costs less than $10 online and can also be purchased at many auto parts stores, plugs into a spark plug cable and then clips to the side of the engine block. It allows you to test whether spark is reaching the spark plug, which allows you to determine whether a coil is working for a particular cylinder in vehicles with distributorless ignition systems with multiple coils. Though testers are available for conventional ignition systems using a mechanical or electronic distributor, a spark plug tester to be used with a multiple coil system should be one specifically labeled as suitable for high energy ignition (HEI) systems.

Oil filter wrench

To remove an oil filter, you will need a specialized wrench. There are several types and all of them are inexpensive. They're discussed fully in a sidebar in Chapter 3.

A "side terminal battery wrench" is a ratchet specifically designed to fit the terminal bolts on the side terminal batteries used by many cars, particularly GM products. It's conveniently small, so it fits the tight area near batteries in many cars and the insulated handle protects against inadvertently causing sparks.

Side terminal battery wrench

"Side terminal" or "side mount" batteries are those with terminals in the side of the battery into which the cables are bolted and are used on many General Motors cars. They can be disconnected with any wrench that fits the 5/16-inch bolt that is used in them, so a special wrench isn't really a necessity. However, special side mount battery wrench ratchets that have insulated handles are available for less than $10. They are a good idea because the insulated handle reduces the risk of shorting the positive terminal of the battery and creating sparks that could potentially trigger an explosion of battery gases.

Battery terminal brush

Designed specifically for cleaning battery terminals, it costs $10 or less at

A battery terminal brush: it's designed so that the outside half cups over a battery post to clean it, while the inside brush can be used to clean the depressions in battery side terminals.

any auto parts store. The tool has two parts, male and female, each with wire brushes. One brush slips over battery terminal posts—twist it and they're clean. The other is a brush that gets into side battery terminals. The two parts nest together for storage.

Impact driver

An "impact driver" transfers the force of an impact on the top of the tool into a twisting force at the bottom of the tool. In other words, you can remove a corroded or rusted screw or bolt by putting the impact driver on the fastener and then hitting the impact driver with a hammer. Impact drivers can be the only effective solution for removing rusted or corroded fasteners. They are not expensive: $25 or less. Typically, the driver comes with both screwdriver bits and sockets. If not, use only specially hardened impact bits and sockets. Wear safety glasses, too.

Disc brake rotors on Japanese and European automobiles are held in place by a screw, usually a Phillips, that threads into the axle hub. This fastener often quickly becomes frozen with rust. The impact driver is the solution.

An impact driver is different than the powered "impact wrench" commonly used in professional repair shops. Though professional versions usually operate on compressed air, you can buy an electric impact wrench for about $200. Impact wrenches are very effective

An impact driver isn't necessarily an air tool. This manual-type is simply struck with a hammer to create the rotating action that loosens stuck screws. It's particularly useful in brake repairs on foreign cars.

at removing rusted fasteners, so you may eventually want to invest in one.

Parking brake cable disconnect tool

See Chapter 12. This is another of those luxury items that you will buy before you attempt to replace a rear brake caliper a second time. You can make do without this tool, but why? You're already saving so much money replacing the calipers yourself. Lisle tools, part number 40800, about $13. Snap-On, stock number BT22A, about $17.

Brake bleeder kit

A bleeder kit consists of a clear plastic hose, a bottle to which the hose attaches. and fittings allowing the other end of the hose to attach to a brake caliper's bleed screw. You can bleed brakes with a hose and a soda bottle, but the kit makes the job easier. Basic kits cost $5 to $20. Make sure that the hose is clear so that you can see bubbles in the brake fluid traveling through the hose. For more about bleeders, see the Chapter 12 sidebar: "Bleeding Brakes."

Very Large "C" Clamp

Bigger than you probably have; one with at least an 8-inch opening. You'll need it for compressing the piston in brake calipers when changing brake pads and doing other brake work. See Chapter 12: Brakes.

This ingenious device allows you to compress the caliper pistons in certain type of disc brakes. The protrusions fit into depressions in the caliper piston. Each side of the tool fits a different piston design. The center holes accept a standard 3/8-inch drive socket extension.

Disc brake caliper piston tool

See Chapter 12. This is a tool that fits on a 3/8-inch drive socket extension and allows you to easily rotate the screw-in caliper pistons on certain disc brakes back into their cylinders. It costs less than $10 and should be available at any auto parts store.

Dead blow hammer

The idea behind a dead blow hammer is that it has all of the weight of a hammer and the force associated with that weight, without any of the rebound. Dead blow hammers are filled with shot encased in a steel canister, itself encased in a plastic shell. The advantage of a dead blow hammer is that it concentrates the force because there is no kickback. Expect to pay between $30 and $50.

An oxygen sensor socket has a slit down the side to accommodate the "pigtail" of electrical wires attached to the sensor. You can't remove or install an oxygen sensor without it.

Oxygen sensor socket

Oxygen sensors have wires that are attached to the end, so a typical socket won't work. An oxygen sensor socket has a long slot in its side to accommodate the pigtail wires. American cars use a 7/8-inch socket while the metric size for European and Japanese cars is 22 mm. Those happen to be almost identical in

size, so the same socket usually works on both domestic and foreign cars. Oxygen sensor sockets cost less than $20.

Quick-disconnect tools

As mentioned already, there are a variety of quick-connect fittings. They are commonly used on fuel lines, oil lines, clutch hydraulic lines, and, occasionally, heater hoses. Some of them require a special tool to disconnect and some do not. When a special tool is required, it is often as simple as a flanged sleeve that slides into the fitting. But the tools differ widely in appearance, depending on the type of fitting for which they are designed. These tools often work on only one manufacturer's vehicles. Moreover, the same manufacturer may use more than one type of quick-connect fitting and each usually requires its own special tool. A set of quick disconnect tools that includes those required for most major makes can be purchased for about $30. Individual tools cost less than $15. A well-stocked auto parts store will carry a selection.

Coil spring compressor

This tool consists of two very large screws with a large hook or claw on each end. One attaches to each side of a coil spring. Tightening the screw compresses the spring so that it can be removed. A coil spring compressor is necessary to remove MacPherson struts. If you buy one for this purpose, get one that is specifically designed for MacPherson strut springs. Though you can spend $150 or more for one, you can buy a good one for about $60 online. You probably don't have to buy it; many parts stores loan coil spring compressors without charge, though there is usually a refundable deposit. They can also be rented.

Trim pad removal tool

Snap-On, stock number A177A, about $30. This weirdly shaped device is listed by Snap-On as a trim tool for GM vehicles and most imports but its uses far exceed trim removal, though I'm sure it does that as well. It is the perfect tool for

You probably won't find a trim pad tool at a hardware store. These tools are designed to remove interior door panels, but they have a variety of other uses. This one is made by Snap-On and has the easily gripped handle typical of that brand.

removing all sorts of plastic fasteners that vehicle manufacturers now use to: a) save weight, thereby increasing fuel economy and reducing greenhouse gas emissions; or, b) save money and simultaneously make it possible to charge you $5 for a replacement. Yes, you can find a similar tool made by someone else for less money (I did), but it doesn't work nearly as well.

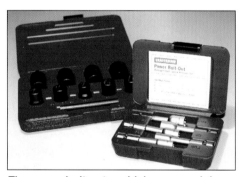

These are bolt outs, which are special sockets designed to grip a damaged bolt head that an ordinary wrench can't grip. This set is Craftsman and was purchased at one of their many sales—a good time to buy tools you may use only occasionally, but for which there's no substitute when the need does arise.

Rescue tools

What do you do when the bolt head is rounded off, and you can't grip it with any wrench? You use a Bolt-Out, a tool specially designed to dig into the damaged bolt head so that you can twist it out. When the screw head is too damaged to hold the screwdriver blade? A screw extractor looks very much like a coarse reverse twist drill bit. Drill a short hole into the screw head and then use a hammer to

lightly tap the extractor into the hole. When drilling into metal, you should use hardened drill bits designed for metal, and light lubricating oil to dissipate heat. Then twist the screw out using the handle from a tap and die set (not a wrench) to turn the extractor. You can also use a screw extractor when a bolt head breaks off. A tap and die set allows you to restore damaged threads on a bolt or in the bolt hole. Craftsman sells Bolt-Out sets from $25 to $50, screw extractor sets for $40 to $60, and a basic tap and die set including both standard and metric sizes costs about $60.

Battery charger

A basic battery charger costs less than $50. Models with more features cost less than $100. It should be designed so that it operates automatically and won't overcharge the battery. It should also have an internal system that automatically senses if the cables have been installed on the wrong terminals and cuts off current.

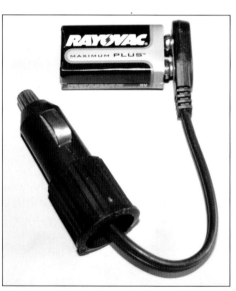

The computer memory saver avoids losing radio presets and memory settings by providing just enough current to the vehicle's electrical system, when the battery is disconnected, that these items don't lose their memories.

Computer memory saver

A little device using a 9-volt battery that plugs into the cigarette lighter

before you disconnect the battery, it is designed to provide just the minimal trickle of electricity to the circuits required to preserve memory settings, such as radio pre-selects. Inexpensive at under $15.

Transmission fluid funnel

See Chapter 11. It is a long, narrow funnel designed to fit into the dipstick tube of an automatic transmission. It's handy for adding automatic transmission fluid to most automatics because the fill opening is often hard to reach with a bigger funnel.

Trouble light

Though a good flashlight is a necessity, many times a "trouble light," sometimes called a "shop light," works better. It can provide brighter light over a broader area, though it isn't as good for peering into the tight spots. Most use a fluorescent bulb, but some use a light emitting diode (LED). The latest thing is the rechargeable trouble light: no cord. At under $65, they're about twice as expensive as the corded light. However, when you're under a car and the cord is

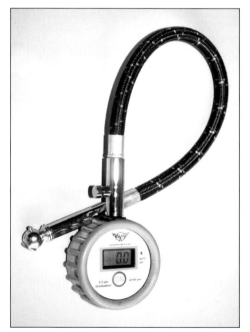

A good tire gauge makes checking the tires much easier. This one lets you bleed air out, so that you can get the precise pressure you want.

Parts

How do you know what part you need?

It seems pretty straightforward, but there are complications. Even within the same make and model, there may be several different versions of a single part, such as a brake rotor. The part actually used depends on the equipment options with which the car was built.

Ideally, you would know the part number. You may be able to find the part number online. Many GM parts can be searched at the ACDelco website at acdelco.com. Ford, Mercury, and Lincoln parts catalogs are available at the Motorcraft website at motorcraft.com. Also, many new car dealers have expanded their parts departments into Internet sales. An Internet search using your vehicle's brand name and "parts" will usually bring up several sites that can provide parts numbers. Some even include exploded diagrams of parts and components.

If you don't know the part number, but you know the pertinent specifications of your car–the engine configuration and size, transmission type, etc.–that will ordinarily be sufficient to identify the correct part, either at the parts counter or at an online parts retailer's website, such as at rockauto.com.

Sometimes you'll discover that you need to know a code, such as "JL9," to determine which part is required. These codes identify a specific option or equipment type installed on the vehicle car when it was manufactured. Different parts may be required for cars with a specific code than those without it. When you look at the parts list and see that there are two choices for your vehicle, one for a vehicle with a specific code and one for the rest, you'll need to figure out which one applies.

The codes applicable to the vehicle are on the "service

Continued on page 18

---

snagged on something so that you can't move the light, you'll consider it money well spent.

Tire Pressure Gauge

See Chapter 13. You need to keep your tires properly inflated, so you need an accurate gauge. The easiest to use has a bleed valve built into the base of the gauge, so that you can overfill the tire, then bleed air down to the correct pressure. Cost: $35 or less.

Coolant Hydrometer

Also called an "antifreeze tester," it is inexpensive, and available at both auto parts and discount stores. It suctions a sample of the coolant into a chamber and reads out with a float to both the freezing point and boiling point of the coolant.

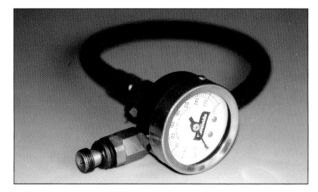

Compression gauge

Used to test cylinder compression, it is a gauge on a hose that screws into the spark plug hole. With it, you can diagnose a variety of internal mechanical engine problems. A good one costs less than $40.

Tool chest

There is no substitute for a good metal tool chest with roller-bearing drawers. The standard-bearer is Craftsman. There are other brands, such as Kobalt, which are equivalent. If it doesn't seem to be as good as a Craftsman, don't buy it. Also, don't buy the really cheap Craftsman tool chests, either; they don't have roller-bearing drawers. If you want to go the eBay route, you can find some unique-themed tool chests, such as those themed with NASCAR drivers.

The compression gauge allows you to verify that the cylinders and valves are in good shape and, if not, isolate which one has low compression and diagnose the reason for the problem.

A quality tool chest must have roller-bearing drawers. The weight of three sets of wrenches in the drawer is more substantial than it might seem. Try the drawers, and then visualize how that drawer will feel loaded.

Typically, tool chests are arranged like pyramids.There is a big one on the bottom, which rolls on large rubber casters, and one or two others (narrower in depth but of the same width) that stack on top of the base unit. The top one has a hinged lid. Watch out for that hinged lid; don't let it guillotine your fingers.

You can approach buying your tool chest in two ways: either buy one unit at a time, as you need and can afford it; or, buy the whole shebang as a set. You will save money if you buy it as a set, and you'll really save if you wait until they are on sale. A Craftsman set with a base unit and two units that stack on top costs between $350 and $500, depending on how many drawers are in each unit. Whatever you do, though, buy quality. If you buy a cheap tool chest, there will always be something more important than replacing it, so those drawers that drag every time you open them will still be in your garage when you're drawing down your 401k.

Parts CONTINUED

parts identification" sticker or its equivalent, usually located on the driver's door jam, under the console lid, on the glove box door, under the trunk lid, or under the spare tire cover.

So, where is the best place to buy the part you need?

You can always go to the dealership's parts department. Original equipment (OE) parts are usually, though not invariably, a safe choice. Unfortunately, they can be the most expensive choice, as well.

Instead of patronizing your local dealer, who will probably quote list price for a part, you can often get OE parts for much less through one of the new car dealers selling factory authorized parts online. Often, you can buy OE parts from an online parts retailer, such as rockauto.com, or at a parts store, such as AutoZone. AC Delco parts are OE on GM vehicles; Bosch is OE for many European vehicles; NGK is commonly OE on Japanese cars; Motorcraft is original equipment on Ford, Mercury, and Lincoln; and, Mopar is a Chrysler parts OE brand name.

Parts stores and online parts retailers also stock OE-equivalent parts. These may not have been manufactured by the OE supplier (though some are), but are designed to meet the same specifications and standards as the OE part. There is nothing wrong with this concept—automobile manufacturers, after all, buy their parts from independent suppliers. Many companies both supply OE parts to auto manufacturers and make OE-equivalent parts for the automotive aftermarket.

Some aftermarket parts are better than OE. Aftermarket performance parts, including brake pads, rotors, and calipers, spark plugs and plug wires, suspension components and springs, are designed to exceed the specifications and capabilities of OE parts. There are also, of course, substandard replacement parts on the market. But parts made by established parts manufacturers and sold by reputable retailers, whether online or at a parts store, should be completely satisfactory substitutes for OE parts.

What about rebuilt parts?

Once again, the key is the company that remanufactures the part. Many remanufactured parts are produced by companies that are also OE new-parts suppliers to automobile manufacturers. For example, Remy Inc. is an OE supplier of starters and alternators to GM, Daimler/Chrysler, Honda, Toyota, and Hyundai under the Delco-Remy brand. But it also remanufactures these components, both under their own Remy brand and under private label brands sold through parts stores.

What if the part isn't available?

What if the manufacturer no longer "services" that part, and it isn't stocked at auto parts stores? Or, maybe the manufacturer does still stock the part, but the car is an older one and the price of the new part equals or exceeds the value of the car. Or, the manufacturer has superseded an old part with a newer one, but the new part is not an exact fit replacement for the old part.

One way to locate that part is through a salvage yard. Type "used auto parts" into an online search engine and you will be introduced to an amazingly sophisticated national network of automobile salvage yards. Salvage yards have created parts-locator services: type in the make, model, and year of the vehicle, contact information for yourself, a description of the part, and submit the form. The inquiry is sent to a number of salvage yards throughout the country, so that those that have the part can respond directly to your e-mail. Their inventories are computerized and they can ascertain in a very short time whether they have the part that fits your car. There are even salvage yards that concentrate on only a single brand of automobile.

Sometimes a manufacturer supersedes an older part number with a newer part. Usually, this means that the newer part is superior to the older one. But, sometimes it's done because the supply of the old part has been exhausted, so the new part is substituted. When this happens, the old part and the new one may not be exactly the same. That can cause problems in installation, especially if the two are not dimensionally the same and clearances are tight. When faced with that choice, you may want to find an Internet forum devoted to that make and spend a little time doing online research. You may be better off getting a used part from a salvage yard than a new one from the dealer.

There are also parts dealers who specialize in "obsolete" parts: new parts no longer stocked by the OE manufacturer. (You may see the term "NOS." It means "new old stock.") Many of these sources can be located on the Internet by searching for "obsolete automobile parts." Also, brand-specific parts-locating guides listing hundreds of parts sources are published in both soft cover and CD Rom formats by the Garden of Speedin, at gardenofspeedin.com, and cost only about $30.

There is also one other possibility: the small business that specializes in rebuilding your old part. There are businesses that rebuild digital instrument panel displays, such as Mr. Whizard at mrwhizard.com. Their website also has a list of symptoms that are common problems for each brand. Some businesses will rebuild power window regulators for a fraction of what a completely new one would cost, such as Window Regulators USA online at regulatorusa.com. If you're faced with a part that's hard to find or maybe just impossibly expensive, spend time on the Internet and you may discover that it can be economically rebuilt.

Supplies

There are some supplies that it is useful to have on hand when working on cars.

Penetrating oil

The best way to loosen rusty fasteners. It is not a magic elixir because it takes time to work, but it is indispensable. Liquid Wrench is the best-known brand, but many swear by PB Blaster.

Dielectric grease

This product does not conduct electricity, so it can be used to lubricate in places where avoiding electrical conductivity is important, such as spark plug insulators. Its primary purpose, however, is as a mosture barrier. Thus it is the perfect coating to protect electrical connections from corrosion, provided that you apply it over the connected surfaces.

High-temperature silicone lubricant

This is what you use to lubricate brake caliper slide pins, but it also works really well as a weather strip protectant (just rub it in).

Silicone spray lubricant and white lithium grease are both basic supplies for lubricating door hinges, hood latches, and a variety of other moving parts.

Brake Cleaner

Brake cleaner removes brake dust, grease, oil, and other contaminants without leaving a residue.

Air intake cleaner

The proper product for removing deposits from the throttle body, which can make an amazing difference in the way the car idles and accelerates. This is not the same as carburetor cleaner, which contain chemicals that can damage oxygen sensors and catalytic converters.

Mass air flow cleaner

An electrical component cleaner and the only safe cleaner for an MAF. Other types of cleaners, especially those that are petroleum-based, can damage the MAF.

Mass air flow sensor cleaner, brake cleaner, and air intake cleaner: each of these is a specialized cleaner designed for a particular purpose and for which there is no substitute.

White lithium grease

A traditional automotive lubricant for sliding parts, such as door hinges.

Hand cleaner

Purpose-made hand cleaners are far better than normal bar soaps at removing the oily dirt that gets on your hands when you're working on a car..

Working on your car doesn't have to mean greasy hands: you can use hand cleaner, but if you wear nitrile gloves you probably won't need hand cleaner. The padding of mechanic's gloves protects your hands while still allowing a good grip on tools.

Nitrile gloves

They're cheap, they're disposable, and they're even better than hand cleaner because they keep your hands clean. They allow you almost as much tactile sensation as bare hands, so you can still feel what you're doing. Because they're not latex, they're safe for those with latex allergies. Even the Saturday morning TV mechanics wear them, so why not you?

Shop Towels

The red towels you may have seen mechanics use. They're cheap: you can buy them in bulk at Wal-Mart, Sam's Club, or Costco, and they're almost indestructible. They also don't give off lint, which is a necessity for jobs such as changing automatic transmission fluid.

CHAPTER 2

HOW TO LIFT YOUR CAR—SAFELY

Some of the tasks described in this book, and many of those to which you will aspire after your confidence has been expanded by reading this valuable tome, require that you get *under* the car.

Parts for this job

None

Tools for this job

Floor jack
Jack stands (four)
Wheel chocks (one pair)
Jack & jack stand pads:
  commercially purchased or hockey
  pucks (one pad for the floor jack,
  four for the jack stands)
4-inch wood lift ramps:
  (pair, self-fabricated if applicable)
Pinch weld adapter:
  (four, self-fabricated if applicable)

Time for this job

Once you've done it a few times, lifting your car won't take more than half an hour. But it is a task that demands all of your care and attention. So, don't rush it and do take the time to double-check that everything is properly positioned before going to the next step.

Advance Planning

You will need to know the "lift points" for your car. Lift points are the places under the car designed to accept the vehicle's spare-tire jack or to be used when raising the vehicle with a commercial hoist in an automobile repair shop. The owner's manual will specify the lift points designed for the spare-tire jack. The factory shop manual, however, will usually specify additional lift points. There will be designated lift points for use with a floor jack, a commercial suspension contact hoist, and a commercial frame contact hoist. A suspension contact hoist lifts the car at the suspension's lower A-arms. Some cars cannot be lifted this way. The designated lift points for a frame contact hoist usually use the same lift points designated for the spare-tire jack.

Also, standard J2184, jointly issued by the Society of Automotive Engineers and American National Standards Institute in 2000, recommends that the vehicle manufacturer attach a label designating the lift points to the car itself, either under the hood or in the glove box, and mark the actual lifting points under the car with a hole, raised area, or depression shaped as an equilateral triangle. Some manufacturers do that and some do not.

Hazard Warning

Getting under a car is dangerous. As discussed in the text, *always* use secondary supports whenever working underneath a vehicle. If there is the slightest doubt in your mind that the car cannot possibly fall on you, don't get under the car.

Never get under a car supported only by a floor jack. Floor jacks can fail, in which case the car will fall on you. Never get under a car supported by the tire-changing jack that came with the car. These jacks are lightly constructed and unstable. A car can easily fall off of one. Don't support a car with cinder or concrete blocks, either; they're not designed for the load and can break apart without warning.

Be sure that the load rating of your floor jack and jack stands is adequate to support the weight of the vehicle. Use twice the actual load as a general rule. In other words, if the car weighs 4,000 lbs., then each of four jack stands will be supporting about 1,000 lbs. A jack stand rated at 2 tons gives you a 100% margin of safety.

Always use common sense when under a car. Some brake and suspension bolts have very high torque values. Before applying significant levels of force to a fastener while you are under the car, double-check the stability of the load and its distribution on the jack stands.

Let's do it

So, how do you lift a car without hurting it? Yes, without hurting the *car*. Modern cars are generally of unibody construction. Lifting at the wrong location can be a very expensive mistake. In a unibody car, there is no separate frame. The body and chassis are one unit, designed to distribute load forces throughout the structure of the car. Most of the areas under a unibody car are not designed to support the car's weight and can be damaged if used as a lifting point. Unibody cars have specific designated lift points that are designed to take the load imposed by lifting the car.

In contrast, on most pick-up trucks, truck-based SUVs, and many older cars the body is bolted to a separate frame (called "body-on-frame" construction). These vehicles can be lifted wherever the frame rails are accessible.

To lift the vehicle, you will need a floor jack and jack stands—two jack stands if you're only lifting one end, and four jack stands to lift the entire vehicle. If you don't have one, the sidebar titled, "How to Buy a Floor Jack and Jack Stands," will help you select the proper one.

Ramps are one way to lift your car, but they're not the best choice.

It might seem easier to use steel ramps to lift the vehicle. Every auto parts store sells them, they're not very expensive, they lift the end of the vehicle about 9 inches, and all you have to do is drive onto them.

Ramps, however, have limitations. First, getting the vehicle onto the ramps can be tricky: if you go too slowly, the ramps tend to be pushed in front of the tires; and, if you go fast enough to climb the tire onto them, there's a risk of overshooting the end of the ramp. Second, you can only lift one end of the car with ramps. Third, ramps do not allow you to perform brake jobs or any other project that requires removing a wheel. Fourth, their height isn't adjustable. Finally, many ramps will not work with sports and performance cars because they are too steep for cars with low ground clearance and too narrow for cars with wide tires. All in all, a floor jack and four jack stands are much more useful than a pair of ramps.

Lifting and Supporting a Vehicle Safely: Secondary Supports

To lift a car safely:
1. Lift only when the vehicle is on a firm level surface.
2. Immobilize the vehicle with wheel chocks; also, unless you will need to

How to Buy a Floor Jack and Jack Stands

Floor jacks come in several different rated capacities, ranging upward from 1.5 tons, and also differ in maximum lift heights. "Low-profile" floor jacks are designed with a lower pick-up height (the height of the jack cradle when the jack is fully depressed) to fit under cars with low ground clearance, such as a Corvette or Viper. Though most floor jacks are made of heavy gauge steel, aluminum "racing style" floor jacks have become very popular. These usually use a roller instead of wheels at the front of the jack. Apart from appearance, their chief advantage is significantly lighter weight than steel floor jacks.

A top-line Hein Werner 2-ton capacity floor jack with a low pick-up height capable of lifting to 20 inches and weighing 98 pounds lists for about $450. It can be purchased online for much less, as low as $300, plus shipping. A Craftsman 2-ton capacity aluminum floor jack that can lift to 18.5 inches and weighs 42 pounds lists for about $200. Cheap 2-ton capacity floor jacks, usually made in China, are available at many stores for as little as $20. Avoid those; they're cheap for a reason.

Jack stands also are made either of steel or aluminum, have different rated capacities, and have different maximum and minimum heights. Jack stands are sold in pairs.

Common jack-stand rated capacities start at 2 tons and go up. Generally, the higher the rated capacity of the jack stand, the taller it will be at both minimum and maximum heights and the more it will cost. But even the best quality jack stands are not expensive: Hein Werner 3-ton capacity jack stands list at $105, but are available on-line and from tool suppliers for as little as $55, plus shipping. Craftsman jack stands of 3-ton capacity list for about $20. Astro Pneumatic aluminum jack stands of 3-ton capacity sell for about $60.

Voluntary safety standards for floor jacks and jack stands, both referred to as "portable automotive lift devices" (PALD), have been issued by the American Society of Mechanical Engineers (ASME) and American National Standards Institute (ANSI), most recently in 2005. Jacks and jack stands meeting the ASME/ANSI-PALD and PALD-4 standards for floor jacks and jack stands, respectively, (including those in the examples given above) have been tested for safety and load-bearing ability. If it doesn't meet those standards, don't buy it.

rotate a wheel, set the parking brake and put the vehicle in gear or in "park."

3. Position jack stands only at the vehicle's designated lift points.
4. Use a jack and jack stands rated to twice the weight they will actually support.
5. Use secondary supports.

The primary protection against a vehicle shifting when it is supported by jack stands is the weight of the vehicle. Two tons pushing down on jack stands is actually pretty stable—*provided* that the surface under the vehicle is level, and *provided* that its weight is distributed among all of the jack stands.

But, what if the vehicle falls? The answer to that's obvious, isn't it? The core concept in safely placing a vehicle on jack stands is secondary supports. *NEVER* get underneath a car on jack stands unless you have at least two infallible ways of keeping it from falling.

To illustrate the concept of secondary supports: suppose you are going to replace the front brake pads. You've lifted the front of the car and placed jack stands on each side of the vehicle at designated front lift points.

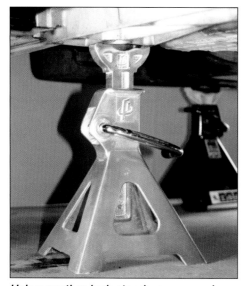

Using another jack stand as a secondary support is also a good idea. It need not be positioned at an accepted jacking or lifting point, as it is not bearing a load. Rather, it's there as an insurance policy.

Instead of setting the tires and wheels off to the side after removing them, slide them under the car directly behind the jack stands. You could even stick a couple of wood blocks between the wheel and the bottom of the car. Instead of removing the floor jack, leave it in place under the car. Relax the jack sufficiently to remove any load from it. But leave it positioned against the lift point, so that the floor jack can bear the load, if it should come to that.

Set another pair of jack stands snugly under the suspension A-arms at their pivot points on the frame. These pivot points bear the vehicle's weight through the suspension, so they should be strong enough to sustain its weight on jack stands.

Should the car slip from the jack stands, there are now three systems that will interfere with gravity: the second pair of jack stands, the floor jack, and the removed wheels and tires.

There are two things to bear in mind when positioning secondary supports. First, because it is unlikely that a jack stand will simply fail, the purpose of secondary supports is to accept the weight of the car if the car shifts position. That means the secondary supports should be located under something large enough that the secondary support will still be positioned to support it even if the vehicle does shift position.

Second, anticipate "dynamic loading." Dynamic loading means that if you drop something onto a jack or jack stand, the force imposed on the jack at the instant of contact may be several times the actual weight of the load. For that instant, the load may substantially exceed the capacity of the jack or stand and it will fail. That means the secondary support jack and jack stands should be positioned snugly against the point of contact with the car. There should not be a gap between them.

However, secondary supports should not themselves be supporting any of the weight of the vehicle. If they are doing that, they are not secondary supports. For example, if a floor jack left in place behind a jack stand is still supporting

some of the vehicle's weight, then it—not the jack stand—has become a primary support. Moreover, the vehicle will probably be unstable, because its weight is not distributed among all of the jack stands.

A vehicle should be lifted only when it is situated on a level surface. That surface should also be strong enough to support the vehicle's weight. If lifting on a blacktopped driveway, it is prudent to place 2 x 2-foot plywood sheets underneath each of the jack stands to prevent them from sinking into the asphalt under the vehicle's weight.

If you plan on removing a wheel once the vehicle has been lifted, break the lug nuts lose before lifting it, just one-half to three-quarters of a turn. This is easier and safer to do before the car is lifted.

Wheel chocks are essential. Don't lift at home without them (or anywhere else, either).

Position the wheel chock snuggly against the tire at the end of the vehicle opposite the end you're raising. Chock both wheels.

To lift the vehicle, first position purpose-made wheel chocks behind the tires at the end of the vehicle opposite the end that will be first lifted. In other words, if you're lifting the front, put the chocks behind the rear tires. The chocks should be positioned to prevent the vehicle from rolling away from the jack. Wheel chocks should be designed so that most of the inclined surface contacts the

the tire. Wheel chocks are far superior to using boards, rocks, chunks of concrete, or some other substitute. Those substitutes only come in contact with the tire at one point on its surface. Consequently, they can easily be pushed out of the way by the tire. Wheel chocks, in contrast, are designed to contact the tire at multiple points on its surface to keep it from rolling. Wheel chocks cost about $10.

After positioning the wheel chocks, set the parking brake, and put the transmission in gear (if a manual transmission) or in "Park" (if an automatic). If the job you'll be performing, such as replacing rear brake pads, requires the parking brake to be disengaged so that the wheel is free to rotate, consider whether you can do that after the vehicle has been placed on jack stands, so that the wheels are immobilized during the lifting process itself.

You will have to position the floor jack under a lift point that will not be used to support the vehicle when it is on the jack stands. Usually, the simplest way to do this is to use the lift points designated for the spare-tire jack or frame contact jack as the locations for the jack stands. Use the lift points designated for a floor jack to raise the car, and then position secondary supports at lift points (if any) designated for a suspension con-

tact hoist. (See "Advance Planning" at the beginning of this Chapter.)

You should be sure to consult the factory shop manual for the lift point locations, but typically the floor-jack lift points will be at the center of a cross-member running across the bottom of the car at the front and another at the back. The spare-tire jack/frame-jack lift points will be at the sides of the car under the rocker panels.

Do not, however, assume that every cross member under the vehicle can be used as a lift point. Merely because across-member looks strong enough doesn't mean it is strong enough, particularly if it is made of an alloy. For example, C5 Corvettes have four similar cross-members under the car, two at the front and two at the back. Of each pair, only one is strong enough to permit lifting with a floor jack. Avoid lifting on any subframe or suspension member that appears to be made of an alloy unless you absolutely know it can bear the load.

It is almost always preferable to lift from the ends of the vehicle, rather than from the sides. Unibody cars will only have two safe lift points to a side, each of which is needed for the jack stands. But even a body-on-frame vehicle is best lifted from the ends because manufacturers often run fuel lines and brake lines

The hockey puck between the jack stand and the jacking point of the car protects the rocker panel from damage that could be caused by the jack stand jaw.

along the interior of side frame rails. These lines can be damaged by a floor jack when lifting from the side.

The "cradle" (sometimes called the "saddle") of a typical floor jack, the part that contacts the car, has teeth that look somewhat like those on a Halloween Jack O' Lantern and are designed to fit around steel frame rails. When using a floor jack, the load should not rest on

Hockey pucks can be used as jacking pads.

Hockey pucks also can be turned into vehicle lift pads, such as these made for a C5 Corvette.

How to Make Your Own Pinch Weld Adapter

If your car has pinch welds running through the spare-tire jack/frame-hoist lifting points, you will need to use an adapter that straddles the pinch weld and fits between the vehicle and the top of the jack stands. Unfortunately, there don't seem to be any that are commercially available for use with jack stands.

But that's not a problem, because you can make adapters from a 4 x 4-inch board that is free of knots. You should be able to make four of them from less than a 1.5-foot long board. For tools, you'll need a saw (preferably a power saw), a chisel, a hammer, and some sandpaper. Do not use anything smaller than a 4 x 4-inch board because it won't be strong enough.

Mark a 4 x 4 to be cut into blocks, but don't cut the blocks. Mark and cut groves in the board.

On the board, measure out four blocks, each about 3.5 inches long. Mark a line across the board at these locations, but don't cut the blocks out, yet. From these marks, measure to the middle of each block and mark the middle. Then measure to the each side of the middle to define the width of the groove that is necessary to straddle the pinch weld on the vehicle. Mark a line at the edges of what will be the groove.

The idea is to cut a groove in the block that will straddle the pinch weld. Exactly how wide and deep that groove needs to be depends on the pinch weld on the car, so you'll have to mea-

Chisel out the wood between the cuts to create the groves that will accommodate the pinch weld.

sure the pinch weld's height and width. When the adapter is straddling the pinch weld, the flat top of the wood block on either side of the groove must rest against a flat surface on the underside of the car to each side of the pinch weld. It's the top of the wood block that takes the car's weight. The groove needs to be deeper than the pinch weld is tall, so that the pinch weld does not rest on the bottom of the groove. The groove needs to be wide enough so that any curvature of the sheet metal at the top of the pinch weld fits inside the groove.

The groove must always run across the grain of the wood. If it were to run parallel to the grain, the block would be more likely to split. For the same reason, the groove should never be cut deeper than one-half the height of the block.

Once you've determined how wide and deep the groove needs to be, secure the wood so that you can cut it. A Black & Decker Workmate or similar portable workbench is ideal for this. But, what's important is that you have a way of holding the board steady while you use both hands to cut it with a circular saw.

Adjust the circular saw blade to the depth that you want for your groove and adjust the angle of the blade so that the groove will be narrower at the bottom than it is at the top. Cutting the groove in something of a "V" shape makes the sides of the groove stronger than if the grooves were cut at right angles and also self-centers the adapter over the groove when you use it.

After you've cut the sides of the groove, use a chisel to remove the wood from the groove. Then cut the blocks out from the board and sand off the rough edges.

What you end up with is a wood block that will straddle the pinch weld and is strong enough to sustain the weight of the vehicle when placed between the jack or jack stand and the car. When you use one of these wood pinch weld adapters, always be sure that the saddle of the jack stand runs across the grain of the wood block to reduce any risk that the block will split. If you should ever detect any sign of a split in one of these pinch weld adapters, discard it and make a new one.

Then cut the board into blocks, and you have blocks that can be used when jacking on a pinch weld.

these teeth; it should rest on the cradle between the teeth.

It may be necessary to protect the car against damage from the floor-jack cradle's teeth and from damage caused by the tops of the jack stands. Polyurethane pads are commercially available to fit any size jack cradle or jack stand. Protech Products, online at protechproducts.net, carries a complete line of both jack pads and stand pads. Jack pads cost from $20 to $30; stand pads about $25 per pair.

But hockey pucks often work as well and are a lot cheaper, at about a dollar each. They can be used as pads inserted between the floor-jack cradle and the jacking location of your vehicle to prevent the cradle's teeth from contacting the sheet metal during lifting.

They can also be used as pads between a jack stand and the car, *provided* that you locate the puck precisely on the jack stand and lower the car carefully and gently, to ensure that the puck will be squeezed at its center. When pressed between a vehicle and a jack stand, however, a properly positioned hockey-puck pad has just enough give to hold itself stably into place on the jack stand saddle.

The frame-hoist lifting points on late-model Corvettes are "shipping slots" under the rocker panels—receptacles that permitted chaining the car down during transport from the factory. Hockey pucks can be modified by inserting a large "eye" screw into the center of each of them so that the eye slides into the slot. Turning the puck then turns the eye per-

pendicular to the slot and retains the puck on the bottom of the car.

On some unibody cars, the designated spare-tire jack/frame-hoist lift points have "pinch welds" running through them. Pinch welds, also known as "panel rails," are two narrow flanges of sheet metal welded together (like upside down praying hands) that run the length of the car directly under the rocker panels. If you put a pinch weld on a jack stand without protecting it, you'll crush the pinch weld.

If the lift point has a pinch weld, an adapter that fits between the jack stand and the car and straddles the pinch weld is necessary. Both Protech Products and The Eastwood Company (online at eastwoodco.com) sell pinch weld adapters designed for use with floor jacks, but there do not appear to be any

Position the jack cradle so that the jaws fully engage the frame member being jacked.

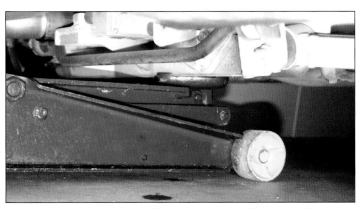

The jack cradle swivels, so it can be arranged in a way that straddles this frame member.

When the jack raises the car, it will naturally crawl on its wheels. It is important that these wheels be able to move as the vehicle is raised.

After the front of the car has been raised and jack stands placed under the side rails behind each rear wheel, at the factory designated jacking point, the rear is raised.

commercially available pinch weld adapters for jack stands. Fortunately, you can make your own pinch weld adapters from wood blocks. The instructions are in Sidebar: "How to Make Your Own Pinch Weld Adapter."

The process of lifting the vehicle is basic. Lift one end with the floor jack sufficiently to locate the jack stands at the designated spare-tire/frame-hoist lift points for that end of the car. Then gently and slowly lower the car onto the jack stands. Check the stands to be sure they are properly positioned at the lift points before lowering the vehicle that last one-half inch that loads the jack stands. If you are going to lift both ends of the vehicle, you'll need to remove the floor jack and repeat the process at the other end.

When positioning the floor jack, raise the cradle to the car and check to be sure it is positioned properly before actually lifting the car. Also, be absolutely sure nothing will interfere with the jack's wheels being able to turn and move. As the car is lifted, the jack must be able to move forward in order to compensate for the change in cradle location relative to the length of the jack body. In other words, the cradle starts at the end of the jack, but when it is fully raised it is in the middle of the jack. Since the car won't move, the floor jack must be able to move as it lifts.

Some cars must always be lifted first at the front and cannot be lifted only at the back. Sports cars, such as late-model Corvettes, often have so little ground clearance under the nose that lifting from the back without first lifting the front will push the nose into the pavement. Advice on how to lift low-clearance vehicles is located in the sidebar titled: "How To Lift Cars With Very Low Ground Clearance" available through this book's page at cartechbooks.com.

When you have lifted the vehicle, place your secondary supports and then give it a good push. Do not push so hard that you actually try to knock the vehicle off the stands, but hard enough that you'll be able to feel it if there is any give, or any sense of instability or shift.

Using a floor jack and jack stands, you can easily lift a vehicle in your garage, where it is convenient to your shop tools and sheltered from the weather. You need only enough surrounding space to be able to pump the floor-jack handle.

Lowering the Vehicle

When lowering the vehicle, position the jack so that the cradle will seat properly as it takes the vehicle's weight. If you can't see, feel around the cradle with your fingers to ensure that the cradle is positioned correctly.

It might seem that lowering the vehicle is merely the reverse of lifting it, and that's basically true. However, there are several precautions that should be emphasized. First, double-check that you've pulled everything out from under the vehicle before you start to lower it, *including* the secondary supports.

Second, double-check that the parking brake is engaged before lowering the vehicle and that the chocks are still tight against the tires. If you've raised both ends of the vehicle, chock the tires on the first end that you lower; you need to be sure that the vehicle cannot roll as it is lowered. The floor jack has wheels, so the vehicle can roll while it is still on the floor jack if the vehicle's wheels are not immobilized.

Third, be sure the jack handle is lowered far enough that the bodywork of the vehicle will not hit it as the car descends. Check that the jack stands have been moved far enough away that it won't hit them, either.

Fourth, if you've had the wheels off, remember to finish tightening the lug nuts to the factory specifications once the car is on the ground. If you've had a wheel off the car, it's remarkably easy to forget this last step and there's no visible reminder. Always finish tightening lug nuts to factory specifications with a torque wrench. It may seem that this is overly particular, but unevenly tightened lug nuts can distort a brake disc sufficiently to create excessive heat in spots, leading to warped brake rotors.

Jack stands are then placed under the rear side rail jacking points, just ahead of the rear wheels. The vehicle is completely supported by the jack stands once the floor jack is removed.

When returning the vehicle to the ground, be careful lining up the floor jack under the jacking point.

ENGINE LUBRICATION

SELECTING AND CHANGING THE OIL AND FILTER

The first step in changing the oil is knowing when to do it. There are many people who believe that the oil and filter should be changed every 3,000 miles. In a survey of professional mechanics conducted by Valvoline in 2006, 60% of them recommended an oil change every 3,000 miles. Only 2% recommended going more than 5,000 miles before changing the oil. Yet, no automobile manufacturer concurs with those opinions.

In the 1950s, 3,000 miles was the typical oil change interval. But that was before multi-viscosity detergent motor oils became common. We've come a long way since then, and both modern engines and modern oils are far better engineered than they were even a decade ago. Changing the oil every 3,000 miles is seldom necessary today.

Many late model cars have an "oil life monitor," a display that shows the "oil life" remaining and tells you when it's time to change the oil. Rather than recommending a specific mileage interval for oil changes, automobile manufacturers recommend changing the oil when the oil life monitor says it's time. These monitors are programmed to calculate the remaining life of the oil based on the mileage and speeds driven, the amount of time idling, engine temperatures, and RPM.

Some car owners are suspicious of oil life monitors. They believe auto manufacturers are prone to specifying long oil change intervals to artificially lower maintenance costs and, consequently, doubt that monitors are reliable. The truth is actually the opposite: manufacturers developed the monitors to lower warranty claims for engine damage caused by sludge and deposits. Rather than recommend oil changes based only on miles driven, oil change monitors allowed auto manufacturers to recommend an oil change based on how the specific car was actually being driven. If your car has an oil life monitor, you should change the oil when it tells you to change the oil.

If your car does not have an oil life monitor, then you need to determine whether your driving fits the definition of "severe service." When the auto manufacturer recommends oil changes by mileage interval, there are usually two categories: normal driving, and "severe service." Check how that term is defined in your owner's manual, but it customarily refers to driving in muddy or dusty conditions, driving where temperatures are very hot, driving short distances in cold weather, and towing. If you do fit the severe service category, then you are one of the minority who should be changing the oil every 3,000

miles. If not, you should feel safe in following the manufacturer's recommendation.

The manufacturer's oil-change recommendation, whether established by a monitor or mileage interval, assumes that you use oil of the proper quality and viscosity. The owner's manual will specify the standards that the oil used in your car must meet. See Sidebar: "Decoding the Oil Label." Regardless of how you decide when it is time to change the oil, you should always replace the oil filter at the same time.

Parts for this job

Oil
Oil filter

Tools for this job

Oil filter wrench
Oil drain pan
Breaker bar
Socket and any necessary adapter
Socket ratchet or box end wrench
Torque wrench
Old newspapers
Mechanic's nitrile rubber gloves
Lint-free rag
Paper towels or shop towels
Empty gallon milk jugs or
    similar containers

Time for this job

As with any auto job, don't do this one the first time when you've got a deadline. Counting the time to lift the car and to clean up afterward, figure it will take at least an hour.

Advance Planning

Buy the oil. Look up the proper oil viscosity in the vehicle owner's manual. Decide whether to get synthetic or conventional oil (see Sidebar: "The Best Oil…"). Check also for any other oil requirements, such as meeting API, ISLAC, ACEA, or specific manufacturer standards, such as GM, MB, MS, LL, or WSS designations (see sidebar below). Oil in one five-quart container is usually less expensive than buying the same quantity in individual quarts.

The owner's manual will also specify the part number for the oil filter. That part number will apply only to filters made or used by the vehicle manufacturer. Filters made by different manufacturers will have different part numbers. However, any store that sells filters can tell you which one you need. Most have a book or electronic display located near the filter display that cross-references parts numbers to the original equipment part number. Filters are not all the same. There are substantial differences in quality.

Last, but not least, you'll need to know the torque specification for the oil pan drain bolt. That's probably not in your owner's manual, but it is in the fac-

Decoding the Oil Label

The label on the oil bottle has lots of useful information, but not enough space to explain it all. Here's what it means:

"Viscosity," sometimes referred to as the "weight" of oil, refers to the oil's thickness and its ability to flow at various temperatures. Oil is affected by heat and cold. Light oils flow better at cold temperatures, but are less able to withstand high temperatures and may then become too thin to maintain lubrication. Oils with more thickness maintain lubrication better at high temperatures, but thicken when cold and may not flow well enough to provide lubrication.

A system, known as standard J300, has been devised by the Society of Automotive Engineers (SAE) to classify oils by viscosity. The higher the number, the thicker the oil. So, a "30 weight" oil is thicker than a "10 weight." Oils that have only one SAE number, such as "SAE 30," are called "straight grade" oils and are today uncommon.

The American Petroleum Institute "starburst" certifies oil is suitable for gasoline engines. Also check for the API service standard on the oil container.

This is the API "donut" gives the oil's viscosity and states which API service standards are met by the oil.

"Multi-viscosity" oils are chemically modified to combine the best attributes of both low- and high-viscosity oils into one oil that flows well when cold, but still lubricates well when hot (see the sidebar that discusses oil filters) The SAE classification of multi-viscosity oils uses two numbers and the letter "W" (for example: SAE 5W-30"). The first number indicates how the oil performs when cold and the second indicates how it performs when hot. The "W" stands for "winter." So, a "5W-30" motor oil has the same properties at 30 degrees Celsius ("C") as a 5-weight oil and the same properties at 100 degrees C as a 30-weight oil.

This system is used for classifying all multi-viscosity oils. However, the cold temperature used by the standard varies with cold temperature viscosity: 0W is measured at −35 degrees C, 5W is measured at −30 degrees C, 10W at −25 degrees C, and 15W at −20 degrees C. The cold temperature used changes with the viscosity because viscosity is not linear. In other words, a 10W-30 oil does not have twice the viscosity when cold as a 5W-30 oil. Rather, the classification system is empirical: it is based on comparing an oil's cold temperature performance to that of a straight-grade oil of a specific viscosity at the same temperature. To make it meaningful, the temperature at which that comparison is made must drop as viscosity is lowered. A 5-weight oil will function at a much colder temperature than a 30-weight. So, to make a meaningful comparison to the cold performance of a 5-weight oil, the temperature at which the comparison is made must be correspondingly colder.

There are also some emblems on the typical oil-bottle label. The American Petroleum Institute (API) certifies that oil is suitable for use in gasoline engines by a "starburst" emblem on the oil label. It also issues API "service standards" specifying minimum properties of motor oil. "API Service SM" is the current standard. The API "donut," an emblem of two concentric circles with a horizontal line dividing the top and bottom, states the API

Continued on page 29

Decoding the Oil Label CONTINUED

service standard at the top, the SAE viscosity in the center, and may state "energy conserving" at the bottom. "Energy conserving" oils have additives designed to very slightly improve fuel economy in comparison to an oil used as a standard. The term is only applied to lower-viscosity multi-grade oil. Though formerly a separate standard, it is now included in the SM service standards. So any oil that meets API service standard SM also will be energy conserving.

API service standards are revised periodically. The second letter of the standard is alphabetical, so that the SM standard supersedes SL, etc. New standards always incorporate the requirements of the old ones, so oil meeting the current SM standard can be used in a car for which SJ or SL was originally specified.

ILSAC GF-4 is the current standard set by the International Lubricant and Standardization Committee, superseding ILSAC GF-3. The ILSAC combines representatives of the major American and Japanese automobile manufacturers with those from the oil companies. Standards set by the ILSAC are more exacting than API service standards.

The European Automobile Constructors Association, known as the ACEA (the acronym corresponds to the French spelling), sets its own standards. A3 is the current ACEA standard for high-performance motor oil for gasoline engines. Unlike API and ILSAC standards, ACEA standards are not consecutive: A1 and A5 standards are different than A3, and A5 does not supersede A3.

Many automobile manufacturers, including BMW (LL, for Long Life), Daimler-Chrysler (MS), Ford (WSS), General Motors (GM), Mercedes-Benz (MB), and Volkswagen (VW), have established their own specifications for oil to be used in their vehicles. These standards cover lubrication, but can also serve other purposes, such as specifying additives that protect emissions equipment. Particularly with synthetic oils, the label may state that the oil meets certain manufacturer standards. However, to get a complete list of manufacturer standards met by a specific motor oil, go to the oil company's website and locate the product data sheet. That sheet will list all of the standards, including manufacturer's standards, met by each motor oil produced by that oil company. So, read the fine print.

---

tory shop manual. Of course, you can just tighten the drain bolt by feel and probably get away with it, but that's not doing the job right. If you don't have the factory manual, your local library may have it or may have another reference that can provide the proper torque value.

Hazard Warning

To get at the oil drain bolt and oil filter, you'll likely need to lift at least one end of the vehicle. There's a temptation just to lift it with a floor jack and reach under it. It's only going to take a minute, right?

Don't. Never get under a car supported by a floor jack or by the car's spare-tire jack. Floor jacks are hydraulic cylinders and can fail without warning. They even fail during NASCAR races, which is why pit crews don't get under a race car until it's on jack stands. Every owner's manual warns against getting under a car supported by the spare-tire jack. They're lightly constructed and unstable. See Chapter 2 for the proper procedure for lifting the car.

Let's do it

Changing oil is simple: drain the old oil, remove the old filter, install the new filter, and fill the crankcase with new oil. Basically, that's it. There are a few nuances, however.

Oil pans are designed with baffles to prevent oil in the pan from sloshing away from the oil pump pickup during cornering, braking, and acceleration. In some cars, if the car isn't level when the oil is drained, the baffles can trap old oil in the pan.

For that reason, it's best to drain the oil while the car is level, at least the first time. If you lift only one end of the car, you should lower it back to the ground while it's still draining to allow any remaining oil to escape. If nothing further drains out when you do that, you can omit this step next time.

Warm oil flows better than cold oil, so drain the oil when it's warm. Do not drain the oil when it is too hot to handle comfortably.

Changing the oil and filter without

getting your hands covered with old oil is impossible. Mechanic's nitrile rubber gloves, which look like surgeon's gloves but aren't sterile, are available at any auto parts store. They allow you to keep your hands clean while still preserving the tactile sensation of working barehanded. They're perfect for this job. When you're done, you just throw them away.

The old oil can be drained into any pan large enough to hold it. However, plastic oil drain pans specifically designed

A proper oil drain pan minimizes the mess and makes disposing of the old oil easier—just pour it into the milk jugs and take it to the recycling center. But put newspapers down anyway.

---

for this job are inexpensive and a lot easier to empty than a foil roasting pan from the supermarket; they're not much more expensive, either. Drain pans have a top that screws off to open the entire pan to catch the draining oil. Then you put the top back on and empty the oil through the pour spout.

It also makes sense to cover the area under the engine with old newspapers. Oil that drips or spills onto the driveway or garage floor could cause you to take a spill.

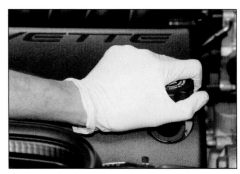

The required oil viscosity is usually specified on the oil filler cap. Loosening the oil filler cap allows air into the engine, which helps drain the old oil. But leave the cap over the fill opening so dirt doesn't get inside the engine.

Start by loosening the oil filler cap, located on the top of the engine. Loosen it, but don't remove it. Loosening it lets air flow freely into the system, so the oil drains faster. Keeping the cap in place is a safeguard against something falling through the oil fill hole and into the engine. Remember Murphy's Law; if it can happen, it will happen.

This is the oil drain plug. On some cars, the drain plug is at the rear of the oil pan. On this car, a C5 Corvette, it is located at the front.

Then remove the oil drain plug bolt. If you are lucky enough to have a C6 Corvette Z06, there are two of them. But, for the rest of us, there's only one.

Loosen the drain plug with a socket and breaker bar, applying even pressure and keeping the wrench straight. Many oil pans on modern cars are aluminum, so apply gradual pressure to prevent damage to the threads.

The oil drain bolt is located at the front or rear of the oil pan, and is usually angled upward from the bolt toward the pan. It is very likely that using a breaker bar will be required loosen it, especially if the last person to change the oil didn't use a torque wrench when tightening it. You will probably need a socket adapter to permit using a 1/2-inch drive breaker bar with the socket that fits the drain bolt, which is probably a 3/8-inch drive socket. Loosen the bolt, but don't remove it.

If someone before you has rounded off the bolt head so that a wrench won't grip it, you can use Vice-Grips. Replace a damaged bolt as soon as possible because

The drain plug is holding back more than a gallon of oil. When the oil starts flowing out, it can knock the very slippery drain plug out of your fingers.

you won't be able to tighten it properly with a torque wrench if the head is rounded off.

Verify that the drain pan is positioned where it will catch the draining oil. When the drain bolt is first removed, the oil flow will arch outward. As the flow lessens, the oil will drip straight down. You may need to reposition the drain pan during the process.

Unscrew the loosened drain bolt by hand. When you remove the bolt, hold on to it. A drain bolt covered with oil has a unique gravitational downward pull, especially when that first spurt of oil

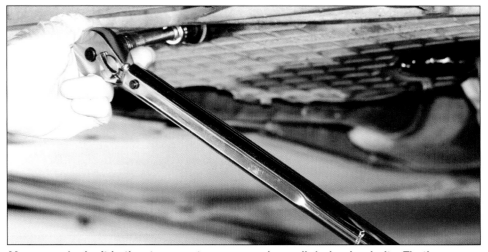

Many people don't bother to use a torque wrench on oil drain plug bolts. That's a mistake, because over tightening the drain plug bolt can damage the oil pan threads. It also makes it unnecessarily hard to remove it at the next oil change.

The Best Oil...

What's the best oil? Four properties are critical to the performance of oil in your car: pour point, shear strength, oxidation rate, and viscosity index.

Pour point is the temperature below which oil will not pour out of a standard container within a specified time. Shear strength is the measure of the oil's ability to keep moving parts from actually touching each other at high temperatures and pressures. Oxidation rate measures how rapidly the molecules in the oil burn and fragment, which diminishes lubricating ability and creates sludge. Viscosity index (VI) measures resistance to viscosity change as temperature changes. A high VI number is better than a low one, because it means less viscosity change.

Synthetic oil outperforms conventional oil in all of these measures. Here's why:

The ideal oil is built from uniformly sized molecules. When molecular sizes vary—which they do in conventional oil—pressure and heat burn the smaller molecules and fragment the bigger ones, ultimately creating varnish and sludge. To offset this, conventional oils require additives. To create multi-viscosity oils, polymer viscosity index improvers (VIIs) must be added to conventional oil. These polymers uncoil as the oil heats, reducing the oil's natural tendency to thin out. But VIIs are destroyed by pressure and high temperature. That means the same conditions that degrade oil's lubricating ability also reduce its resistance to viscosity change.

The size of molecules in synthetic oil is much more uniform than the molecules of conventional oil. That's why synthetic oil pours better when cold, handles high heat and pressure better, and maintains viscosity better. Synthetic oil also lasts longer than conventional oil, both because its molecular structure better resists oil breakdown and because it requires fewer additives. The best oil, therefore, is synthetic oil.

What's the best synthetic oil? To answer that question, review the product data sheets. Every oil company posts on its website a product data sheet for each oil they produce. It lists all the data discussed here, so you can compare competing brands according to the criteria you consider most important.

One other thing: don't use aftermarket oil additives. Aftermarket additives are combinations of detergents, solvents, friction reducers, zinc compounds, and viscosity thickeners. Many of these are already included in multi-viscosity oil, so you already have them. Most will lower the VI number by making the oil heavier, which will also increase oxidation. None will prevent oil breakdown. Spend your money on a better oil filter, instead.

comes draining out. So, try not to drop it. Wipe the drain bolt off with a clean lint-free rag and set it aside someplace that is clean.

Allow plenty of time for the old oil to drain out. The baffles inside the engine oil pan can lengthen the time it takes for oil to drain completely. For this reason, some performance cars have minimum recommended drain times. On late model Corvettes, for example, it is considered so important that the recommended drain time is actually cast into the alloy engine-oil pan.

Once the old oil has completely drained, wipe off the area around the drain hole with a clean lint-free rag. Reinstall the drain bolt and finger tighten it. Then tighten the drain bolt to the auto manufacturer's specification using a torque wrench.

Using a torque wrench to tighten the drain bolt may seem like an unnecessary precaution, but there is a reason for it. On many modern cars, the engine oil pan is made of aluminum or some other relatively soft alloy. The drain plug, however, is steel. You can strip the threads out of the oil pan if you over tighten the drain plug. Moreover, aluminum and steel expand at different rates when heated. An over-tightened drain plug stresses the aluminum during these cycles. If the aluminum threads aren't stripped when the steel drain plug is over-tightened, they might strip when it is removed. If you must tighten the drain plug bolt without a torque wrench or you don't know the specified torque, be gentle.

It is now time to remove the oil filter. You may just be able to unscrew it by hand, but you probably will need to use an oil filter wrench to loosen it. There seem to be an almost infinite variety of oil filter wrenches on the market. For help with this, see Sidebar: "Selecting the Perfect Oil Filter Wrench."

If the oil filter is on so tightly that it just won't budge, take a piece of large grit sandpaper and fold it in half so that the grit is exposed on both sides. Put the sandpaper between the filter and a band-style wrench or just twist the filter with your hand while holding the sandpaper against the filter. If all else fails, you can always resort to an old mechanic's trick: hammer a big screwdriver into the side of the old filter, and twist it off with that. Before removing the oil filter, position the drain pan underneath it.

Once you have the filter loosened, unscrew it the rest of the way with your hand. As the filter is unscrewed to the point that it can be removed, it will dump whatever oil was directly above it on your hand. If this catches you by surprise, you will let the now slippery filter drop from your hand and fall into the drain pan with a very big splash. So, be prepared.

Continued on page 34

...Deserves the Best Filter

The best oil filter captures very small impurities without impeding oil flow and it does so for a relatively long period of time. It doesn't matter how long your oil can last if your filter can't be effective for just as long.

If you hold an oil filter in your hand and look at its base (the part that screws up against the engine), you'll see holes. Oil flows from the engine into the filter through the smaller outer holes and flows back into the engine through the big hole in the center. Inside, going from the top to the bottom of the filter, is the element, which is made of pleated cellulose and polyester paper or pleated synthetic fiber media. When oil enters the filter, it flows between the filter housing and the filter element, through the filter element into the center of the filter, and then back into the engine.

The oil filter on the right, which uses synthetic fiber to filter particles from the oil, cost about $5 more than the filter on the left, which uses paper.

Oil filter performance is measured by standardized test procedures established by the SAE, including "single pass efficiency" and "multiple pass efficiency." Most oil filter manufacturers list one or both of these, expressed as a percentage, on the filter packaging. But the numbers can mislead the uninitiated. Better efficiency is important, but the filter must also have the capacity and durability necessary to maintain efficiency for the life of the oil. A cheap filter with high efficiency numbers may plug up quickly. If the filter element then collapses under oil pressure, the engine can starve for oil, pieces of the element can get into the engine, and the filter housing can burst.

Studies show that most engine wear is caused by the smallest particles in the oil (less than 20 microns in size) immediately after start-up, when oil pressure is low. These particles evade filtration by paper element oil filters because a paper element sufficiently "efficient" to trap them would also quickly clog.

The best oil filters use synthetic fibers, rather than paper, as the filtering medium. Because synthetic fiber elements have more passages than paper elements, they trap more and finer particles while still maintaining oil flow and filter longevity.

An average paper element oil filter, such as the orange one pictured, costs seven or eight dollars. For an extra five dollars, you can buy a top-of-the-line synthetic fiber filter, like the other one pictured here. If you're using synthetic oil, you should be using a synthetic fiber oil filter.

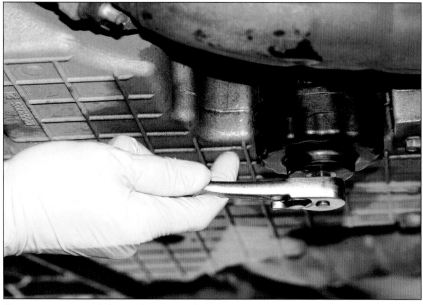

A cap-type wrench is made to match a specific brand and size of oil filter. It fits onto a socket ratchet or breaker bar.

Whatever wrench you choose; use it only to loosen the filter. Remove it with your hands.

While you wait for the oil to drain, "prime" the new filter by filling it with fresh oil. That way, oil flows into the engine as soon as it is started.

Selecting the Perfect Oil Filter Wrench

The perfect oil filter wrench is the Holy Grail of auto mechanics. The variety of oil filter wrenches seems almost limitless, but the three most commonly available types are band-style wrenches, cap-style wrenches, and pliers-style wrenches.

Band-style wrenches are the most popular. They have a band that closes around the filter as the handle is levered outward. The handle swivels up and down, so the filter can be turned with the handle at an angle. This makes it easier to fit the wrench into tight spaces around an oil filter. Also, if you have to, you can tighten an oil filter with one. Yes, theoretically, you should hand-tighten an oil filter. That theory, however, assumes you didn't get oil on the outside of the filter while priming it or installing it.

Band-style wrenches are manufactured in different sizes, but most stores carry only a large size. That can be a problem; if it is too big, it may be difficult to position it to close enough to grip the filter. KD Tools (online at kd-tools.com) makes band-style oil filter wrenches in four sizes and Sears sells the set for under $50. Or, you can buy them individually for less than $15 on the Internet (search "KD" and "oil filter wrench"). In some instances, a strap wrench (similar to a band-style) will also remove an oil filter, if there is enough room for the handle to be perpendicular to the filter.

Cap-style wrenches fit over the filter end and are designed to accept a socket ratchet. They are, in essence, big sockets designed for an oil filter. The cheap ones are made of plastic. The better cap-style wrenches are metal. These wrenches have two drawbacks. First, they are brand-specific and filter-specific. The wrench that works on the Fram filter for the Chrysler Town & Country won't fit the AC filter on the Chevrolet Suburban, because the filter ends that fit into the wrench are of different sizes and shapes. Second, they are prone to slipping, particularly the ones made of plastic.

A variation of the cap-style wrench is the three jaw wrench. Like the cap-style wrench, the three jaw wrench fits over the end of the filter and is designed to be turned by a socket ratchet. The difference is that it has three jaws, which progressively tighten around the filter end as the wrench is turned. Three jaw wrenches are usually not stocked by auto parts stores, and Sears doesn't sell them. However, tool dealers sell them on the Internet (search "three jaw oil filter wrench").

The third choice is the pliers-style wrench, also called an adjustable jaw wrench. These look much like a giant Channel-Lock tool with the pliers end shaped to fit around the filter body. They have excellent grip; if you can reach the filter, you can remove it. The problem with these wrenches is clearance; on some cars there isn't enough room around the filter for the jaws.

There may never be the perfect oil filter wrench. Fortunately, they typically cost only $5 to $10, so you can afford to have more than one.

Lightly coat the rubber gasket on the base of the oil filter with fresh oil, so that it will seal better when installed.

This is what the oil filter screws onto. Wipe it clean with a lint-free rag and make sure that no bits of the old filter gasket are stuck to it.

Once it has been removed, empty the oil filter into the drain pan. Even after you've dumped it out, the filter will still retain oil because it has an internal valve designed to keep oil from flowing backward into the engine. Hold the filter with the base upright to allow it to refill with the trapped oil, and then dump it again; do that several times and you'll get most of the oil out. To completely drain the old filter, which you should do before disposing of it, puncture it at the rounded end.

Now examine the rubber gasket on the old filter to see if the gasket is intact. If it is not, then some of the gasket material has stuck to smooth face of the engine block where the filter installs. That residue will have to be removed to prevent an oil leak. It may not be easy to see the face of the filter mount on the engine block, so examining the gasket on the old filter is a simple way to check it. Set the old filter aside, open end up.

Remove the dipstick, unless your car is one of the few that now use electronic sensors instead of a dipstick. Wipe the dipstick clean, and reinsert it.

If the oil filter's installed position is vertical, "prime" the new filter by filling it with oil before installation. This will speed delivery of oil to the engine on start-up. Fill the filter by turning it with the open end up and setting it in its own box. Let the box support the filter as you pour the oil into it. If the filter installs in a horizontal position or at an angle, omit this step.

Though some of the highest-quality oil filters have self-lubricating gaskets, the rubber gasket around the base should be lubricated on all other filters. Coat the gasket lightly with motor oil before the filter is installed. Just dip your fingertip in clean oil and rub it once around the gasket.

Using a clean lint-free cloth, wipe off any old oil that remains on the smooth surface of the engine against which the oil filter presses when it is installed. If you can't see that surface, run your finger over it to feel any irregularities. If any old gasket has stuck to this surface, work it off with a lint-free cloth dipped in WD-40 or similar solvent. Don't use a screwdriver or metal blade; the scratch you make will become an oil leak.

Hand-tighten the new filter until the gasket comes into contact with the engine, and then turn it another 3/4 of a turn. Over tightening the filter can actually cause leaks.

Screw the new filter into place, by hand. When the gasket begins to touch the smooth engine surface, note the position of the filter and then turn it an additional 3/4 turn, unless the filter manufacturer specifies differently. This should be possible to do by hand, but you can use a band-type filter wrench if the filter is slippery.

Do not over-tighten the filter. Not only will that make it much harder to remove at the next oil change, but it can distort the shape of the gasket, which will cause leaks. Lower the car to the ground, following the procedures discussed in Chapter 2.

The air inside the engine has to escape as the oil is poured in, so pour slowly. Check the dipstick before adding the last half-quart.

Remove the oil filler cap, insert a funnel into the oil fill hole, and pour new oil into the engine. Don't be in a hurry. Gravity has to carry the oil through the engine to the oil pan. When you have all but about a quart of the stated capacity poured in, check the dipstick. If, despite your best efforts, any old oil did remain in the engine, a full fill would overfill it. Then slowly top off to the "full" mark, and replace the oil fill cap.

Verify the oil level with the dipstick. Don't forget to write down the mileage or reset the car's oil life monitor, so that you'll know when it's time to do this again.

Start the engine, let it idle for a few minutes and then shut it off. The oil pump pressure will work any trapped air out, and the oil level may drop a bit. Check the dipstick again and add oil as needed to bring the level to "full."

The only thing remaining is to clean up and recycle. Pour the old oil into a container—empty milk jugs work perfectly—so that you can take it for recycling.

Most communities require recycling used motor oil and have collection sites. Also, many auto parts stores accept used oil for recycling. If you don't know of a recycling collection point, you can find one on the American Petroleum Institute's recycling website at earth911.org.

Most communities do not require recycling used oil filters, so usually you can throw that in the trash. The Filter Manufacturer's Council provides access to state-by-state filter recycling regulations online at filtercouncil.org, but the filter should be completely drained before disposing of it. To do that, the Environmental Protection Agency recommends punching a hole through the filter's rounded end or through the rubber anti-drain valve at the screw-on end (it's the rubber you see through the little holes), and then draining the filter for 12 hours at 60 degrees F or warmer.

The final step is to reset the oil life monitor following the directions specified in the owner's manual. If the car doesn't have an oil life monitor, make a note of the mileage on a piece of paper and keep it in the glove compartment. That way, you'll know when it's time to do it again.

CHAPTER 4

THE MODERN IGNITION SYSTEM
DISTRIBUTORLESS IGNITION SYSTEMS, SELECTING AND REPLACING SPARK PLUGS AND DIAGNOSING COIL FAULTS

The ignition system fires the spark plugs. It takes 12 volts from the battery, transforms it into high voltage in the "ignition coil" (or coils), and then distributes it to fire the spark plugs. How all of this works is explained in the Sidebars, "Mechanical, Electronic, and Distributorless Ignition Systems," and "The Coil: The Heart of the Ignition System."

Ignition systems once required regular and frequent maintenance. But modern vehicles use "distributorless ignition systems" that require only occasional replacement of the spark plugs. Moreover, many manufacturers specify a 100,000-mile replacement interval for spark plugs. So, in modern cars, replacing the spark plugs is the only routine maintenance needed for the ignition system; but it is, nonetheless, needed.

Spark plug electrodes erode with use, increasing the distance between the center and side electrodes. That increases electrical resistance, weakens the spark, and increases the voltage in the spark plug wires. The result is diminished performance and fuel economy.

Think of a hose with a nozzle at the end. Reduce the size of the opening and the volume of water emitted by the hose decreases while pressure in the hose rises. Electrical resistance caused by an increased spark plug gap is the same concept. There is more information on this in Sidebar: "Anatomy of a Spark Plug."

Because modern distributorless ignition systems use very high voltages, they will fire worn spark plugs. But the engine will not perform as well with worn plugs as it will with new ones. Even platinum-tipped park plugs are likely to have significant electrode erosion by 50,000 miles Though you may not notice the resulting gradual loss of power, you'll feel the difference the first time you drive the car after replacing them.

Parts for this job

Spark plugs
Anti-seize compound
    (for spark plugs)
Dielectric grease

Tools for this job

Spark plug socket
Breaker bar
Socket extensions, as required
U-joint socket connector or
    flex-drive connector (if needed)
Socket ratchet
Torque wrench (ft-lb or in-lb;
    see text)
Spark plug gap gauge and
    gapping tool
Can of compressed air
    (computer keyboard cleaner)
Fender cover
Computer memory saver
    (if applicable)

Time for this job

How long it will take to do job depends entirely upon how difficult it is to access the spark plugs. This can be an easy and quick job or it can make you want to rethink the entire concept of working on your own car. So, the first time, pick a day when you don't have to

Mechanical, Electronic, and Distributorless Ignition Systems

There are three types of ignition systems: "mechanical," "electronic," and "distributorless" (DIS). Almost every modern car uses a distributorless ignition system.

Many books and magazine articles fail to distinguish between the systems, which can cause confusion because they are very different.

A mechanical system uses a "distributor" containing "breaker points" and a "rotor" to send the coil's current to the individual spark plugs. In a distributor, lobes on a shaft turned by a camshaft at 1/4 engine speed would push open a spring-loaded electrical contact, called breaker points, when a spark plug was to fire. This would interrupt current flow to ground in the coil and create the current required to fire the spark plug. A cable from the coil went to the center of the cap of the distributor, where it made contact with a "rotor," i.e., a rotary switch turned by the distributor shaft. When the breaker points opened, current flowed from the coil to this rotary switch and from it, as the rotor turned, to each of the contacts for the spark plug cables, firing the spark plugs in sequence.

These systems were used for over 50 years, up until the late 1960s. While simple, they were high maintenance: a "tune-up" to replace the "plugs and points" was routine about every 12,000 miles.

Electrical ignition systems are very similar to the mechanical system, except they substitute electronic, optical, or magnetic switches for the breaker points. There is still a distributor, rotor, and distributor cap, so there remain a number of moving parts that can wear. But the absence of breaker points reduces the level of required maintenance. These systems were common in the 1970s and 1980s.

Distributorless systems were introduced in the early 1990s and are common in modern vehicles. As the name implies, the distributor—together with all of its moving parts—is eliminated. All of the functions required to fire a spark plug are controlled by a computer.

A spark plug must be fired before the piston reaches the top of its upward travel in the cylinder to ensure that the "flame front"—the point furthest from the spark plug, at which actual combustion has occurred—meets the piston moving in the opposite direction at precisely the right time. This is called the spark "advance." If the spark plug fires too soon, you hear pinging: there hasn't been enough compression and the fuel/air mix explodes, rather than burning very quickly. If the spark plug fires too late, there isn't time for all of the fuel/air mixture to burn before the piston starts to descend. In extreme instances, there is backfiring, because combustion is still occurring when the exhaust valve opens.

Mechanical ignition systems were very limited in how they determined the proper degree of spark advance. They used a combination of engine vacuum from the intake manifold acting on a diaphragm attached to the distributor and centrifugal weights to physically advance the spark by moving the points in relation to the lobes on the distributor shaft. Electronic systems were similar. In effect, these systems calculated spark advance based only on engine speed and load.

In contrast, because the engine management computer fires the coils in a distributorless system, the computer can calculate the proper spark advance based on any factor that is relevant. The factors can include intake air temperature, engine coolant temperature, the density of the air, and many other factors, as well as engine speed and load. It can also adjust spark timing in milliseconds, literally between firing one spark plug and the next. Moreover, by controlling current flow into the coils, it can control the voltage used to fire the spark plugs, minimizing wear on the plugs while simultaneously assuring adequate voltage to the plugs for any given engine load.

use the car again that day, and when there is no pressure on you to get this job done on a deadline.

Advance Planning

You will need to know the vehicle manufacturer's recommended spark plug "gap," i.e., the specified distance between the tips of the center and side electrodes of the spark plug. This may be stated on the "emissions sticker" located in the engine compartment. It may be listed in the owner's manual. Otherwise, it can be found in the factory shop manual or equivalent reference.

Spark plugs must be tightened to the manufacturer's torque specification, so you need to look this up before starting the job. The factory shop manual will, of course, have this information.

It's also a good idea to spend some time in advance under the hood figuring out how to reach each of the spark plugs. Sometimes a component must be loos-ened or removed to gain access to one or more plugs.

You may have a car with a "coil-on-plug" (COP) ignition system—one with a coil or coil assembly located directly on or over the spark plug. If it bolts to the engine block (as opposed to sliding into the spark plug recess or screwing to a bracket), you will need to know the torque specification for these bolts. You will also need to know the factory-specified sequence, if any, for removing and installing them.

The Coil: The Heart of the Ignition System

The ignition coil is the heart of the ignition system. It transforms the 12 volts from the battery into 20,000 or 30,000 volts, even as much as 100,000 volts, at the spark plugs.

In old-style mechanical ignition systems, there would be one coil for the entire engine. In modern distributorless ignition systems, there will be one coil for every two cylinders or one for every cylinder. But, however many coils there are, their function is the same as it used to be: creating the spark at the spark plug.

Essentially, an ignition coil is a transformer. That is, it transforms electricity of one voltage to electricity of another voltage by use of a principle known as Faraday's Law of Induction. It is the same theory used by electrical transmission transformers to get electricity from the generating plant to your house.

An ignition coil consists of two coils of wire, one inside the other, both wound around an iron or steel core. Each loop of wire is called a "winding." The outer coil of wire, which is called the "primary winding," is made of thicker wire with only a few hundred loops, or windings, around the core. The inner coil of wire, the "secondary winding," is made of many thousands of windings of much thinner wire around that same core.

When current flows into the primary winding from the battery, it creates a magnetic field around that winding that encompasses the secondary winding. This creates—"induces," in electrical vernacular—a voltage in the secondary winding and a consequent current flow from it.

How much voltage is created in the secondary winding depends on how many more windings it has than the primary winding. In a typical automotive coil, the primary winding will have several hundred windings; the secondary coil will have 15,000 or more windings. This "steps-up" the voltage in the secondary

winding far above 12 volts. Consequently, the current flow from the secondary winding is high. But it is not high enough to overcome the resistance created by the gap in the spark plug.

So far, this is exactly the same concept your power company uses to "step up" and "step down" electricity as it is routed to your house from the generating plant

The power company, however, tries to avoid voltage spikes. In a car, a voltage spike is intentionally created to fire the spark plug.

When current flow into the primary winding is suddenly cut off, the magnetic field collapses. That collapse creates a voltage spike in both windings, primary and secondary. But the voltage spike in the secondary winding is vastly higher, because the much higher number of windings has already substantially stepped up the voltage.

Voltage is, in essence, the electrical pressure that creates current, current being the flow of electricity through a conductor. The voltage spike in the secondary winding causes a surge of current strong enough to overcome the resistance created by the gap between the spark plug's electrodes, and push electricity across that gap. That is the spark.

So why do they use four, six, or eight coils instead of one? "Saturation." Saturation is the extent to which the magnetic field has built to its potential full force. It takes time for the current flowing into the primary winding to create the magnetic field. More time allows the current to build a stronger magnetic field (i.e., greater saturation). The stronger the magnetic field, the higher the voltage will spike when that field collapses. Using multiple coils permits greater saturation and that makes for a stronger, "hotter" spark.

Hazard Warning

Modern distributorless ignition systems employ much higher voltages than older-style mechanical systems, the kind that used a distributor. Many diagnostic techniques that worked with mechanical ignition systems—for example, checking for spark by holding a spark plug cable an inch or so from the engine while it was running—will cause a massive electrical shock if tried with a distributorless system. Do not attempt to trouble-shoot a distributorless ignition system with the engine running. Also, be sure to disconnect the negative battery cable at the

The Cadillac Northstar V-8 engine presents most of the challenges involved in changing spark plugs: it is a transversely-mounted V-8 engine with aluminum cylinder heads, dual overhead camshafts above the spark plugs, and coil-on-plug ignition.

battery before attempting to remove any component of the ignition system, other than the spark plugs themselves, including coils and coil packs.

Let's do it

Be sure the engine is cold before attempting to remove spark plugs. On many modern cars (and some not-so-modern ones), the cylinder heads are aluminum. The threads on spark plugs, however, are always made of steel. Steel is stronger than aluminum by mass. Steel and aluminum expand at different *Continued on page 41*

Anatomy of a Spark Plug

Spark plugs are commonly thought of merely as the ignition source in an internal combustion engine. In reality, they're a lot more—something of an engineering marvel, in fact.

First, they are a means of sealing the cylinder head against the pressure imposed by compression and ignition of the air/fuel mixture.

Second, but less obviously, spark plugs are an integral part of the engine's cooling system: they draw heat away from the combustion chamber and transfer it to the cylinder head, where it can be further dissipated by the coolant.

Third, spark plugs are an electrical contact. The spark is created as part of a process in which electrical current flows to the vehicle's body ground and back to the battery's negative battery cable through the base of the spark plug and the cylinder head.

And fourth, of course, the spark plug ignites the air/fuel mixture. But, even this obvious task turns out to involve some clever engineering to ensure that the spark lasts long enough and is "hot" enough, i.e., has enough current flow, to do the job.

In their basic construction, all spark plugs are the same. There are, however, variations among spark plugs to accommodate the specific requirements of particular engine and cylinder head designs.

A spark plug is constructed around a steel "center shaft," which is rod that runs from the top of the spark plug to the bottom. At the very top of this shaft is the "terminal," which is the electrical connection point for the spark plug cable's boot.

At the very bottom of that center shaft is the "center electrode." The top of the electrode butts up to the bottom of the center shaft. Center electrodes are usually made of copper surrounded by nickel alloy, but can also have tips made of platinum or iridium attached to them.

The center shaft is surrounded by the "insulator," which runs from the bottom of the terminal into the bottom of the spark plug and extends over the upper portion of the center into the combustion chamber, leaving only the lower part of the center electrode uncovered. Though the insulator appears to be porcelain, it's actually specially made to resist high engine pressures while still conducting heat well.

Between the center shaft and the insulator there is an airtight sealer that also serves to hold the center electrode in place. The part of the insulator that extends into the combustion chamber is called the "insulator leg."

The "housing" surrounds the lower part of the insulator. It is made of steel, threaded at the bottom, and has a hex bolt top. This is what screws into the cylinder head. Many, but not all, spark plugs also have a gasket that surrounds the housing right above the threads and is designed to be crushed between the housing and the cylinder head when the spark plug is installed to assure a tight seal against leakage of combustion gases.

The "ground electrode," sometimes called the "side electrode," is welded to the bottom of the housing and extends under the center electrode, but doesn't touch it. The distance between the two electrodes is the "gap."

Spark plugs also have "resistors." A "resistor" spark plug is not a different design, but simply uses a metal for the center shaft that prevents current flow over the gap from tailing off as current flow subsides. This prevents radio static and radio frequency interference, which is important in cars run by computers. Any quality spark plug will be a resistor spark plug.

Within these basics, there are a number of variations in spark plug design. The extent to which the insulator leg extends into the combustion chamber affects how much heat it will absorb and dissipate, i.e., the plug's "heat range." The longer the insulator leg, the more heat the plug will retain (a "hot" plug); conversely, the shorter the insulator leg, the less retained heat (a "cold" plug). A certain amount of heat is necessary to burn away deposits from the insulator leg and the electrodes. Too much heat, however, can fuse deposits to those surfaces. That's why replacement spark plugs should always have the same heat range as the original equipment spark plugs.

There are also a number of different metals used for electrodes. Iridium spark plugs have a very thin iridium tip welded to the bottom of the center electrode. Platinum plugs have a platinum pad fused to the bottom of the center electrode. So-called "dual platinum" spark plugs also have a corresponding platinum coating on the ground electrode. Conventional spark plugs have a copper center electrode that is coated with nickel alloy.

Additionally, there is variety in the design of the ground electrodes. There are spark plugs that have two ground electrodes, some have a groove cut into the ground electrode, and some that have split the ground electrode into a fork. There are spark plugs with multiple ground electrodes and there are even spark plugs designed for rotary engines in which the bottom of

The anatomy of a spark plug, as described in the text. Though all follow the same basic principles, there are myriad variations in the design and construction of spark plugs.

Anatomy of a Spark Plug CONTINUED

the spark plug housing is extended to act as a 360-degree ground electrode.

Most modern cars use platinum tipped spark plugs as original equipment. There are some cars that have iridium spark plugs as original equipment, either for higher performance due to the stronger electrode material (Corvette) or the increased plug life it allows (certain Toyota models, among others).

When purchasing replacement spark plugs, iridium tipped plugs may be a very good investment, even though they are more expensive than platinum tipped spark plugs. Iridium is a scarce metal that is even harder than platinum. Iridium plugs can stand higher heat and voltage levels and will last longer. On many cars, it is difficult to access at least some of the spark plugs, so the extra cost for iridium plugs is more than offset by longer service life.

In contrast, conventional spark plugs, sometimes called "copper" plugs, are usually not a good choice, even though they are the least expensive. They have a service life that is less than half that of typical platinum-tipped spark plugs.

While upgrading the spark plug tip material is a good idea, switching to a spark plug with a ground electrode of a different design is probably a poor idea, particularly in cars with distributorless ignition systems. The concept underlying multiple or modified ground electrodes is that increasing the electrode

area lowers the electrical resistance created by the gap, so less voltage is needed to fire the spark plug. Back in the day when gasoline contained lead, lead fouling was a problem and increasing electrode area helped by giving the spark more places to which it could jump.

Distributorless ignition systems with multiple coils are designed for spark plugs with a large gap and, consequently, high resistance. That large gap creates a physically longer spark and the higher voltage generated by the coils creates a hotter spark, one that is physically bigger because more current is flowing. Reducing spark plug resistance undermines the design.

You may also hear about spark plug "indexing." This is aligning all of the spark plugs with their electrodes pointing in the same relationship to the intake valves to promote flame travel through the fuel/air mixture. The idea was developed in racing long ago. Even then, it was probably more psychology than science.

Indexing serves no purpose in a modern vehicle's engine. That's because the computer has everything covered. Fuel injection gives engine designers precise control over fuel/air "swirl" (turbulence created within the fuel air mix as it flows into the cylinder). Distributorless ignition systems provide a hot spark, perfectly timed to the engine's needs.

To access any part of the engine, the decorative shroud must be removed. This one is held in place by two small nuts.
Its technical name is the "intake manifold service cover."

With the two nuts removed, the shroud lifts off. This is one of the ways that decorative engine covers are attached.

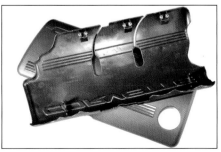

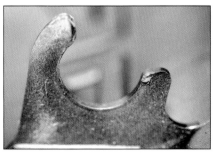

This is the bottom of a fuel rail cover from a Corvette. Like an engine shroud, fuel rail covers are a decorative way to conceal parts of the engine. These install by clipping onto the fuel rails underneath then.

This is one of two clips on each fuel rail cover. The cover pulls off and pushes on. If there are no obvious fasteners holding a decorative engine cover in place, it may simply pull off.

Trouble-Shooting Distributorless Ignition Systems

Problems in distributorless ignition systems divide into two types: it won't start, and, it runs poorly. Proper diagnosis requires the aid of the factory shop manual, which has both the necessary specifications and trouble-shooting procedures specific to the engine. However, here are some general trouble-shooting tips for distributorless systems.

Usually, if a no-start condition is not caused by a battery problem, it is caused by a defective crankshaft position sensor, camshaft position sensor, or a problem with the connections of one of these sensors. If the computer controlling the engine—whether called the "powertrain control module" (PCM), "electronic control module" (ECM), or something similar—does not get a signal from the crankshaft sensor, the computer has no way to know which spark plug to fire or when, so it fires none. For similar reasons, most cars won't start with a bad camshaft sensor (though some go into a "limp home" mode when there's no camshaft sensor signal).

NOTE: Some vehicles have two crankshaft position sensors. Two sensors feed information to the PCM sooner at start-up than one sensor, so the PCM can start firing the spark plugs after only 180 degrees of engine rotation.

However, don't overlook the possibility that the problem is in the sensor connector, not the sensor itself. Many crankshaft position sensors are magnetic, so they attract iron and steel particles that can turn into rust or cause corrosion if they get into the connector. But, regardless of the type of sensor, dirt, grease, or moisture in the connector can cut off power to the sensor or block its signal, as can damage to the wiring from the connector.

If the engine starts, but is "missing" (not firing in a cylinder) either intermittently or regularly, the problem may be the coil. Because distributorless ignition systems have multiple coils, a defective coil will only affect the spark in the cylinders it serves. There are several ways to check this possibility. There is also one way, which will be discussed, that you should never use.

Starting with a cold engine, start it and let it idle for a few minutes. Then feel the temperature of the exhaust manifold at each of the spark plug locations. If the coil isn't firing at all, the manifold near those cylinders will be cold while the remainder of the manifold will be warm. You can also switch the suspect coil with another. If the "miss" moves with the coil, then you've isolated the problem.

Alternatively, you can use a "spark tester" or "spark checker," which is a device that plugs into the spark plug cable and then attaches to a ground on the engine block. With distributorless ignition, you should use only a spark tester specifically designated for use with high energy ignition (HEI) systems. Install the spark tester and then turn over the engine while watching for a spark.

Never, however, check for spark in a distributorless system by holding a spark plug cable near the engine with your hand while cranking. If you do, you are in for a terrible shock, literally. This obsolete technique dates back to mechanical ignition systems generating much less voltage than today's multiple coil distributorless systems.

Coils can also be tested with a digital multimeter (DMM), using the "ohm" (resistance) function. To do this, you connect the multimeter across (i.e., from one to the other) the primary terminals of the coil (which checks the primary winding) and then across the secondary terminals (checking the secondary winding). The lowest range on the DMM should be used when checking resistance in the primary winding, because it should be less than 2 ohms in most vehicles. Resistance in the secondary winding should be much higher, and 6,000 to 30,000 ohms is not unusual.

The factory shop manual will provide specifications for proper resistance in both windings. It will also identify the connector terminals for the primary and secondary windings. If the coil does not meet the resistance specifications, it should be replaced.

You can also test the spark plug wires. Remove the wire. Using the ohm setting on the DMM, put the positive lead on the coil end of the wire and the black lead on the plug end of the wire. Measure the resistance and then check the factory shop manual for the correct specifications. Resistance increases with the length of the conductor, so the manual will likely quote the specification in $k\Omega$ per foot. A resistance below specifications indicates a short circuit; above spec suggests internal deterioration.

Last, but certainly not least, check for diagnostic trouble codes (DTC). A misfire in a cylinder will set at least one DTC, and possibly more than one. The code won't tell you "the coil's bad." But it will tell you what problem occurred and in what system. That can help you isolate the problem or, perhaps, eliminate the coil as a possible cause. See Chapter 10 for more on retrieving and interpreting DTCs.

Sometimes the coil is blamed for problems caused elsewhere. A coil that doesn't create enough voltage can fail to fire a spark plug. But a defective or loose spark plug cable can cause the same result.

The factory manual will identify the trouble codes and detail trouble-shooting procedures specific to the model. It will also provide the service procedures for removal and replacement of defective sensors and coils.

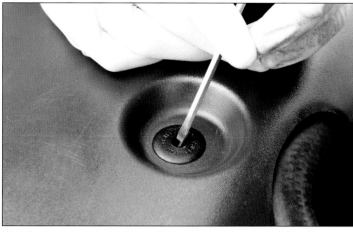

Plastic fasteners hold the radiator shroud in place. The stem must be pushed inward to release it. Generally, fasteners release either by pushing in, like this one, or pulling out.

With the fasteners released and removed, the radiator shroud lifts off. The shroud must be removed to gain access to the lower row of bolts holding the coil rail assembly to the cylinder head.

rates when heated. If it is a contest between the strength of the threads on the spark plug and those of the aluminum cylinder head, it will be the aluminum threads in the head that distort and fail first. An attempt to remove a spark plug when the engine is hot invites irreparable damage to the threads of the aluminum cylinder head.

To get to the spark plugs, it may be necessary to remove an engine shroud or the fuel rail covers. Sometimes these are attached with small hex bolts or Allen bolts. Often they are held in place by small plastic clips molded into the underside of the shroud and are detached by firmly but gently pulling upward. If it is necessary to remove the oil filler cap to lift off the cover, be sure to put the cap back on immediately so that dirt and objects are kept out of the engine. On cars with transverse engines, it also may be necessary to remove the shroud located above the radiator. If a car has a coil-on-plug (COP) ignition system, the coil or coil pack must be removed to access the spark plugs.

Modern "distributorless" ignition systems have multiple coils, one for every two spark plugs or one for every spark plug. These coils are sometimes arranged all in one "coil pack" located on the side of the engine, with spark plug cables running to the spark plugs. In other designs, individual coils will be located directly on the spark plug (COP) or close to the spark plug and a short cable will lead from the coil to the plug ("coil near plug": CNP). Sometimes COP ignition is made part of a coil pack that fits directly over several contiguous spark plugs. In some systems, one coil fires two spark plugs simultaneously; one that is on the compression stroke and another that is on the exhaust stroke. That's called a "wasted spark" system; the spark in the exhaust stroke is wasted.

All distributorless ignition systems are considered "high energy ignition"

Disconnect the negative terminal of the battery before removing the coil rail assembly. Only the negative cable must be removed to break the circuit. In this car, the battery is under the back seat.

The coil rail assembly (this is the bottom) has four individual coils, one for each spark plug, held in one unit. The four metal terminals protruding from it fit into boots that fit over the spark plugs.

(HEI) systems. Spark plugs in high energy ignition systems usually employ a much larger gap than those in old-style mechanical ignition systems. Also, HEI systems carry much higher current through the spark plug cables than mechanical systems. For those reasons, only spark plug gap gauges and spark plug testers designated for HEI use should be used with these systems.

Before disconnecting or removing a coil pack or COP coil, disconnect the negative (i.e., black) battery cable at the battery. Unfortunately, disconnecting the battery can erase your car's radio presets and memory settings and trigger the radio's anti-theft lock. For less than

ten dollars, you can buy an automotive "computer memory saver" that plugs into the cigarette lighter and uses power from a 9-volt battery to save those settings.

After disconnecting the battery, the next step if the car has COP ignition is disconnecting the electrical connector between the coil and the ignition control module. These are usually plastic male and female ends, with a snap clip that holds them together. It is usually disconnected by lifting the snap clip slightly, so that it will clear a tab in the male part of the connector as the parts are separated. There are at least three ways to accomplish this: use your fingers to lift the clip as you pull the connector ends apart; use a small screwdriver to raise it; or, get a specially designed "electrical connector

separator tool" made by Lisle, part number 13120, for less than $10.

Then the COP unit itself must be removed. It may attach to a bracket or it may bolt to the engine block. Some COP units are part of the rubber boot that fits over the spark plug insulator and into the same recess in the cylinder head as the plug. If it is a coil rail assembly, i.e., a coil pack that covers a group of spark plugs as a unit, there may be a factory-specified sequence for removal and reinstallation of the bolts attaching it to the engine. This sequence must be followed, as well as factory-specified torque values for those bolts.

When removing most bolts, after initially loosening it, you can feel what you're doing better by using only the extension and socket.

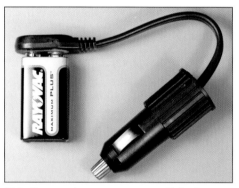

This "computer memory saver" device plugs into the cigarette lighter to preserve radio presents and accessory memory settings when the battery is disconnected.

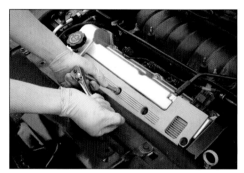

There are eight bolts attaching the coil rail assembly to the cylinder head, which are to be removed and installed in a specific sequence. Every car has repair procedures unique to it, which is why having a factory shop manual is so important.

To remove the electrical connector to the coil rail assembly, depress the plastic tab (in the middle of the picture) and, while holding the tab down, slide the connector apart. Once the tab clears the locking stud on the other end of the connector, it should slide off. Some tabs are designed to lift up to release; some push down.

The bottom row of bolts is located underneath the upper radiator hose, which must be pushed out of the way to reach them. Mounting engines transversely allows auto engineers to use engine compartment space efficiently, but often compromises accessibility.

With all of the bolts removed, the coil rail assembly can be lifted out. The terminals are wedged into the spark plug boots, so it takes a bit of a tug to free it.

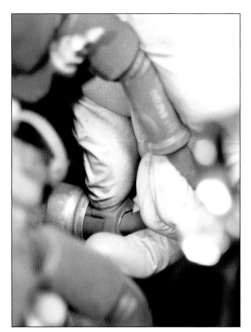

This Corvette engine uses coil-near-plug ignition and has spark plug wires. This is how to remove a spark plug boot: twist the boot (not the wire) as you pull it outward. It may have to twist almost 180° to break loose.

If your car does not have COP ignition, it has spark plug cables. That means you must next remove the spark plug boot, i.e., the end of the cable that covers the spark plug. Some COP systems also use spark plug boots, though without any cable.

Removing the spark plug boot can be a real challenge, especially if the plug is difficult to reach. Engine heat can tightly fuse the rubber boot to the spark plug's

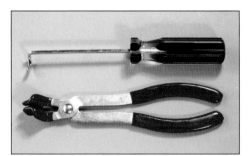

Two of the many types of spark plug boot pullers: one looks like a screwdriver with a bent end, the other is a pliers designed to grasp the boot. There are others. Few work well, and none on more than a handful of vehicles.

porcelain insulator. To remove the boot, twist it on the spark plug insulator a half-turn or so and then pull it upward while continuing to twist. You should be able to feel when it comes unstuck. If the plug cable is short, such as those used on coil-near-plug arrangements, it may help to disconnect the other end so that the entire cable is free to rotate. But twist and pull only on the spark plug boot itself, never on the cable. Twisting or pulling on the cable can damage the internal electrical connection between the cable and the boot.

You may be tempted to buy a "spark plug boot puller." There are many different designs on the market: some are pliers-type designs, others look like a simple corkscrew, and one type looks like a screwdriver with a bent end. Unfortunately, many pullers will not fit into the available space around the spark plugs on modern engines. There are, however, some pullers designed for specific engines. Schley Products, Inc., for example, makes a puller, product number 98180, specifically designed for Volkswagen and Audi vehicles. KD Tools, Snap-On, and Lisle all make several pullers designed for specific engines.

As adoption of electronic engine management systems eliminated frequent spark plug replacement, and emissions mandates required optimal spark plug location in the combustion chamber

This is the "air injection reaction vent solenoid." To change the rear cylinder bank spark plugs on this car, it must come off because it straddles the coil pack. Several of the nuts cannot be seen from any direction, so the process must be done by feel. In most cars, changing spark plugs will require disassembling one or more of the other components to get access to some of the spark plugs.

ber, spark plug accessibility became a secondary consideration. Unfortunately, the subject doesn't get much discussion in many factory shop manuals; they may say little more than unscrew the old plug and screw in the new one. Don't feel you're missing something if it looks as though you'll have to take something apart to get at all of the spark plugs. Check out the following examples:

On many Chrysler, Dodge, and Plymouth minivans, access to the rear bank of spark plugs is easiest from underneath the vehicle.

On some compact S-10 Chevrolet pick-up trucks, access to the passenger's side spark plugs requires removing the right front wheel and tire and reaching through the wheel well.

On the 750i BMW, the starter connector and remote battery terminal must be removed (which requires using a U-joint socket with an extension) to get access to the rear-most spark plug.

On some vehicles, including certain Subarus and Toyota Tundras, access to the rear spark plugs is facilitated by removing part of the intake manifold.

On certain Toyota minivans, the wipers need to be removed to access the rear-bank spark plugs.

On certain Lexus models, the cruise control module must be removed from the throttle body and the throttle body then removed to access the rear spark plugs.

This list is merely designed to show that if it looks as though something has to come off to gain access to a spark plug, you're probably right, even if it is hard to believe they'd design it that way.

Here are some ideas that may help:

Consider whether it's easier to reach it from under the car. V-8 and V-6 engines are narrower at the bottom than at the top, so there may be more room below.

Rethink your tools. Can you use a U-joint socket connector (i.e., flex-drive) and a different combination of extensions to reach the spark plug? Extensions come as long as three feet.

Buy another tool. Spark plug sockets are made with the U-joint as part of the socket. Even more flexible, S-K Tools makes a "double swivel spark plug socket" (S-K product number 33303 for a two-socket set) that has two swivel joints, each of which can flex over a greater variety of angles than the typical U-joint.

Consider whether a component can be shifted without disconnecting it. Often hoses can be moved slightly to afford clearance. The alternator can be moved, though that may require re-tensioning the serpentine belt afterwards. But be sure keep track of the sequence in which components were removed and how they were aligned when installed. Also, be sure to disconnect the battery negative cable if you are working around electrical connections.

Disconnect it and take it out. If it's obvious that it can be removed, go ahead. Just be sure you know what it is before you start disassembling it and, again, disconnect the negative battery cable if you're working around electrical connections.

Search the Internet. There are forums for many auto and truck brands. If there is one for your car, the odds are that someone has posted an answer to the problem. Don't take this information as gospel because sometimes it's just plain wrong. But it may show you the way, or at least give you the needed clue.

Two additional tips: first, when you're removing components, if it's not going to be obvious how to put it back together, snap a few photos with a digital camera as you disassemble it so that you've got a reference for reassembly. Second, have a magnetic pick-up tool

The spark plug boots fit into the depression in the cylinder head leading to the spark plugs. Clear away any dirt or debris before removing the boots.

handy, so that you can retrieve anything that slips out of your fingers and into some inaccessible spot.

Even if your car does have COP ignition, you may still have spark plug boots. They just don't have wires. They still have to come out, and the process is the same: grasp the boot by its edge and remove it with a twisting motion. Now it is time to remove the old spark plug.

A "spark plug socket" is specially designed to remove and install spark plugs. It has a rubber donut inside the socket that grasps the spark plug insulator and holds the spark plug within the socket until it is threaded into the cylinder head, after which the socket can be pulled free. Spark plug sockets come in different sizes, to accommodate the different bolt sizes used in spark plugs. Most 3/8-inch and 1/2-inch-drive socket wrench sets include spark plug sockets in the two most common sizes: 5/8-inch and 13/16-inch. Modern cars typically use the 5/8-inch size. Older cars, garden tractors, and lawn mowers often use the 13/16-inch size.

It is best to remove and replace spark plugs one by one, rather than removing all of them and replacing all of them. In old-style systems with distributors, this avoided the risk of replacing the spark plug cable on the wrong spark plug.

A universal joint allows the socket to work at an angle to the extension. Using a U-joint may allow removing some spark plugs that appear obstructed by other engine components.

The spark plug boot used in the COP Northstar has no wire because the coil rail assembly fits directly into it. In some COP ignition systems, the spark plug boot and the coil are a single unit.

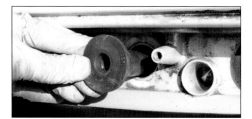

The boots can be pulled out with your fingers using the twist-and-pull technique to break any bond between the boot and the spark plug insulator.

A spark plug socket has an interior rubber gasket designed to fit around the plug's porcelain insulator. The gasket holds the spark plug in the socket during installation and removal of the spark plug.

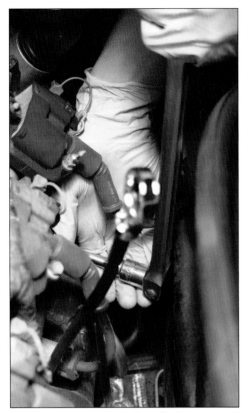

Some spark plugs are installed at an angle to the cylinder head, as in this Corvette. Always be sure the socket is fully seated on the spark plug and, unless using a universal joint, that the breaker bar handle is at a right angle to the extension.

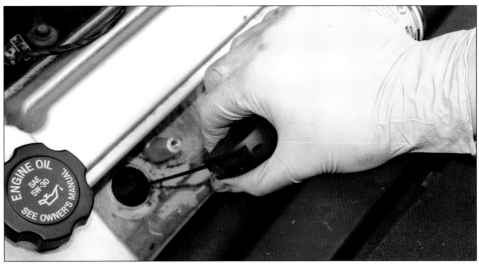

After loosening the spark plug, but before removing it, blow out the hole with canned compressed air, so that no dirt or debris remains in the hole to fall into the cylinder through the spark plug hole once it has been removed.

There's less risk of that with distributor-less systems, but it is still a good idea to do one plug at a time. It minimizes the amount of time there is an opening in the cylinder head that dirt or a foreign object could fall through.

Initially, use a breaker bar to loosen the old spark plug. A breaker bar gives you more leverage, which gives you more control over the level of force you're applying and allows you to apply smooth, even pressure to loosen the plug. Because spark plugs are typically recessed into the cylinder head, an extension will be needed between the socket and the breaker bar. Be sure that the socket is firmly seated on the spark plug. Unlike ordinary sockets, it is necessary to push a spark plug socket onto the plug to seat it because the rubber donut must be pushed onto the plug insulator. Loosen the spark plug, but don't remove it.

Once the spark plug is loosened, blow any dirt or debris from the recess with compressed air. Removing the spark plug will leave a hole at the bottom of the recess, so it's important to get dirt out first. Canned compressed air sold at office supply stores to clean dust from computer keyboards is perfect for this task. It is usually packaged with a plastic tube that fits into the nozzle, which is ideal for blowing out the bottom of the spark plug recess.

After you've blown out the spark plug recess, you can remove the spark plug itself. Remove the spark plug by hand.

After you have loosened the spark plug with a breaker bar and/or socket ratchet enough that it turns freely, remove the breaker bar or ratchet from the spark plug socket and extension and turn the extension/socket with your fingers. Done that way, it is easier to feel when the spark plug is out of the cylin-

Loosen the spark plug with the spark plug socket, an extension, and a breaker bar. A breaker bar allows you greater leverage than a ratchet, so you can apply even force. Do not remove the spark plug yet.

Carefully remove the spark plug and set it aside for later examination, keeping the removed plugs in order so that you can match them to the cylinder in which they had been installed.

der head and easier to lift it out. It also eliminates the risk that you'll damage threads just in case your socket was not securely seated on the spark plug.

As you remove them, lay the old spark plugs on a table or bench in the same order as they were installed in the car, so that you can examine them for clues about the engine's condition. A light-brown coating on the electrodes is a sign of normal combustion. Black deposits indicate incomplete combustion. In the old days, that could be caused by a carburetor set too rich or a bad spark plug cable. Today it may indicate that an oxygen sensor is wearing out, a fuel injector is defective, or the coil for that cylinder isn't firing. See Chapter 9 for more about electronic engine management. See Chapter 10 for oxygen sensors, and the sidebar in this chapter, "Trouble-Shooting Distributorless Ignition Systems."

This is also the time to inspect the spark plug cables and boots for corrosion in the terminals or deterioration in the rubber insulation. Corrosion can interfere with current flow and deterioration of the insulation usually means deterioration of the core inside the cable. Eventually, the spark plug will foul and misfire, setting a diagnostic trouble code

and illuminating the "check engine" or "service engine soon" light.

Before installing the new spark plug, check the gap with a spark plug gap gauge, which consists of a series of small wire loops of specific sizes. These cost about two or three dollars. The wire loop of the correct dimension should pass through the gap with just the slightest touch of drag.

Do not force the gap gauge through the spark plug gap. You can actually damage a spark plug with a gap gauge if you force the gauge through the gap. Platinum and iridium plugs have a coat-

ing or "puck" of the respective metal applied to the tip of the center electrode and the corresponding area on the side electrode. Forcing a gap gauge through the plug can damage or remove that metal. Also, the center electrode of an iridium plug is quite thin and is easily broken.

If the gap is incorrect, it can be adjusted. The gap gauge includes a tool with slots designed to bend the side electrode to increase or decrease the gap. But, for reasons just stated, be careful of the center electrode and don't bend on the area of the side electrode directly below the center electrode.

After verifying the gap, apply a light coat of anti-seize compound to the spark plug threads. Anti-seize should be

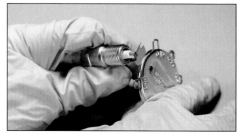

The side electrode can be gently bent to increase or decrease the gap between the side and center electrodes. It can also be bent to center the end of the side electrode over the center electrode. On platinum or iridium plugs, stay away from the end of the side electrode because it has a pad of precious metal on it that will be damaged by the tool.

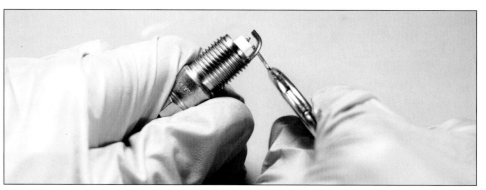

Verify the gap with the gauge, but do not pull the gauge between the electrodes. That would damage the precious-metal pad on the side electrode of platinum and iridium plugs and could break the center electrode of an iridium spark plug. This gauge is designed for high energy ignitions and has gauges with larger dimensions than gap gauges for engines with conventional coils.

Always use anti-seize compound when installing new spark plugs, especially in aluminum cylinder heads. Put it on the threads, but don't get it on the bottom of the plug.

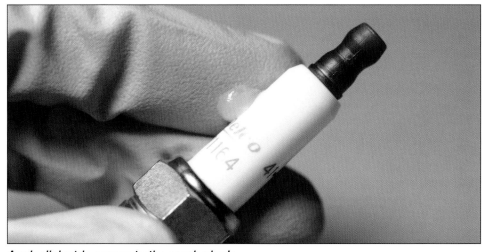

Apply dielectric grease to the spark plug's porcelain insulator. This will diminish the bond that engine heat creates between the insulator and the rubber spark plug boot so that it's easier to remove in the future. Dielectric grease does not conduct electricity.

the vehicle, always use a new gasket if the spark plug originally used a gasket. Spark plug gaskets are designed to crush when the plug is tightened and will not seal as effectively if reused. Also, replace a spark plug in the same cylinder from which it was removed because the pattern of deposits on the insulator leg will be unique to the spark plug. Putting it in a different cylinder can result in accumulating excessive deposits as a new pattern of deposits is added to the old one.

Apply a light coating of dielectric grease to the porcelain insulator of the spark plug, to make it easier to remove the spark plug boots the next time. Do *not* put dielectric grease on the top of the plug. The top is where current flows into the plug. Dielectric grease is *non*-conducting. The spark plug is now ready to be threaded into the cylinder head.

Thread the plug in by hand, the same way you unscrewed it; use the spark plug socket and the extension without the wrench. Doing it by hand, you can feel whether or not the threads are properly engaged, so that you don't cross-thread it. When the threads are properly engaged, the plug should turn freely and you should be able to finger-tighten the plug fully into the head, leaving only the final tightening to be done with a torque wrench.

applied upward from the third ring of threads from the bottom, so that no anti-seize gets into the cylinder when the plug is installed. Use an anti-seize compound that specifically states it is intended for use with spark plugs installed in aluminum cylinder heads. Anti-seize compounds can create electrical resistance between the base of the spark plug and the cylinder head, but anti-seize compounds made with fine copper particles are conductive.

By the way, if you reinstall a spark plug that was previously removed from

Install the spark plug. Use only the extension and the socket and hand thread the spark plug into the socket, tightening it by hand as far as it will comfortably go. Using your hands is the best possible insurance against cross threading the plug, which would damage the threads in the cylinder block.

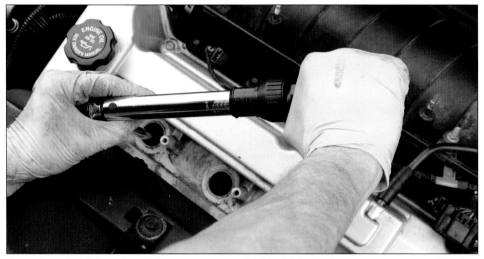

Complete the tightening with a torque wrench. Diminish the factory torque specification by approximately 25% below the dry specification because anti-seize has been used on the threads.

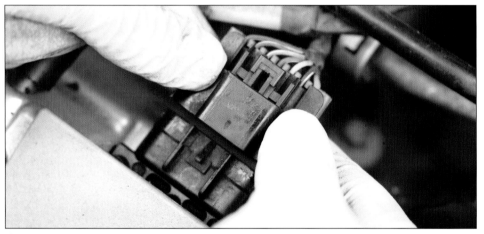

Once all of the spark plugs have been installed, and the coil pack has been reinstalled (tightening the bolts in the correct sequence), it's time to reconnect the electrical connector at the coil pack. Push it on until the tab clicks.

Now it's time to do some math. Unless otherwise stated in the factory shop manual, torque values are always quoted for clean and dry fasteners. Using anti-seize on a fastener means the torque value must be reduced, because anti-seize has lubricating properties and will increase actual torque by about 30% over the reading on the torque wrench. In other words, if a fastener to which anti-seize has been applied is tightened to a reading of 25 lf-lbs, the tension on the bolt is actually equivalent to 33 lf-lbs. So, when anti-seize is used the fastener should be tightened to a reading about 25% below the dry fastener specification.

About 19 ft-lbs with anti-seize is equivalent to 25 ft-lbs without anti-seize.

Finish tightening the spark plug with a torque wrench. When the torque specification is low, as it will be with aluminum cylinder heads, you may find it easier to use a torque wrench that reads in in-lbs, rather than ft-lbs. The shorter handle of a torque wrench reading in in-lbs may be easier to use in the confined spaces of the engine bay. To convert a ft-lb torque specification to in-lbs, simply multiply by 12 to get the in-lb specification.

Socket extensions may be used when tightening with a torque wrench. The basic rules are these: an extension that runs perpendicular to the handle of the torque wrench is just an extension of the fastener and does not affect torque values; however, anything that has the effect of extending the length of the torque wrench handle will distort torque values and should not be used.

Universal joint extensions should never be used with torque wrenches. Universal joints will either add to or diminish from the reading on the torque wrench, depending on the angle of the joints. That means that the reading on the torque wrench has almost no chance of being right when a universal joint is used and there is a good chance of over tightening.

So, how do you tighten a spark plug that you couldn't remove without using a universal joint? Here's how: leave it for last. Tighten all of the other spark plugs first. Tighten each by hand to the point that the spark plug is contacting the cylinder head and you can no longer comfortably tighten the plug further with your hand alone. Then count the number of turns given the plug to further tighten it to the specified torque specification. When you get to the plug that could only be removed with a universal joint, tighten it by hand until the spark plug contacts the head. Then tighten it the same number of additional turns that you turned the other spark plugs.

One by one, repeat the process for each spark plug. Reinstall any components that you removed to gain access to the plugs, as well as the spark plug boots, coil or coil pack, or coil rail assembly. When reinstalling the coil pack, be sure to tighten fasteners in the factory-specified sequence to the factory specified torque, if those are specified in the factory manual. Reinstall the engine shroud or fuel rail covers, and you're done.

It is a good idea to keep a record of the mileage at which you changed the plugs. That way you'll know when it's time to do it again or, alternatively, know when it's time to sell the car so you don't have to go through the experience twice. Just kidding—it's always easier the second time.

CHAPTER 5

MAINTAINING AND SERVICING THE AIR INTAKE SYSTEM

The induction system is often overlooked in performing routine automotive maintenance, but dirt in either the air intake or the fuel delivery can severely degrade engine performance. It is maintenance that is easy to accomplish, but can pay large dividends by preventing trouble. If the induction system has been ignored for a long time, cleaning the intake system will also give you an immediate and noticeable improvement in engine response and smoothness.

Whether controlled by a computer or a carburetor, all automotive induction systems operate on one basic principle: they seek to supply air and fuel in the proportion required by the engine at that moment. Analytically, an internal combustion engine is an air pump. Each time a piston descends with an intake valve open, the engine pulls air into a cylinder. Each time a piston rises with an exhaust valve open, it empties the cylinder so that it can repeat the process.

Airflow into the engine is regulated in the same manner as it was a century ago: with a "throttle valve." This is a large butterfly valve, which progressively opens and closes to admit or reduce airflow into the engine. When cars had

carburetors, the throttle was located in the "throat" of the carburetor, the big hole in the middle that allowed air to be drawn into the engine. In most of today's fuel injected cars, the throttle is located at the front of the intake manifold.

Fuel delivery, in contrast, is controlled in modern engines with great precision. The engine computer—the "powertrain control module" (PCM), "engine control module" (ECM), "engine control unit" (ECU), or similarly named device—opens the fuel injectors at the precise moment, and for the exact duration of time, required to match fuel delivery to airflow for optimum power and economy.

When the throttle is closed, it blocks most airflow to the engine. This creates a vacuum because the piston descending on the intake stroke cannot get enough air to fill the cylinder. When the throttle is fully open, there is no restriction to airflow. So, there is no vacuum. Air flows freely into the engine, and the rate of airflow increases as the RPM increases.

Correctly calculating optimum fuel delivery requires knowing how much air is actually flowing into the engine. When automobiles used carburetors, airflow had to be estimated based on

throttle position. Modern automobiles, however, measure it directly with an airflow sensor. The "mass airflow sensor" (MAF) is the most common type, and is located in the air intake, just ahead of the throttle body.

Here's how a typical MAF works: A filament of thin wire is strung across the intake just ahead of the throttle. Electrical current is then sent through the wire. Due to electrical resistance, the wire is heated to a predetermined temperature, such as 200 degrees C. Air flowing past the wire cools it, which lowers its internal electrical resistance. This allows more current to flow through the wire, which reheats the wire as the increase in current encounters resistance. By keeping the wire at the preset temperature and measuring the change in current flow, after obtaining data from other sensors about intake air temperature and humidity, the PCM can calculate airflow from the current change. For obvious reasons, this is referred to as a "hot wire" MAF.

Though the hot wire MAF is most common type, there are two other types in use on some newer cars. A variation of the hot wire sensor, sometimes called a "cold wire" MAF, incorporates a second, unheated wire to measure intake air temperature. The "thin film" MAF operates on the same basic theory, but uses two thin films of conductive material, such as platinum or silicon nitride, instead of hot and cold wires.

If you don't find an MAF on your vehicle, you many not be overlooking it. Even though most vehicles use an MAF, not all do. Vehicles manufactured since 1966 generally use a "manifold absolute pressure" sensor (MAP) to measure air density in the intake manifold, information used with mass air flow to calculate intake air oxygen content. However, because MAP provides what is essentially engine vacuum information, some vehicles omit the MAF and use MAP data with air temperature and RPM to infer airflow.

Older cars may use a "vane airflow meter" to measure intake airflow or a "Karman Vortex air flow meter." Both of these, for example, were commonly used by Toyota. Technically, these are not MAFs because they measure airflow mechanically—for example, by pushing a door against a spring to activate an electrical signal to the PCM.

Keeping the throttle, throttle body, and MAF clean is critical to the efficient operation of the engine, and good engine performance. Even though these systems are downwind of the air cleaner, they still get dirty. The air cleaner cannot block all dirt from entering the engine because it must not filter so completely that it unduly restricts airflow. Crankcase fumes are vented into the intake system and are another source of intake deposits.

The throttle is designed to leak a certain amount of air past at idle, when it is "closed." In conjunction with the "idle control valve," which is a valve that opens a passage around the throttle at idle to admit air to the intake, this assures that the engine receives enough air to maintain idle speed.

A dirty throttle and throttle body alter idle air flow, and eventually create a lumpy and irregular idle. When the throttle is suddenly opened, there is a great rush of air into the engine. That creates an initial hesitation when the throttle is opened and, if the throttle is really dirty, can actually cause the engine to stall.

A dirty MAF provides incorrect information to the PCM. Dirt coating the hot wire filament acts as an insulator. It retains heat in the wire and protects it from the cooling airflow. Airflow past the wire has less cooling effect, so less current is required to maintain its temperature. That leads the PCM to believe airflow is lower than it actually is, and reduce fuel accordingly, creating a lean condition. Eventually, this will become far enough out of sync with data the PCM receives from the sensors in the exhaust to set a diagnostic trouble code. This will illuminate the "service engine soon" or "check engine" light on the instrument panel. See Chapters 9 and 10 for more information on how electronic engine management uses data to calculate fuel flow and determine engine malfunctions.

So, you should periodically clean the throttle, throttle body, and mass airflow sensor. First, though, review any references or pertinent information in your factory owner's or service manual.

Parts for this job

Air filter (if needed)
MAF cleaner
Air intake/throttle body cleaner

Tools for this job

Lint-free towels or shop rags
Screwdriver

Time for this job

Cleaning the MAF and the throttle body are easy jobs. Most of the time is consumed in dissembling the air intake in order to gain access to them. You should be able to do the whole thing in an hour, even the first time.

Advance Planning

The supplies for cleaning the MAF and throttle body are designed for those purposes and no other cleaning products should be used. So, you'll need to go to the parts store to acquire them.

Hazard Warning

Products designed to clean the mass airflow sensor are flammable. They should not be used when the engine is hot, though they are designed to be used when the engine is warm. Take care not to spray this cleaner on hot engine surfaces. Similarly, shop towels used with these products become highly flammable. Keep the area in which you work well ventilated, keep open flames away from the work area and have a fire extinguisher within reach, as a precaution. Afterward, wash the shop towels as soon as possible.

Let's do it

To clean the mass airflow sensor, you must remove the intake assembly that leads to it, including the air filter. Once you have removed it, you will have exposed the throttle body, so you might as well clean that, too.

Removing the Air Intake Assembly

The mass airflow sensor is located in the air intake. It is part of the snorkel between the air filter and the engine. It is usually a square metal piece about the size of a sandwich sitting crosswise in the air intake assembly.

To clean the MAF, it is easiest and best to remove the air intake of which it is a part. This will simultaneously make it easier to clean the throttle body because it will get the air intake assembly out of the way.

Start by putting a fender protector over the fender. Be sure the fender is clean before covering it with the fender protector. A fender protector on a dirty fender has the same effect as sandpaper: the dirt between the protector and the fender will leave tiny scratches.

Then remove the air intake assembly. The intake assembly connects to the throttle body with a very large screw-type hose clamp. Disconnecting the assembly from the throttle body is simply a matter of loosening the hose clamp

To access the throttle body, loosen the screw holding the air intake assembly in place.

Disconnect the manifold absolute pressure sensor.

Loosen the air cleaner hold downs.

These connectors fasten with a clip that must be lifted to disconnect them.

Disconnect the intake air temperature sensor.

and then gently working the assembly off the throttle body using a gentle side-to-side motion. The clamp doesn't need to be removed, just loosened.

The next step is disconnecting the wiring leading to the air intake assembly. This includes disconnecting the wiring leading to the mass airflow sensor.

Engine wiring connectors are designed to stay connected and keep out moisture. To those purposes, they have male and female ends with a gasket on the male end that is compressed as the connector seats. The female end of the connector has a tab molded into the plastic housing.

Most connectors are designed so that the male end has a springy clip that slides up over that tab and then snaps down to hold the two ends of the connector tightly in place. Within that generic group, however, there are differences in species. Some connectors are designed so that the end of the spring clip is to be lifted to disconnect the two halves of the connector. Some are designed so that the opposite end of the clip is pushed downward, toward the connector, to raise the other end and allow the clip to slide over the tab, thereby separating the connector halves. There are also some connectors on which the function of the clip is performed by a slide that pushes down to connect and pulls up to disconnect.

The fear, of course, is that you'll break a connector in the process of taking it apart. That would be nasty, and probably expensive, because it will probably require replacing whatever leads to the connector, as well.

Fortunately, the plastic used in these connectors is not easy to break. That

doesn't mean you couldn't do it. It just means they're not as fragile as they may look.

Your fingers are the best way to lift the spring clip and separate the connector halves, but that isn't always feasible, because sometimes there really isn't enough room under the clip's lip to slide a finger under it. There are commercially available tools for disconnecting automobile electrical connectors. However, you can also use a small screwdriver to lift the clip enough to slide it over the tap. Use the screwdriver to lift the clip, rather than sliding the screwdriver blade between the clip and the tab. Of course, you have to also be pulling the connector ends apart while you're doing this, but the technique becomes pretty easy once you understand the construction of the connector.

There may also be hoses routing into the air intake assembly. These, too, must be disconnected to remove the assembly.

One type of hose clamp commonly used on smaller-diameter hoses that route air, rather than fluids, within the engine compartment is made of plastic and has teeth that slide over each other as the clamp is pushed together. The teeth are mounted under tabs that keep tension on them once the hose clamp is fully tightened, preventing it from loosening.

Disassembling these clamps is an example of thinking outside of the box. These connectors cannot be pulled apart and there is no release tab. Rather, the

The jaws of this plastic hose clamp should be slid sideways in opposite directions to release it.

Remove the plastic fittings pressed into the air intake assembly by pulling on the plastic fitting itself, not the rubber hose attached to it.

Remove the air filter element.

The entire air intake assembly may now be removed.

The throttle body shows accumulated deposits around the throttle plate.

These deposits exist on the throttle plate itself, as well.

ends simply slide apart, sideways. Use the tip of a screwdriver blade to push the teeth of one end sideways, out of the teeth of the other end. When the teeth separate, the connector is released.

There may also be a small rubber hose that is connected into the air intake assembly by a small plastic fitting that inserts into the air intake assembly. These fittings should be removed from the hard rubber of the air intake assembly by grasping the assembly firmly and pulling. This is a better approach than attempting to remove the small rubber hose from the fitting. Because those hoses are exposed to all of the heat of the engine compartment, they can get quite brittle, particularly where stretched to fit over the end of the fitting. Attempting to remove the hose from the fitting is likely to result in tearing the hose. To replace it, you'll end up having to buy the assembly of which it is a part.

Next remove the air cleaner. Take out the filter element and anything else, such as the cover that goes over the filter element, which will come off. Check the condition of the filter in the process, of course. You should now be able to remove the entire air intake assembly from the car.

Cleaning the Throttle Body

Air intake cleaner is packaged as an aerosol, with a little tube to fit into the spray nozzle. It is a specialized product made for cleaning the throttle body. It is not the same as carburetor cleaner. Air intake cleaners are specifically formulated so that they will not affect other sensors downstream of the throttle body, such as the MAP sensor and HO_2 sensors. For cleaning the throttle body, carburetor cleaners should be avoided because they may not be safe for all sensors in the air intake system and for the oxygen sensors in the exhaust. Some carburetor cleaners are labeled safe for oxygen sensors, but that leaves open the issue of safety to the other sensors. The

Shoot air intake cleaner on a lint free rag and swab out as much of the throttle body and throttle plate as your fingers can reach.

Shoot air intake cleaner into areas that you cannot reach.

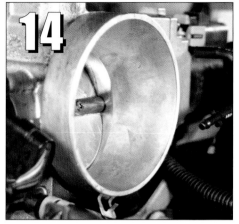

The view after cleaning shows no deposits to interfere with air flow and engine performance.

purpose-made air intake cleaner is the preferred product for this job.

Air intake cleaner will work best on a warm engine, but it isn't essential that the engine be warm to do this job. Moreover, warm is not the same as hot. You will end up with your fingers in the throttle body itself, so you don't want a hot engine (especially as you'll probably be leaning on other parts of the engine in the process).

Running the engine for only a few minutes will put enough temperature into the throttle body deposits to make them easier for the cleaner to dissolve.

Start by spraying an ample amount of cleaner on a lint-free towel or shop rag. Push the throttle with your fingers into an open position, and wipe down the throttle body and the throttle itself with the cleaner-soaked rag. Do not use paper towels. Sometime in this process the throttle plate, which is spring-loaded, is going to shut on the rag. If it were a paper towel, it could tear and you could get paper fiber into the intake.

Get as much of the accumulated deposits off as possible. Reach as far as you can into the throttle body to clean out deposits on the engine side of the throttle. Clean the underside of the throttle plate (the side facing the engine when the throttle is closed).

Once you have cleaned as much as can be removed with the rag, use directed spray from the aerosol nozzle to spray into the throttle body and around the ends of the shaft on which the throttle rotates. The cleaner should dissolve deposits in areas that you cannot reach. However, the area of the greatest accumulation will be the circumference of the throttle body where the throttle seats when closed. Those are the deposits that affect idle and can cause stalling. When it looks clean, you're done.

Cleaning the Mass Airflow Sensor

A specialized cleaner is *essential* to cleaning the MAF. Using carburetor cleaner or throttle body cleaner on the MAF will damage the fine filament wires that are the core part of this sensor, necessitating replacement of the unit. This is a very expensive part. It is also somewhat delicate, and care should be taken to avoid subjecting it to hard shocks.

The MAF is the square metallic object about the size of a sandwich located just after the air cleaner housing in the air intake assembly, between it and the throat that leads to the throttle body. One of the electrical connectors that were detached to allow removal of the air intake assembly went to the MAF.

There is a practical reason for removing the MAF. The easiest way to work on the MAF is at a workbench, where you can see what you're doing and move the air intake assembly into a convenient position.

In order to access the MAF, you will need to further disassemble the air intake assembly. Large hose clamps hold the MAF in place on the filter housing and the remainder of the air intake assembly. Loosening one of those allows removing that portion of the assembly, exposing the MAF to view.

Once the hose clamp is loosened, the MAF can be detached from the air intake assembly, but it won't just come apart in your hands. In order to assure a tight air seal, there is rubber collar that fits over the connection between the air intake assembly and the MAF. The way to separate the pieces is as follows; first, turn back the collar with your fingers all the way around its circumference; then, push the tip of a fairly large screwdriver between the rubber collar and the lip of the air intake assembly. A broad screwdriver blade is better than a narrow one, because it distributes the force more evenly. The plastic from which the assembly is made is lightweight and rather soft, and could easily be torn by too much force.

Using the screwdriver, gently pry the intake assembly away from the MAF until you can pull it apart by hand. Be very careful prying, because if the screwdriver should slip, it could slide into the body of the MAF and destroy the elements.

This collar assures no air will leak into the MAF, but it must be turned back to expose the seam connecting the MAF to the air intake assembly.

Use a screwdriver to gently pry the MAF and intake assembly apart.

Then pull them completely apart with your hands.

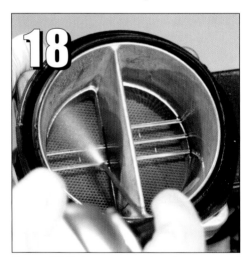

Spray MAF cleaner onto the elements and inside the MAF, but don't touch the wires with anything.

The MAF cleaner will remove any accumulated deposits.

The arrow points in the direction of air flow when the MAF is properly reinstalled.

For purposes of cleaning, it doesn't matter which side of the MAF is exposed. However, there is an advantage to removing the part of the assembly that is behind the MAF. That way, when you clean the MAF you also dislodge any debris that has become embedded in the protective screen that is located in the MAF just ahead of the sensor elements.

Using the aerosol nozzle with the accompanying tube inserted, spray the MAF wires. Do not let the nozzle, or anything else, touch these wires.

That's all there is to it. When the wires look clean, you're done.

If you should take the entire MAF out of the housings, there is a helpful sign to follow when replacing it. The arrow on its body shows you the direction the air should be flowing when it is installed.

Many MAFs are equipped with a mesh screen. This does not serve to protect the sensor. It is there to smooth the airflow. There is a prevailing myth that removing the screen will increase performance. It won't. The screen does constitute a restriction on airflow. But, for that exact reason, removing it reduces the velocity of the airflow. Reducing the speed of the air passing over the hot wire of the

MAF reduces the air's cooling effect, which will be interpreted by the PCM as lower airflow. Hence, the PCM would then decrease fuel supply. So, removing the screen actually hurts performance.

One last thing: In an effort to prevent dirt accumulation on the MAF, many manufacturers incorporate a "burn-off" circuit in the MAF that automatically raises the wire's temperature to about 1000 degrees C for a few moments whenever the engine is turned off. This is designed to burn away any contaminants on the wire. If the MAF has a burn-off circuit and the wire has nonetheless become dirty, the burn-off circuit may not be working. By removing enough of the air intake to expose the MAF to view, starting the engine, and then turning it off to activate the burn-off circuit, you should be able to verify its operation. If the wire doesn't glow red, a relay in the burn-off circuit is probably defective.

THE CHARGING SYSTEM

MAINTAINING, DIAGNOSING, AND REPLACING THE BATTERY AND ALTERNATOR

The "charging system" generates and stores the electricity used by the vehicle. The system has three components: an alternator creates the electricity; a voltage regulator controls how much electricity is created; and, the battery stores the electricity until it is needed to power the starter, fire the spark plugs, illuminate the lights, lower the power windows, or perform any other electrical function.

All automobiles and light trucks manufactured for sale in the United States and Canada since the mid-1950s use 12-volt electrical systems. In most modern cars, the voltage regulator is a part of the alternator and neither can be individually serviced; if there is a problem with either, you buy another alternator, new or rebuilt. In older cars, the voltage regulator may be a separate component.

The charging system is distinct from the "ignition system." The ignition system draws electricity from the battery, increases the voltage of that electricity, and then distributes the current it generates to the individual spark plugs in the correct sequence. The ignition system is the ignition coil (or coils), the distributor (or its equivalent), and the spark plugs. It is covered in Chapter 4.

The charging system is also distinct from the starting system, which consists of the starter motor and a starter solenoid or relay. A solenoid is a plunger, like the bolt on a door latch, which moves when an electrical field is created around it. In effect, it is a powered switch: a small electrical current throws the switch, which then allows a much larger current to flow. A starter relay is similar.

Of course, all of these systems use electricity, so we can collectively call them the electrical system, except that wouldn't be complete. The electrical system also includes the headlights, tail-lights, and the power everythings that make you really, really know you've arrived.

So, references in this and subsequent chapters to the "electrical system" are global. That includes the cigarette lighter, er, "power port," the spark plugs, and everything else that uses electricity. But, when the reference is to the charging system, it is to the battery and the alternator, including the voltage regulator, and the wiring between them.

Many of us don't fully understand electricity. So, we don't feel comfortable working on the electrical system in a car. If this describes you, take a few minutes to read Sidebar: "What You Need to Know About Electricity." It explains volts, amps, and ohms, and how electricity works. Once you understand the basics, the rest is merely logical application of the basic principles.

Keeping the charging system healthy doesn't require much effort or much time, and it pays dividends every time you turn the key in the ignition. But, just in case, you can see Sidebar: "Jump Starting a Car With a Dead Battery." Also, to find out what to do, see Sidebar: "It Won't Start!"

Parts for this job

Baking soda
Distilled water
Battery (if replacement is needed)

Tools for this job

Nitrile gloves
Battery terminal brush
Scrub brush
Old toothbrush
Socket ratchet with extensions
Side-mount battery wrench
  (if applicable)
Digital multimeter
Battery charger (as needed)

Continued on Page 59

What You Need to Know About Electricity

Many people don't understand electricity. It's invisible, so you can't figure it out by looking at it. Because we don't understand it, electricity sometimes seems to do unexpected things, which makes it kind of scary, too.

But, electricity makes your car run. If you don't understand electricity, you will be limited in working on your car. Electricity is very logical and predictable. You just need to understand its rules.

Electricity starts with the atom. An atom has three components: a "proton" and a "neutron," which, together, form the atom's "nucleus," i.e., its center; and, an "electron," which orbits around the nucleus. As the names suggest, the proton is positively charged, the electron is negatively charged, and the neutron has no electrical charge.

In this state—equal numbers of protons and electrons—the atom is "electrically balanced." An electrically balanced atom has no electrical charge. It is neither positive nor negative because the equal number of protons and electrons cancel each other out. But, if there are more of one than the other, it takes on a positive or negative charge accordingly.

An atom will always strive to maintain electrical balance or return to it. It can have any number of protons and electrons, but the atom will always try to add or subtract electrons as needed to be electrically balanced. An atom that is electrically imbalanced is an "ion."

Electrons are lighter than protons and certain electrons orbit further away from the nucleus than others. These "free electrons" can easily detach from one atom and attach to another, as the atoms seek electrical balance.

You now know what is required to understand "voltage," "current," and "resistance:" the three concepts on which the automotive electrical system operates. "Voltage" is the storage of atoms with too many electrons. "Current" is the flow of electrons from atoms with too many electrons toward atoms with too few. "Resistance" is anything that impedes the ability of the electron to move to the atoms with too few electrons.

There are three other terms that you should also understand: "conductor," "circuit," and "ground." A conductor is something that directs the flow of electrons, such as a wire, and is what the electrons move through to get to the negative ions (the atoms with too few electrons). A circuit is the route electrons must travel to get to the end of the journey and find an atom with too few electrons. The ground is the point in an electrical circuit that has zero voltage. To understand the concept of a ground, it helps to understand that voltage is not an absolute measure of how much. Rather, it's a measure of how much more. When there are no atoms that have more electrons than other atoms, that's zero voltage.

The customary analogy for electricity is to liken it to water.

If you have a horizontal pipe connecting the bottoms of two water tanks, with one tank full and the other empty, water will flow from the full tank through the pipe and into the empty tank, until the two tanks are each half full.

By analogy, voltage is the pressure created by the water in the full tank that pushes water through the pipe. Current is the water moving in the pipe. If we make one section of the pipe smaller in diameter than the rest of the pipe, that's where resistance occurs. Zero voltage is reached when the water level in each tank is equal.

Of course, it helps to be able to measure all of this. The "volt" is the measure of voltage. Current is measured in "amperage," sometimes just termed "amps." Resistance is measured in "ohms." Volts, amps, and ohms are sometimes abbreviated by scientists as, respectively, E, I, and R. But more commonly (and in this book), the symbols used are: V, A, and Ω.

Volts, amps, and ohms interrelate. If you know any two, you can solve for the other: $V = A \times \Omega$; $A = V \div \Omega$; and, $\Omega = V \div A$. This is "Ohm's law," and knowing it will be useful when diagnosing electrical systems with a digital multimeter.

There are two types of current: "direct current" (DC) and "alternating current" (AC). The electrons in direct current flow only one way. In alternating current they rapidly flow back and forth. All automotive electrical systems use direct current. The "alternator" (see Sidebar), generates AC (because it's easier) and then converts it to DC before sending it to the battery.

There are two types of circuits: "series," and "parallel." A series circuit is one in which each segment of the circuit leads to another, i.e., the segments connect end-to-end. A parallel circuit is one of two circuits, both leading to the same place from the same place. Resistance in a series circuit slows all current in the circuit. Resistance in a parallel circuit shifts current to the other circuit.

In an automobile, current flows from the positive terminal of the battery to the negative terminal of the battery. That's why the number-one safety precaution when working on an automotive electrical system is to disconnect the battery at the negative cable. Disconnecting the negative cable eliminates the possibility of current flowing through any circuit in the vehicle.

Of course, if you've been a really sharp reader, you've noticed that electrons flow to—not from—the positive terminal of the battery, because they're flowing toward the atoms with more positrons than electrons. So, why do we say current flows positive to negative?

It's partly because the terminology was adopted before scientists completely understood electron flow. But mostly, it's because the terms accurately describes how the electrical charge acts: as a result of this electron flow, the electrical charge flows from the positive to the negative.

Jump Starting a Car with a Dead Battery

There is a right way and a wrong way to jump start a car that has a dead battery. The following details the right way, with step-by-step warnings of the wrong way.

Check that the ignition key in the car with the dead battery is in the "off" position. If the key is on, connecting the cars' batteries can cause a sudden voltage surge that can damage instrument panel digital displays and similar electronic components. Be sure the vehicles are not touching.

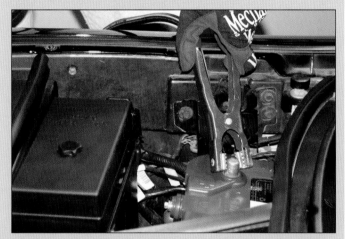

When jump starting a car, connect the positive cables first, to the positive battery terminals on each car.

With the engines both "off," connect the red jumper cable to the positive terminal of the dead battery and the other end to the positive terminal of the good battery. After the positive terminals are connected, connect one end of the black jumper cable to the negative terminal of the good battery and the other to a ground on the engine block of the car with the dead battery.

The last connection of the negative cable should be made away from any fuel lines, moving parts, and away from the dead battery itself. It should be made to steel, not aluminum.

Connecting the negative jumper cable to an appropriate metal part of the car completes the circuit. Because the dead battery is itself grounded to the vehicle frame, the negative battery cable attaches to the vehicle frame.

Start the car with the good battery. Then start the car with the dead battery.

After the car with the dead battery has been started, the cables should be removed in the reverse sequence of installation. Removing the negative jumper cable, which had been last attached to a ground, breaks the circuit. That's why it should be removed first.

In practice, it can be very difficult to locate a suitable place to make the ground connection for the negative jumper cable. Many engine components are made of aluminum, which won't serve as a suitable ground. Limited space in the engine bay also makes it hard to find a location into which the large clamp end of a battery cable will fit, or which doesn't come dangerously close to a moving engine part. This connection shouldn't be made to anything that's not a heavy steel part.

If it is impossible to find a suitable ground location elsewhere, you can make the last negative jumper cable connection directly to the negative terminal on the dead battery. The risk of battery explosion is much reduced with modern sealed batteries and, of course, you should be doing this only in a well-ventilated area. It is probably better to run that risk than to risk physical injury trying to remove a battery cable that's attached near moving engine parts.

There are two caveats concerning jump starting, in addition to following the proper procedure: First, in batteries with removable caps, check the electrolyte level before attempting to jump start (or charge) a dead battery. If the electrolyte is low, fill with distilled water to the proper level. Low electrolyte is more likely to create explosive gases during charging.

Second, never attempt to jump start (or charge) a battery that is frozen. That can create gases inside the battery that will crack the battery case, expelling electrolyte and creating the risk of explosion. A fully charged battery has a freezing point of −77 degrees F. One that is only 50% charged freezes at −10 degrees F. A battery that is only 25% charged freezes at 5 degrees F, and a fully discharged battery freezes at a mere 20 degrees F. Be sure the battery is not frozen before attempting to charge it.

Make the last connection of the jumper cables to a ground on the car being started, rather than to the negative battery terminal. This reduces the risk of sparks igniting the hydrogen gas that batteries can produce when charging.

Engine Won't Start!

When the car won't start, nine times out of ten the problem is caused by corrosion, the battery, or the alternator, and not by the starter. But, there's always that tenth time.

If all that happens when you turn the key is a brief groan from the engine, then nothing except, perhaps, clicking sounds from the engine compartment, get out the battery terminal brush and battery charger or jumper cables. The immediate problem is that the battery doesn't have enough voltage to power the starter. The tests outlined in the text of this chapter will probably track down the problem.

But, if the starter engages and then disengages before the engine starts, or the charging system checks out but nothing happens when you turn the key, then there's a good chance the problem is in the starter, starter solenoid, or starter drive.

The two types of starters most commonly used in modern vehicles are the "gear reduction starter" and the "planetary reduction segment starter." Both types are designed to be compact and produce high torque.

All starters operate on the same basic principles. Because the amperage required to power the starter motor is very high, that current is not routed through the ignition switch. Instead it is routed through a solenoid, which is an electromagnetic switch. When you turn the key, you send low amperage current to the solenoid, where it enters a coil (winding) that creates a magnetic field. This magnetic field moves a plunger against a spring. Either directly or through a mechanism, the movement of the plunger moves the shaft of the starter drive, at the end of which is a "pinion gear."

A pinion gear is a small gear that drives a large gear, in this case the "ring gear" of the crankshaft. The movement of the plunger pushes the pinion gear into engagement with the teeth on the ring gear, connecting the starter drive to the engine's flywheel.

The movement of the plunger simultaneously closes the circuit between the battery and the starter motor by moving a copper disc into contact with both terminals inside the solenoid. Current flows to the starter, the motor turns, and the engine is then supposed to start. When it does, a clutch mechanism allows the pinion gear to freewheel until the ignition key is released. This simultaneously collapses the magnetic field in the solenoid, opens the circuit to the starter motor, and withdraws the pinion gear as the plunger is pushed back to its resting position by a spring.

When you hear a clicking sound as you turn the key, but the starter doesn't engage, that's the plunger in the solenoid. Low battery voltage supplies enough current to create the magnetic field, but closing the circuit from the battery to the starter created a voltage drop. The voltage drop diminishes current flow to the solenoid through the ignition switch, so the magnetic field collapses, then rebuilds as the voltage in the battery spikes up. The process repeats itself as long as you hold the key in the "start" position.

The clicking sound does, however, tell you that the problem is not in the ignition switch. It is also not in the "neutral safety switch" or "clutch safety switch" designed to prevent starting the car in gear.

When the starter engages, but then disengages before the engine starts, the diagnosis depends on whether the starter remains running after it disengages. If it does, the starter drive is slipping. If it does not, the solenoid is defective. If the starter drive remains running, it means current continues to flow through the solenoid. Similarly, if the starter spins, but doesn't engage, the problem is with the starter drive pinion gear or with its clutch.

If, however, the starter ceases running as the starter drive disengages, the solenoid plunger is breaking the battery/starter circuit. That simultaneously withdraws the pinion gear from the ring gear. The problem is either in the wiring to the alternator from the ignition or from the alternator to ground—including faulty, lose, or corroded connections—or in the solenoid itself.

To test the battery cable from the battery to the starter solenoid, disable the fuel system so the car won't start by removing either the fuse controlling the fuel injection or controlling the fuel pump, then connect the red lead of a digital multimeter to the battery end of the cable and the black lead to the starter end, and have an assistant crank the engine briefly. The voltage reading should be 0.5 volts or less.

Next, test the ground circuit from the starter, by connecting the red DMM lead to the starter motor's housing and the black lead to the negative battery terminal and having an assistant crank the engine. If the voltage drop is more than 0.2 volts, there is excessive resistance.

If the battery has proper voltage and there is no excessive voltage drop, but absolutely nothing happens when you turn the ignition key to "start," the problem is usually either the solenoid or the starter itself. One old trick in this situation is to tap the back of the starter with a hammer. If the car then starts, the starter motor is bad. Starter motors have bushings similar to those described in Sidebar: "How the Alternator Works." Tapping the starter can move worn bushings just enough that they'll make contact one more time. The factory shop manual will have a trouble-shooting protocol for the starter, specific to the make and model of vehicle. It's worth pursuing that protocol, as there are other possible problems, such as a defective neutral safety switch (which prevents starting the car in gear) that can create the same symptoms.

While modern starters function better than older, bulkier starters, one side-effect of making starters smaller is making it more likely that the starter, starter drive, and/or starter solenoid will be available for replacement only as a unit. However, on older cars and some newer vehicles, you may still be able to buy a replacement starter drive or starter solenoid separately from the starter motor. Also, many auto parts stores will "bench test" a starter and starter solenoid for you, without charge.

As with alternators, it is very difficult to access the starter on a number of modern vehicles, particularly those with front wheel drive. Before beginning to remove a starter, be certain to disconnect the negative battery cable. Removing the starter itself is a matter of disconnecting the various electrical connections (it's wise to label them as they're removed) and removing the bolts holding the starter in place. Getting to the starter, however, can require removing other components, so having a factory shop manual before starting this job is a very wise idea.

Time for these jobs

Most of these jobs can be accomplished in less than 30 minutes.

Advance Planning

If you think you may need to replace the battery, test it first, as described in this chapter. If you conclude it is necessary to replace the battery, look at the labeling on the old battery to determine the cold cranking amps (CCA), reserve capacity (RC), and group number, so that you can buy the appropriate replacement (see Sidebar: "What to Look For in a New Battery", and Sidebar: "Who Makes It?" on this book's page at Cartechbooks.com). If the old battery was not the original equipment battery, determine the manufacturer's battery specifications from the factory shop manual (or the owner's manual, if it contains that information—many do not).

Hazard Warning

The hazards when working on or around a vehicle's charging system are hydrogen explosion, sulfuric acid burns, electric shock, and bodily injury. Here are the precautions needed to minimize those hazards:

Always work in a well-ventilated area away from any flame source, lit cigarette, cigar, or pipe, or natural gas-fired heater.

Disconnect the negative battery terminal and pull the ignition key before working on any electrical components.

Always disconnect the negative battery terminal before disconnecting the positive; always connect the positive terminal before connecting the negative. That way, there is never a circuit existing when you are disconnecting or connecting the positive terminal, which reduces the chance of creating a spark.

Wear safety glasses and nitrile or rubber gloves.

Batteries create hydrogen gas as a byproduct of charging, whether by the alternator or a battery charger. Hydrogen gas is highly explosive (the *Hindenburg* was filled with hydrogen). That's why the garage door should be open when charging a battery, why a spark or flame near a battery is dangerous, and why you shouldn't allow smoking near a battery.

Next, there's sulfuric acid. The fluid inside a wet cell battery—"electrolyte," sometimes called "battery acid"—is 36% sulfuric acid (the rest is distilled water). It is sulfuric acid that creates hydrogen gas. But even in its liquid state, sulfuric acid is nasty stuff. It can cause burns on the skin and blindness if it gets in the eyes. That is the reason for wearing safety glasses and nitrile gloves whenever working on a battery. If electrolyte does get on your skin, flush with water immediately. If it gets in your eyes, immediately flush with a mild solution of baking soda and water to neutralize the acid, then head to the urgent care center. If you get electrolyte on your clothing, expect to see holes after they're washed.

Finally, there is electric shock. The risk of electric shock when working on a car is vastly overrated.

To get a sense of exactly how little you have to worry about, go out to your car, open the hood, and then take hold of the positive terminal of the battery with one hand and the negative terminal of the battery with the other hand. There will not be a shock, even if you do it with the engine running.

That's because your body has about 10,000 ohms of resistance, which is more than enough to block all but a negligible trickle of current from flowing out of a 12-volt battery. It is current, not voltage, that causes electric shock.

There are very few places in an automobile where the current is high enough to hurt you. The two most obvious are the starter and the ignition system circuits. The current in either can easily exceed the 30-amp level that is normally considered the threshold for electrocution.

But, not to worry; current cannot exist in the absence of a circuit. A circuit, in a car, is the route current travels from the positive terminal of the battery back to the negative terminal of the battery. Cut off that circuit, and there can be no current. No current, no shock—it's that simple. So, always disconnect the negative terminal of the battery before working on the charging system.

One other point: Be sure the ignition switch is "off" and the key is pulled before disconnecting the negative terminal of the battery. If it is in the "on" position, even though the car is not running, disconnecting the battery can create a voltage spike, which momentarily increases current and overloads semi-conductors in the car's computers. Being sure the key is physically pulled from the car is the best way to be sure it's not inadvertently left in the "on" position.

There are some tests that require the battery to be connected and the engine running, such as testing alternator output. In those instances, be very careful that you are not wearing loose clothing that could get caught in a belt or pulley. Also, do not wear jewelry, such as a bracelet or watch band that would be a conductor if it came in accidental contact with a positive terminal.

Finally, when using a digital multimeter be sure that you know the maximum current rating of the DMM—printed by the amp ports—and do not exceed it. Also, see Sidebar: "A Tour Around the Digital Multimeter," and any cautions specifically applicable to its use.

Let's do it

Battery Maintenance: Why It Matters

Battery maintenance is keeping the battery, its terminals and the battery cables clean and free of corrosion. It also involves, for some batteries, checking the level of the electrolyte. There are differences among the various battery types. For explanations, see Sidebar: "How Batteries Work: 'Wet Cell,' 'Gel,' & 'AGM.'"

When a car's battery isn't able to start the car, the most likely cause is corrosion on the battery cables and terminals. Corrosion is the flakey white or blue-green stuff you sometimes see growing like fungus around the battery terminals. Corrosion is caused by sulfuric acid vapor vented from the battery and condensing on the battery terminals during the charging process.

It might seem that a little bit of corrosion couldn't stop current flowing from the battery to the starter, but, it can. If your starter requires 100 amps (most starters pull 100 to 250 amps), the starter will operate as long as the total resistance in the circuit, i.e., the starter motor's load and the resistance in the wiring from the battery to the starter, does not exceed 0.12 ohms. If resistance is 0.10 ohms, and corrosion increases it by a mere 0.03 ohms, current flow is cut

How Batteries Work: "Wet-Cell", "Gel", and "AGM"

Most batteries are "wet-cell" lead acid batteries, in which an electrolyte of 36% sulfuric acid and 64% distilled water surrounds alternating grids, or "plates," made of lead dioxide (negative) and lead (positive), each separated by a porous mat. All of the negative plates are connected together, as are all of the positive plates. A group of plates make up a "cell." In a 12-V battery, there are 6 cells, each producing about 2.1 volts. These cells are connected to one another "in series," i.e., the negative of one cell is connected to the positive of the adjoining cell, thereby cumulating the voltages of the individual cells to create the voltage of the battery.

When an electrical load is applied to the battery, acid from the electrolyte combines with material on the plate material to create lead sulfate and release electrical energy as a product of this chemical reaction. When the battery is charged, the opposite occurs: the lead sulfate converts back to the plate material, in effect storing electrical energy.

"Sulfation" occurs when the lead sulfate crystallizes. When this occurs, it is no longer possible to convert the lead sulfate into the plate material and the capacity of the battery is accordingly reduced. This can occur over a period of time as a result of repeated charge/discharge cycles or it can occur when a battery has been allowed to remain fully discharged for an extended period of time.

All automotive batteries, whether the traditional wet-cell (including "maintenance-free" and "sealed'), "gel," or "absorption glass mat" (AGM), operate upon these same basic principles. The differences among the battery types lie in their construction and way in which the electrolyte is applied to the battery plates.

A "gel" battery is similar to the wet-cell battery just described except that silica is added to the electrolyte to convert it from a liquid to a gel. Gel batteries are generally designed for "deep cycle" use. Deep cycle means that the battery is designed to be essentially fully discharged and then recharged, repeatedly. Gel batteries have one very big disadvantage: they must be recharged very slowly. Rapid recharging can destroy the battery.

However, most batteries that are called "gel" batteries actually are not. The term is often imprecisely used to refer to batteries that are actually of the third type: AGM batteries.

Absorption glass mat batteries absorb the electrolyte into a fiberglass mat, which is wound between the plates, which are themselves ordinarily formed as cylinders. Optima is perhaps the best-known brand of AGM battery. AGM batteries are less sensitive to vibration than wet-cell batteries, cannot spill battery acid, and may have longer life expectancies in daily use. They can be recharged at a typical rate, though recharging at a very high rate can damage an AGM battery.

Unless it is a deep cycle battery, however, AGM batteries are more likely to die if completely discharged than wet-cell batteries. These batteries are not a good choice for a car that will be stored for an extended period of time, such as a collector car in the winter. If an AGM battery is not to be used for a period of time, it is a good idea to connect it to a Battery Tender—a special charger that maintains battery level, but is not a trickle charger—that will automatically maintain the charge.

to 92 amps, which isn't enough to spin the starter.

That's why it is important to keep the battery terminals and cables clean. Corrosion can occur under the battery cable ends or between the cable end and the terminal post, where it isn't easily seen. But even unseen corrosion can increase resistance enough to leave you stranded, particularly if the battery is a few years old and weaker than when new.

As well as at the battery terminals, corrosion can occur at other electrical connections in the circuit: the connection of the negative battery cable to the ground at the vehicle's frame; the connections at the alternator and at the starter solenoid or relay; and, the starter ground. These connections can be cleaned the same way as the battery terminals. However, *never* attempt to clean connections to the starter without first disconnecting the negative terminal of the battery.

Dirt and grease on the top of the battery can also affect battery performance. A dirty battery top can create a path for current to flow between the positive and negative battery terminals, creating a low amperage drain. By itself, that small electrical drain might not have mattered, but factor in an older battery that's not holding a full 12-volt charge, a little extra resistance in the starter circuit due to corrosion, and all you hear when you turn the key is the clicking sound a starter solenoid makes when it's not getting enough current.

Battery Maintenance: Cleaning & Adding Water

There are two types of battery terminals: "post" terminals and "side terminals" are common on General Motors vehicles and sometimes called "side mount" terminals. Some aftermarket batteries designed to suit more than one make and model have both types of terminals, including the one pictured in this chapter.

Conventional post-type battery clamps look like a "C" that has been squeezed together to grasp the battery post. To release the clamp, loosen the bolt that holds the tips of the clamp together. Then put the tip of a large screwdriver in the gap between the tips and twist. The twisting action of the screwdriver pushes the clamp ends apart sufficiently that you should be able to lift the clamp straight up and off the post.

Occasionally post-type battery terminals and clamps become so corroded that the bolt won't turn, the bolt head rounds off, or the clamp is just stuck. Should that happen to you, do *not* pry against the top of the battery or battery case. That could rupture the battery and cause an explosion that sends sulfuric acid everywhere. Instead get a "battery terminal puller," which is available at any auto parts store for $10 or less. It has two arms to go around the side of the battery clamp while an auger-threaded foot in the middle pushes down on the terminal itself. Battery posts are tapered from top to bottom, so it loosens the clamp as it pulls the clamp upward. Because it is pushing the post through the clamp, this puller can't damage the battery.

Never pound on battery cable ends to force them onto the battery. That can cause internal damage to the battery, as well as damage to the battery case. If a cable end cannot be tightened sufficiently to hold on the battery terminal, the cable end should be replaced.

The cables on a side-terminal battery bolt into the battery on the side of the battery case. To remove the cable, loosen the bolt. The bolt remains in the cable when the cable is removed. You can use a box-end wrench of the proper size or the special "side terminal battery wrench" already discussed in Chapter 1. But avoid using an adjustable wrench. These bolts have small heads that can be rounded off easily if the wrench is loose or slips.

If the bolt on a side terminal battery cable is too damaged to remove with a wrench, you have no choice but to use Vise-Grips, but be sure to wear safety glasses. The terminal itself is held in place by the plastic of the battery case. Too much force on a frozen side mount can twist the terminal in the case, damaging the battery and releasing electrolyte. If the bolt is frozen, tap it lightly with a hammer; use penetrating oil, and some patience. One other trick is to try tightening the bolt, just slightly. Sometimes that is enough to release internal corrosion and allow for removing the bolt.

The simplest and easiest way to clean battery terminals and cable ends is with a battery terminal brush, available at any auto parts store. This device has two nesting parts, each of which is a wire brush. One part fits over post-type battery terminals and the other fits

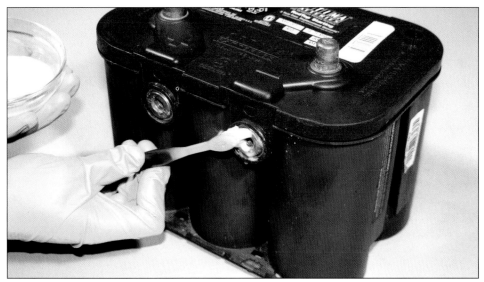

Baking soda and water will clean corrosion from battery terminals. This is an Optima battery, an absorption glass mat battery manufactured by Johnson Controls.

inside the recessed terminals of side mount batteries.

If there is already corrosion on the terminals, you may not be able to remove all of it with a battery terminal brush, especially corrosion inside the threaded terminals of a side mount battery. In that situation, you can use one of the commercial products for removing battery corrosion that are sold at auto parts stores. Or, you can make your own by mixing a 1:2 or 1:3 proportion of baking soda and distilled water in into a paste or slurry and then painting it onto the terminals with an old toothbrush.

After allowing time for the solution to react to the corrosion, scrub the terminals and cable ends with the toothbrush and rinse with distilled water. The same mixture can also be used to clean the battery top and case. Be sure to use distilled water, which you can find at any supermarket. Tap water can leave mineral deposits on the battery, which can create a new low amperage drain between the positive and negative terminals.

Corrosion may also be present on the battery "hold down"—the bolt and clamp that keep the battery in place—and on the tray in which the battery sits. If so, remove the battery and clean these with the baking soda and distilled water solution. There are two types of hold-downs: one uses a clamp across the top of the battery that bolts to a rod alongside the battery; the other uses a rubber wedge that bolts over a lip at the bottom of the battery case. The wedge type unbolts, as well, but you'll need a socket ratchet with extensions to loosen it. Once the battery is out, clean the entire battery case as well.

When reinstalling the battery, take care not to over-tighten the battery hold down bolt. The battery should be held firmly in place, but over-tightening the bolt can crack the battery case.

Also, there are a few vehicles in which the battery is not located under the hood, but is either in the trunk or underneath the back seat. Unless an AGM battery is used, these batteries must be vented. Vented batteries have an opening for a small hose that leads from the battery to vent hydrogen gas to the outside of the vehicle. If the hose is removed during cleaning, be sure to reattach it.

Most batteries today are "sealed" or "maintenance free" and do not need water added to them. These batteries are designed so that there is an area within the battery that allows battery gases to re-condense into electrolyte, thereby avoiding the need for replenishing. These batteries, however, have safety valves that will allow emission of hydrogen gas if the internal battery pressure exceeds specified levels. Some maintenance free batteries actually do not have liquid electrolyte, including the advanced "absorptive glass mat batteries," commonly, though incorrectly, called "gel" batteries (see sidebar in this chapter).

There are, however, still batteries that are not sealed: that is, they have removable caps, either the screw-on type or the kind that push into the battery top, and you do need to check electrolyte level periodically. It can be difficult to determine whether a battery is sealed or has caps. If there are two panels, each covering three battery cells and separated by some form of gap from the rest of the battery, those are probably caps and can be removed by gently prying the panels up with a screwdriver. If, however, the battery is completely smooth on top, it probably is sealed.

To ascertain the level of electrolyte in a battery with caps, after removing the

The "hold down" is what keeps the battery in place. Corrosion can build up around the base of the battery and be visible in the area of the hold down clamp. This makes it easy for the battery to develop "case drain."

Many cars have the battery in the trunk or, as here, under the rear seat. This protects the battery from engine heat, and also provides better weight distribution. From an engineer's perspective, however, it allows reducing the size of the engine compartment or putting other things into it.

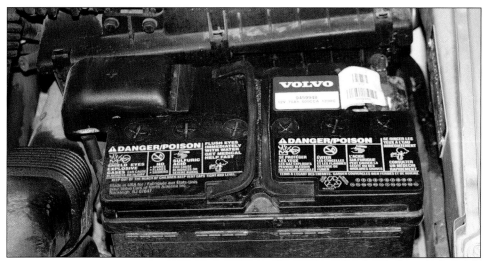

This battery may look similar to sealed, maintenance free batteries, but if you look closely, you'll see that it actually has removable caps. Batteries with lids or caps that can be removed should be checked periodically to assure that the electrolyte is at the proper level.

caps look for a visible "full" mark. Add distilled water to each cell to that mark. If there is no mark, add only enough distilled water to keep the fluid level above the tops of the plates in each cell, but about 1/8 inch below the bottom of the fill hole. Also be sure that any vent holes in the caps are clean and open.

When checking electrolyte level or adding distilled water to a battery, always wear safety glasses and be sure the area is well ventilated. Add water very slowly and don't overfill the battery. There are special battery fillers available at auto parts stores, or you can use a turkey baster or small pitcher. Always, however, use distilled water. Tap water will react with chemicals in the battery and shorten its life.

Your battery may have an "eye": a little plastic lens in the top of the battery, also called an "indicator eye." The eye has a color, usually green, to indicate that the battery is OK. If it's red or black—the color varies with manufacturer—it's not OK. These eyes actually measure the electrolyte level and charge, but they are far from being reliable. The eye only reports on the condition of one of six cells, assuming they're all the same. If, however, another cell is dead, the eye will not report this. Even if the cells are all the same, a battery can show

a green eye even though it is only holding a 25% charge and is in such bad shape that a 25% charge is the most it can hold.

Technically, that battery isn't "dead," but, it has absolutely no margin left for starting the car when conditions are not ideal and should be replaced. That's why taking half an hour to test your battery with a digital multimeter—as outlined below—is such a good investment of time. You'll know when it's time to replace the battery: you won't waste money doing it too soon, and you won't find out when it's too late, either.

You may see articles suggesting that you can prevent corrosion in battery terminals and cable ends by applying dielectric grease or petroleum jelly before reattaching them. That is very poor advice: dielectric grease does not conduct electricity. Applying dielectric grease or petroleum jelly to the mating surfaces of an electrical connection just increases resistance to current flow. Dielectric grease is designed as an oxygen and moisture barrier. It should be applied only to the outside of the terminal and cable connections, never the mating surfaces. Used that way, it can protect against corrosion and current drain by sealing the terminals from the atmosphere.

Once you have cleaned the battery, test it to determine whether it needs charging. If you cleaned corrosion off the battery, chances are good that it is not fully charged.

Testing the Battery with a Digital Multimeter

Testing the battery with a digital multimeter is usually the logical first step in trouble-shooting any problem in the charging system. It's also a fine way to figure out whether you're due for a new battery.

There are, however, two things to remember before beginning these tests: First, the charging system is integrated, so what causes a problem in one part of the system can be a problem in another part of the system. A prematurely dead battery may have been killed by a defective battery cable, or a loose alternator drive belt. Just because you found one problem doesn't mean you've cured the patient. You may have only applied a band-aid. That's why it makes sense to test the entire system.

Second, the voltage and amperage specifications accompanying these tests are typical for 12-volt systems, all of which are essentially similar. But the best practice remains checking the factory shop manual for the exact specifications applicable to your vehicle, because there is some variation among manufacturers in the ranges deemed "normal."

There are other ways to test a battery, including commercially available dedicated battery testers, of which the Midtronics brand is the best known. Any professional auto repair shop will have one. But, they start at about $200 and go up from there, averaging well over $400. Most of the functions of professional equipment can be duplicated with a digital multimeter. In fact, professional battery testers include many of the functions of a DMM.

You may also hear about battery "carbon pile load testers." Consumer versions of these are available on the Internet and in some auto parts stores for about $100 and up. Basically, these

A Tour Around the Digital Multimeter

It is the single most useful electronic diagnostic tool you can have: the digital multimeter (DMM). It's not expensive. While cheap ones can be found for as little as $20, a completely satisfactory DMM can cost less than $60. You can spend more, but you don't need to.

All digital multimeters have the same basic settings and controls, and the same basic jacks. These are related to the three basic functions of a DMM: measuring voltage, measuring current flow, and measuring resistance. That's why it is called a "multimeter." It combines the functions of a voltmeter, ammeter (amps), and ohmmeter (resistance) all in one instrument. It's a "digital" multimeter because it reads out the results in numbers, not as a dial with a moving needle. A multimeter with a dial and needle is an analog multimeter.

Do not use an analog multimeter on a vehicle. First, it can give false readings when measuring current and voltage. An analog multimeter has less resistance than a DMM, which means that it can actually permit more current to flow than the component it's supposedly measuring. Second, when measuring ohms, an analog multimeter sends out a much larger voltage than does a DMM. An analog meter sends out enough voltage to damage solid-state components (i.e., integrated circuits, transistors, and diodes, including light emitting diodes and liquid crystal diodes). Now for the tour.

There are four areas on the front of the DMM: the display, the range selector, the mode selector, and the input jacks. There are also two leads, a red one and a black one, and there may be other accessory leads, as well. Many multimeters also include a clamp with red and black leads to it. This is an "inductive pick-up" clamp. It can be clamped onto a spark plug wire to calculate engine RPM.

The display gives you the actual number being measured. The display will show whether it is measuring AC or DC (alternating current or direct current) and the unit of measurement, i.e., volts, amps, or ohms. The DMM display will also show "O.L" or "over-limit" (or something similar) when the measurement exceeds the range of the multimeter.

Letters are used in conjunction with the electrical abbreviations in the display to indicate the range: "m" stands for "milli," i.e., 0.001 or 1/1000 of something; "k" stands for "kilo," which is 1000 times as much, i.e., multiply by 1000; "u" is "micro, 1/one millionth; and, "M" stands for "mega," which is multiplying by one million. So, 2 kV is 2,000 volts, 2 mA is two one-thousandths of an ampere.

For each type of measurement, there are choices of the "range" in which the result should be displayed. For example, if you are measuring resistance (ohms) you could display the result with a range of 0 to 40 Ω, 0 to 400 Ω, 0 to 4 kΩ, and up to 0 to 40 kΩ.

Most DMMs have "automatic ranging," which means that you can let the DMM automatically select and display the range appropriate to the measurement. In the example, if the DMM reads 700 ohms, it automatically selects the kΩ range and shows the measurement as 0.700 kΩ. This reads out the result to the maximum number of decimal places, so the result is as accurate as possible.

Starting with the mode selector, there is an "off" position and positions for AC Volts (V with a ~ above it), DC Volts (V with a solid and dashed line above it), millivolts (mV with a solid and dashed line), ohms (Ω), diode check (→⊦), amps/milliamps (mA, A), and microamps (uA). Working on vehicles, you will likely have no need for the microamp setting.

Finally, there are the input jacks. "COM" stands for common ground (the electrical ground). The black negative lead always goes in the COM jack. It never goes in any other jack. The read lead is positive and it is plugged in to the jack appropriate to the measurement involved: the V jack when measuring voltage or resistance, and the A jack when measuring current (amperage). There may also be a jack for milliamps and microamps, mA and uA. On some DMMs, there may be one combination jack for V, A, and Ω.

Digital multimeters all specify a maximum current level that should not be exceeded when using the unit. The maximum current level is printed on the face of the unit, at the amperage jacks. DMMs also have one high amperage jack, such as 20 A. Avoid using it because it has no fuse.

The level of protection that a DMM offers against sudden transitory overloads is reflected in its International Electrotechnical Commission rating. IEC CAT-III is the lowest rating you should buy, and you should also be sure that the DMM you select is approved by the Underwriter's Laboratory as meeting its standard 3111-1. An IEC CAT-III rating translates to protection against a voltage spike of 8,000 volts with only 2 ohms of resistance, which translates to 4,000 amps. These ratings, admittedly, are of more concern when using a DMM on household current than to using a DMM on a car, because unexpected lightning strikes can cause voltage spikes in household electric systems. But, there are two reasons to buy a CAT-III DMM: first, if you do use it in the house, it's protection you should have; second, those who make quality DMMs meet this standard, so it's an easy way to assess quality.

Voltage is always checked with a digital multimeter by setting up the DMM as a parallel circuit. Amps and ohms are always tested by using the DMM as part of a series circuit.

When you connect two parallel circuits to a voltage source, such as a battery, you get a larger current flow than would be the case if it were a series circuit. That is because, all things being equal, a parallel circuit has less total resistance than a series circuit. Amperage and resistance are inversely proportional, so when you cut resistance in half, you double amperage.

The difference between serial and parallel circuits is important when using a digital multimeter. If you try to test amperage or resistance by creating a parallel circuit, you will get an inaccurate result (overstating current, understating resistance), you may blow a fuse in the DMM or damage it (some amperage ranges may not be fused), and you may overload the circuit in

the car, potentially frying something expensive, such as a integrated circuit. So, be sure you know the circuit before hooking up a DMM.

After you're familiar with the functions of a DMM, there are obviously many more tests that you can perform with it than are described in this book. A good place to find more information is the factory shop manual. It will have a wiring diagram for every circuit in the car and accompanying trouble-shooting charts for each potential problem that tell you exactly what to test to isolate the fault.

devices create a very high amperage circuit directly from the positive to the negative terminals of the battery, with a very large resistor in that circuit. The device then measures the drop in battery voltage as this artificial load is placed on the battery. Used improperly, a "carbon pile" can overload the battery and damage it internally.

There is also an old-fashioned battery-testing device called a battery hydrometer. This is a device that looks like a turkey baster with a float inside. It measures the specific gravity of electrolyte. From that, it is possible to roughly calculate the state of charge of the battery. A battery hydrometer is available at any auto parts store for around $10. However, it isn't very accurate and is useless for sealed or maintenance free batteries that do not allow access to the electrolyte.

In contrast to these, the DMM is a reasonably priced instrument that gives accurate results, is easy to use, and can be used to diagnose almost any automotive electrical system problem. Plus, you can use it on the household electrical system, too.

To test the charging system with a digital multimeter, start by measuring the battery's "open circuit voltage." This is done with the engine not running and the ignition "off." It measures the voltage the battery is holding, i.e., the level of battery charge.

If the battery has just been charged, turn on the headlights for one minute. This removes so-called "surface voltage" from the battery: essentially, a form of magnetic field. Then turn off the headlights and the radio and all accessories.

Select a voltage range that includes 12 volts. If the DMM has it, select the autoranging feature.

Plug the negative (black) lead of the multimeter into the COM port. "COM" stands for "common ground."

NOTE: Black wires and cables are always negative; red wires and cables are always positive. The "ground" is that

part of the route current takes that leads back to the battery's negative terminal from whatever used the current, such as the starter. The route from the positive battery terminal to the negative terminal is a "circuit."

The black lead on a DMM always plugs into the COM port because it is always the ground wire. It never, ever, ever goes in any other port. Moreover, no matter what test is being performed, the black lead will always be attached to the circuit at a point that is closer to the negative battery terminal than wherever the positive lead is attached. This can be

Before doing any other tests, check the battery to see if it is fully charged. The tests require a fully charged battery to provide the most valid results.

a bit confusing, because some tests require attaching both leads to the return part of the circuit, which is negative (and black). Just remember that current always flows into the DMM through the positive and out through the negative, which is why the black lead must attach closest to the negative battery terminal.

Now plug the positive (red) lead of the DMM into the "V" port. V and Ω are the accepted symbols, respectively, for volts and ohms; amps is "A." Attach the red lead to the positive battery terminal. Then attach the black lead to the negative terminal.

The reading on the DMM is the battery's actual voltage, at that moment: 12.60 V or above—fully charged; 12.45 V—75% charged; 12.30 V or above—50% charged; and, 12.15 V—25% charged. If the reading is less than 12.0 volts, you have a dead battery.

That may not seem as though it adds up: it's a 12-volt battery, but 12 volts is dead. Actually, an automotive battery is a 12.6-volt battery. It is comprised of six separate cells, linked together. Each cell should have about 2.1 volts, which gives a total of 12.6 volts for a properly functioning, fully charged battery.

NOTE: These voltage readings assume the ambient temperature is about 70 degrees F. Battery voltage drops as temperature drops because the chemical reactions inside the battery are slowed and resistance rises. At 0 degrees F, a 12-volt battery's amperage will be reduced by 35%, at –20 degrees F it's 50% lower. In cold weather, it may be necessary to remove the battery and warm it overnight before these tests can be validly performed. Similarly, if the battery is excessively hot, due to engine heat or a high ambient temperature, the battery should be allowed to cool. High heat turns some of the electrolyte into gas and weakens the battery until the gas condenses.

If the battery is not fully charged at this point, you should use a battery charger to bring it to a full charge. Validity of the remaining tests depends upon a fully charged battery.

Once the battery is fully charged, disconnect it from the charger. It can be tested for "battery drain," also called "parasitic drain" or "parasitic load":

Plug the red lead into the amps port, marked "A," on the DMM. .

Set the DMM to the lowest range and disconnect the negative battery cable.

Then connect the positive lead of the DMM to the negative battery cable and connect the negative lead to the negative battery terminal. That way, current flows through the DMM from the negative cable to the negative battery terminal.

Now wait 30 minutes, with the DMM connections in place. In many cars, disconnecting the battery actually increases parasitic drain within the system because it activates circuits within automotive computers that have stored electricity and those computers will continue to demand current until internal timers shut them down. If you don't wait for these to shut down, about 30 minutes, there may be extra current loss and the test readings may be erroneously high. If you have a computer memory saver, do not use it during this test because it introduces current, albeit very little, into the system.

After waiting 30 minutes, turn on the DMM and check the reading. That is the battery drain. Most modern cars continue to use some current from the battery

If the battery isn't fully charged, put it on a battery charger before testing the alternator. The alternator is designed merely to maintain the level of charge in the battery. To completely charge a battery, a battery charger is the proper tool.

Once the battery is fully charged, further tests are possible, starting with the battery drain test. This car passes, no problem.

when the car is not running to maintain the memories in electronic components. That drain should only be about 0.020 amps (20 mA). A battery drain of 0.035 amps (35 mA) indicates a short circuit (i.e., a short-cut in the circuit allowing current to the ground before it is supposed to) somewhere in the electrical system.

Turn off the DMM and disconnect it from the battery's negative cable and terminal. Then, reconnect the negative battery cable.

You can now test for "battery case drain," which is current drain across the battery case from the positive terminal to the negative terminal. Plug the positive lead into the V port and select the lowest volt range on the DMM. The positive lead should be clamped to the top of the battery case and the negative to the negative battery terminal. If the reading is more than 0.5 volts, there is an excessive drain across the top of the battery and it needs to be cleaned, as above.

The remaining battery tests require disabling the vehicle so that it won't start. That can be done in one of two ways, depending on the age of the vehicle and the type of ignition and fuel system it has.

Most modern vehicles have an electric fuel pump because they use fuel injection systems that require pressurizing the fuel lines. To prevent the car from starting, simply remove the fuse for the fuel pump. Start the car—it will start because there is some residual pressure in the lines that will supply fuel momentarily—let it die, and proceed with the testing. Alternatively, locate the fuse for the fuel injection and remove it, which will have the same effect.

The owner's manual will describe the location of the fuse blocks and provide a diagram that shows the identity of the various fuses. That information is also in the factory shop manual.

In older cars, especially those that use a carburetor rather than fuel injection, the fuel pump is mechanically operated by the engine. Vehicles of this age generally use a conventional distributor to send current to the spark plugs and can be disabled by removing the rotor from the distributor. Trace the spark plug wires back to their point of origin on the distributor cap, locate the two slotted, spring-loaded screws that hold it on, and twist them as you push down to release the cap. You should be able to pull it off without disconnecting the wires. The rotor is the plastic disc or beam with a metal contact at the center and one end that fits on the shaft inside the body of the distributor. Remove it and then reinstall the cap. The ignition is now disabled.

If the battery cables clamp onto posts on the battery, you can now perform a "voltage drop test" of the connection between the cable and post. This test is not practical on a side terminal battery because the clamp entirely covers the battery terminal.

The DMM should be set at the lowest volts range, the positive lead should be plugged into the V port, and the positive lead should be touching the positive post. The negative lead should be touching the positive battery clamp. While holding them in place, have an assistant crank the engine. The reading should be 0.0 volts. That means that all of the

Next is a test for "battery case drain," which is a flow of current from the positive to the negative terminal over the battery case itself. This battery is very clean, so it's not surprising that it shows no voltage leakage.

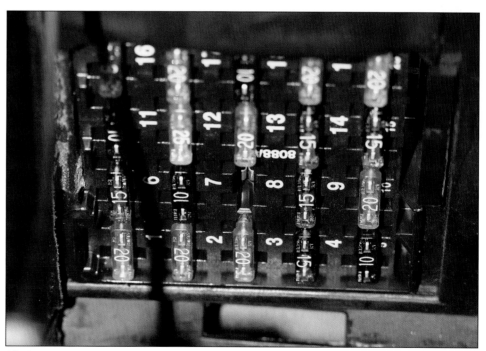

Modern cars with electronic fuel controls can be disabled from starting either by removing the fuse that controls the fuel pump or removing the fuel injection fuse. In this case, the fuse box is located in the glove box, under a cosmetic cover. However, many cars have several different fuse box locations.

current is flowing through the post and clamp, none through the DMM. In turn, that means there is no resistance in between the post and clamp. If there were resistance, some of the current would take the path of least resistance through the DMM. A reading above 0.0 V indicates corrosion or dirt.

This is only one example of a "voltage drop test," which is a test that measures resistance inferentially by comparing voltage under load at two points on a circuit. It is particularly useful for measuring resistance in low resistance circuits. Battery cables, for instance, are low resistance circuits. Because current flow is inversely proportional to resistance, getting high amperage in a circuit mandates having low resistance. When you see big, thick cables in the car, those are low resistance circuits; all things being equal (voltage, material, length) a big fat wire has less resistance than a thin one, so it permits more amps.

DMMs have an ohms function designed to test resistance by sending a small level of current through the circuit and measuring how much gets through. But this function isn't valid for a low resistance circuit because the cur-rent flow is too small to encounter resistance in a circuit of that type. A voltage drop test can indicate resistance in such circuits. The same theory underlies the tests that are used to measure resistance in battery cables, covered later in the chapter.

The last battery test is the "cranking voltage test." This test puts the battery under load turning the starter and measures the change in voltage. It, too, is done with the engine disabled, so that it cannot start.

Set the voltage range to a range that includes 12 volts or select the autoranging feature. Plug the red DMM lead into the V port and attach the lead to the positive battery terminal. Attach the black lead to the negative battery terminal.

Now, have an assistant crank the engine for 15 seconds. Observe the voltage reading during the last three of those seconds. As the engine cranks, the voltage reading will go down. If, in the last three seconds of the test, the reading is 9.6 V or higher, then the battery has sufficient cranking voltage. A reading of 9.5 V or below means that either there is resistance in the battery cables or that the battery does not have enough cranking capacity.

Testing the Negative Battery Cable with a Digital Multimeter

The negative battery cable runs from the negative battery terminal to a ground on the vehicle's frame. The positive cable runs between the battery and the alternator, attaching at the output terminal, sometimes referred to as the "B" terminal. A branch of the positive cable also runs to the starter solenoid or relay.

If the voltage reading when performing the "cranking voltage test" or any of the other battery tests is low, that could be due to a fault in the negative battery cable. To test the negative battery cable, the engine must be disabled so that it will not start, as described above.

With the positive lead again plugged into the V port and the range set to the lowest voltage range or to autoranging, attach the negative lead to the negative battery post (to the post, not the cable—on a side mount, attach it to the bolt head). Attach the positive to a good ground, such as the engine block or the frame.

Have your assistant crank the starter again and observe the reading. Expect a reading of 0.1 V. A reading in excess of

The "cranking voltage test" measures the battery's performance under the heavy load of starting. This battery is well above the lowest acceptable level.

Set up for testing the negative battery cable by using a voltage drop test measuring cable resistance by creating a parallel circuit to ground. Of course, you have to first find a ground. This car has a heavy metal bracket (designed for lifting the engine) that is easily accessible, so that's the ground that will be used.

0.2 volts means there is excessive resistance in the negative battery cable or its connections. Either the connections are loose, they're corroded, or there is an internal deterioration of the negative battery cable itself and you should replace it. Be sure to retest after replacing the cable, just to be sure you've corrected the problem.

This test measures the voltage drop over the negative cable. By bridging from the body ground to the battery negative terminal, you create a circuit parallel to that of the battery negative cable. Current returning to the battery flows through the ground to the negative battery cable and through the cable to the negative battery terminal. By creating a second circuit parallel to the battery cable and measuring the voltage difference at each end, it's possible to calculate resistance in the primary circuit. That's because some of the current is going through the DMM instead of the primary circuit. Current takes the path of least resistance, so if some flows through the DMM, it means that there is resistance in the primary circuit, at least enough to discourage some of the electrons from flowing through it.

You cannot expect a 0.0 V reading on this test, unlike testing for resistance between the battery terminal and clamp. Some resistance is inevitable simply because the circuit includes a cable: length is one factor creating resistance, so a connection by cable always has more resistance than a direct connection. But this is supposed to be a low resistance circuit, so the resistance should be minimal. At this point, replace the fuel pump fuse or distributor rotor, so that the car can be started.

Testing the Alternator and Positive Battery Cable

The easiest test to perform on the alternator is output at the battery. The test verifies the performance of the positive battery cable at the same time, so if the output is within proper specifications, it means both alternator and cable are performing properly.

To test the alternator output at the battery, plug the positive lead of the DMM into the V port and connect it to the positive battery terminal. Connect the negative lead to the negative battery terminal. You should, of course, be getting a fully charged reading of 12.6 V or near that. Have an assistant start the car with all accessories off and idle the engine at a fast idle of about 1,500 rpm. The voltage reading should increase by about 2 volts, but a reading between 13.2 V and 15.2 V is within normal range.

Then increase engine speed to between 1,800 and 2,800 rpm. The voltage reading should not change from the idle-speed reading by more than 0.5 V.

Turn on the lights and accessories that were previously turned off. The voltage reading should not drop below 13 V.

A reading above 16.0 volts on the first test indicates that the voltage regulator has failed and the alternator is overcharging the battery. Overcharging creates excessive heat in the electrolyte. That causes electrolyte to gas and vent away and also damages the ability of the lead plates within the battery to perform the chemical reaction necessary to store electricity, so the battery soon fails. The

alternator must be replaced (unless the car is old enough to have a separate voltage regulator).

A reading below these specifications indicates either low alternator output or too much resistance in the circuit. Assuming the battery terminals and cable connectors are all clean and free of corrosion, the next possible cause to check is the alternator drive belt.

"V" belts—the kind of belt that has a "V" cross-section shape—are notorious for slipping. As the belt wears, it stretches and the surface that meets the pulley burnishes and becomes smoother. The end result is the belt slips. Also, centrifugal force will lift a loose belt away from the pulley as speed increases. So a belt that doesn't slip when you're inspecting it at idle can slip when RPM increases. That's why a squealing sound as you rev the engine is a classic sign of a slipping drive belt. Adjust the V belt and check alternator output again.

Serpentine drive belts—the ones that are wide and have a series of grooves on one or both sides—can also slip. Though these are automatically tensioned, the belt can slip if the belt is worn or the tensioner is improperly adjusted, or failing.

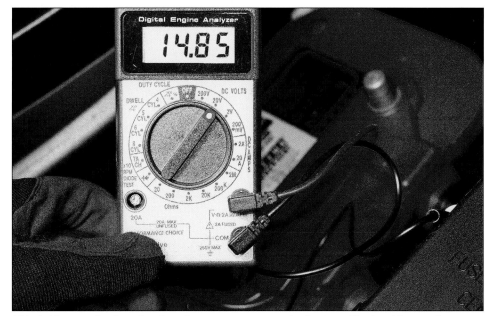

This is the result of testing for alternator output at the battery. The healthy reading gives the alternator, the voltage regulator, and the cables a clean bill of health. The alternator is designed to exceed battery rated voltage, but not by too much—only by enough to create the chemical reaction in the battery that allows it to store electricity.

How the Alternator Works

An alternator, sometimes referred to as an "AC generator" (with AC standing for "alternating current"), creates electrical current by using magnets. Passing a magnet over a wire creates voltage. There are two types of alternators: the conventional alternator used on older cars, and the newer "compact high speed" alternator used on modern cars. But, they both work essentially the same way.

An alternator consists of a "stator" (sometimes called an "armature") and a "rotor" which rotates within the stator. The stator is a circular iron frame several inches wide that is covered with many yards of looped wire. This wire is arranged in three groups, each covering 120 degrees of the stator's circumference. Technically, this is termed a "three phase" alternator and produces alternating current in a series of overlapping pulses easily converted to direct current.

The rotor consists of a shaft around which are mounted a series of opposing iron fingers. Each finger fits into the slot between the two fingers immediately opposite it, but none of the fingers touch. When the rotor is mounted inside the stator, these fingers are arranged across the width of the stator almost, but not quite, touching it.

The rotor is turned within the stator by a belt (serpentine on newer cars, a "V" belt on older cars) that turns a pulley on the outside of the alternator. The rotor is driven by the engine crankshaft at two or three times engine speed (the alternator pulley is smaller than the pulley on the crankshaft).

When the ignition switch in the car is turned to the "on" position, electricity flows from the battery through a voltage regulator to "brushes" inside the rotor. A brush is a carbon pad that serves as a contact point between a wire attached to the brush and a rotating shaft. The brushes are pressed by springs onto a "slip ring," which is an encircling ring of conductive metal that is part of the shaft. Electricity flows through the brushes to the rotor shaft and to a separate set of wound wires inside the rotator assembly called the "field winding," sometimes called the "rotor coil." "Rotor coil" should not to be confused with an "ignition coil," which is the part of the ignition system that creates high voltage to fire the spark plugs.

Current flowing into the field winding creates a magnetic field around the rotor. This makes the iron fingers "electromagnets." When the rotor is spun, this magnetic field spinning in proximity to the stator generates voltage. Because the iron fingers are positioned in alternating opposite directions, one becomes a North pole and the next becomes a South pole, all the way around the rotor.

Because the rotor is an electromagnet, the amount of voltage produced by spinning it within the stator can be controlled by controlling the amount of current flowing to the rotor. This is the function of the "voltage regulator." The voltage regulator measures the voltage output of the alternator and adjusts the much smaller "field current" flowing into the rotor to achieve proper output and prevent overcharging. If the alternator and voltage regulator are functioning properly, the alternator's voltage output will be between 13.5 and 14.5 volts. Below 13.5 volts, the car will be discharging the battery. Above 14.5 volts, it will be overcharging the battery. However, the alternator in a 12-volt system is designed to produce more than 12 volts of current because additional voltage is required to overcome the electrical resistance of the battery and charge it. In modern alternators, the voltage regulator is located within the alternator body and cannot be separately serviced.

The alternating arrangement of North and South electromagnets on the rotor creates alternating current (AC). Direct current (DC) constantly flows in one direction, while alternating current goes back and forth constantly. A light bulb doesn't care which direction the energy it is using flows, but a car battery is storing electrical power, not using it. It requires current that only flows one way: in through the negative terminal and out through the positive terminal, creating a circuit.

It may seem odd that car manufacturers would create AC when the car requires DC, but there is a reason. Alternators are less complicated, cheaper, more durable and less prone to failure than DC generators. So, automakers use alternators and then convert the output to direct current with diodes. A typical alternator has two diodes for each group of looped wires on the stator, i.e. six diodes. A diode is essentially a filter that allows only current going in one direction through, blocking the current going in the opposite direction. By using diodes, the alternating current created by the alternator is converted to direct current that can flow to the battery.

When the ignition switch in the car is turned to the "on" position, you should see the alternator warning light illuminate. It should then go off as the engine starts. This is because the warning light is actually part of one of the alternator circuits. It draws battery current on its positive side when the ignition is on, but the alternator is not charging, which is why it goes on. When the alternator is running, it receives offsetting current through a diode from the alternator on the negative side, which extinguishes the warning light.

As with a V belt, a squealing serpentine belt is a sign that it's slipping; but, just because it's not squealing doesn't mean it's not slipping. Serpentine belts, tensioners, V belts, and their adjustment are covered in Chapter 8.

If, after checking all of these possibilities, the alternator output still fails to reach the proper level, then the source of the problem is either the positive battery cable, i.e., the alternator output cable to the battery, or the alternator itself.

To test the positive battery cable/alternator output cable, plug the positive lead of the DMM into the V port and connect it to the output terminal, i.e., the "B" terminal of the alternator. You may have to move a rubber boot on the terminal to access it. There may be a letter "B" cast into the alternator housing near the terminal. Connect the negative lead of the DMM to the positive terminal of the battery. Start the engine and bring the RPM up to about 2,000—somewhat more than a fast idle.

The reading on the DMM should not more than the specification listed in the factory shop manual, which is usually about 0.2 V, though some GM vehicles permit a voltage drop of as much as 0.5 V. If the voltage drop exceeds specifications, there is resistance in that circuit—either the terminals, including the alternator terminal, or in the cable itself.

If the terminals are clean and corrosion-free, then replace the cable and retest.

The alternator is grounded through the alternator frame, which bolts to the engine. Together with the output cable, this ground completes the output circuit of the alternator. In order to charge the battery, the alternator must provide sufficient current to slightly exceed the 12.6-volt maximum capacity of the battery. There must be a current flow through the battery from positive to negative to cause the chemical reaction between the electrolyte and lead plates in the battery that makes it possible for it to store the electrons, i.e., hold a positive charge.

Thus, this "negative circuit ground test" compares current flowing to ground at the battery negative terminal to that flowing to ground from the alternator. If more current is flowing to ground from the battery negative while the alternator is charging than from the alternator, it indicates resistance in the alternator ground circuit.

With the positive lead in the V port, connect the DMM positive lead to the negative terminal of the battery. Then connect the negative lead to the alternator frame or housing.

Again, start the engine and bring RPM to about 2,000. Expect a drop in voltage of 0.1 V. 0.2 V or more is indicates excessive resistance in the ground circuit. Because the alternator ground is through the engine block and frame, rather than through a cable, resistance on this test is usually an indication of corroded connections or a loose cable.

If both the insulated side of the alternator output circuit and the ground side show minimal voltage drop, then the problem is with the alternator. It will need to be replaced.

There is an alternative (unintended pun) to testing the alternator on your own. In some instances, this alternative may also be the only safe way to test it.

Many auto parts stores will "bench test" the alternator for you, free of charge. Bench testing means you take the alternator off the car and bring it to them, and they put it on a specialized machine that does a variety of different tests in a matter of a few minutes, including some tests that you can't run without having that special equipment, such as testing diodes in the alternator.

Alternators can also be tested on the car. Some auto parts stores are now offering to do this as well, usually without charge. The machines that do that have been in existence for over 25 years (the Sun VAT 45 is the most prominent of these, to the point that it is actually referred to by name in some factory shop manuals), but the newest models, such as the Snap-On MicroVAT, are small enough to be hand-held. These testers require only three connections—both battery terminals and an induction clamp around the negative battery cable—and can fully test the battery, alternator, and starter in less than a minute. At $900 for a MicroVAT, these are too expensive for the consumer but are practical investments for parts stores.

In fact, this may be the only way to test the alternator in your vehicle. In some cars, particularly those with front wheel drive and transverse engines, it's difficult to even see the alternator, much less to attach the leads from a digital multimeter to it. It may even be necessary to remove other components, such as the radiator, to access the alternator. It makes a lot of sense, if you have one of those cars, to find a parts store than can test the alternator for you on the car.

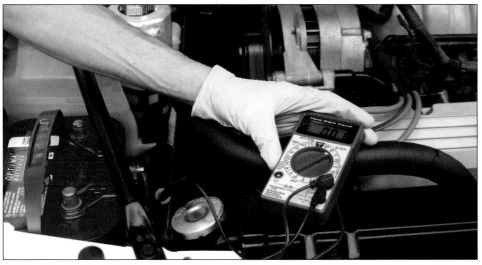

Testing the positive battery cable with a digital multimeter is just a matter of setting up a voltage drop test between the output terminal of the alternator and the positive terminal of the battery, into which current flows from the alternator.

Also, don't overlook the help you can get on cars manufactured for model years 1996 and after from OBD-II diagnostic trouble codes. Most internal faults in an alternator will set a code. If there is a code, that gives you a big lead on finding the cause. If there is no code, check the factory shop manual for the possible alternator-related codes, anyway. If you know what could set a code and no code has been set, you should be able to assume that system is functioning properly.

Diagnostic trouble codes are covered in Chapter 10. If a code has been set, the shop manual will provide a diagnostic procedure to further trace the cause of the fault, as well as repair procedures.

Removing & Replacing the Alternator

To remove the alternator, disconnect the negative battery cable, and then the positive cable. Then disconnect the electrical connections at the alternator. If the vehicle drives the alternator with a V belt, there are usually two bolts holding the alternator in place, one of them in a slide and the other bolted to the engine as a pivot. Loosen the one in the slide and remove the V belt, as described in Chapter 8. If the alternator is driven by a serpentine belt, remove the belt by pushing the tensioner away from the belt, as also described in Chapter 8. Once the belt is

off, then remove the bolts holding the alternator in place and remove the alternator. This is, incidentally, a good time to replace those belts if they appear worn.

Even if you need to replace the alternator, you may not need a new one. Many companies that manufacture original equipment alternators, such as Delco-Remy, also rebuild alternators. A quality rebuilt alternator should be a completely satisfactory replacement, at a much lower price than a new alternator.

Installing a replacement alternator is the reverse of removing the old one, the exception being that the V belt (if equipped) must be properly tensioned. To tension the V belt, using a long screwdriver to pry against the alternator with the V belt in place, hold the belt tight as you tighten the slide bolt. The tension is correct when the belt can be depressed approximately its own width at the point midway between the two pulleys furthest apart. That is, push on the middle of the belt where the distance between pulleys is the longest. Recheck the tension after the engine has been running for fifteen minutes or so.

It is very important to make sure that the pulley on the alternator aligns with the other pulleys, so that the belt is not being pulled to the side as it turns. Misaligned pulleys wear belts prematurely, resulting in belt slippage and noise. Checking pulley alignment is discussed in Chapter 8.

If the charging system is operating properly and the battery can be fully charged, any loss of battery voltage is likely due to a fault in the wiring, which is causing a parasitic loss. Many automobile dealer service departments and professional repair shops are equipped with instruments that can locate a short that is causing a battery drain. You can, of course, attempt to isolate it with a multimeter if you suspect the cause. Otherwise, it makes sense to delegate the job to someone with the proper tools.

Looks new, but it's actually rebuilt, perhaps by the same company that made it when new. The key to quality in a rebuilt part is the remanufacturer, just as quality in a new part depends on its manufacturer.

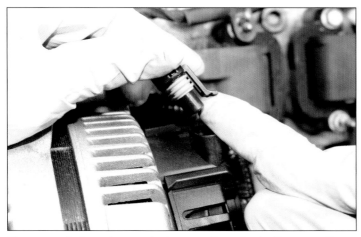

The second step when replacing an alternator is disconnecting the various electrical connectors. The first step, however, is even more important: disconnecting the battery.

Then, removing the alternator is merely a matter of loosening and removing the mounting bolts. The alternator on this Corvette is very easily accessed, but some alternators can only be removed from underneath the car.

CHAPTER 7

COOLING SYSTEM EFFICIENCY

ANTIFREEZE, RADIATOR HOSE REPLACEMENT AND DIAGNOSIS

The cooling system's function is transferring heat from the engine to the atmosphere. Coolant is circulated by a pump located in the engine (the "water pump") through passages within the cylinder block and cylinder heads and then to the radiator. The radiator is comprised of finned tubes through which the coolant passes, releasing heat to the atmosphere. Fans, which are usually electrically powered in modern cars, pull air through the radiator when the vehicle's speed isn't sufficient to maintain adequate air flow. Most radiators today are made of aluminum. The water pump is driven by an accessory drive belt or by the serpentine drive belt, which is powered by a pulley on the external end of the crankshaft.

The cooling system is also designed to heat the engine. When a cold engine is started, a thermostatically controlled valve cuts off coolant flow to the radiator to promote engine warm-up. As the coolant reaches operating temperature, the valve opens until it is completely open by the time normal operating temperature is attained. This valve, called the "thermostat," is typically located in the engine block, in a coolant outlet housing to which one of the radiator hoses con-

nects. Coolant is also circulated through smaller diameter hoses to the heater core, which is essentially a small radiator through which air is circulated to warm the passenger compartment.

"Coolant" is a mixture of antifreeze and distilled water, almost always in a 50/50 proportion. There are several different types of antifreeze, and they are not compatible with one another (see Sidebar: "Dex-Cool, G-05, and the Green Stuff." Antifreeze protects against coolant freeze-up and also raises the coolant's boiling point. Cooling systems are closed, so that pressure within the system increases as the coolant heats. This pressure further raises the coolant boiling point. Typically, a cooling system will have a pressure of about 15 pounds per square inch at operating temperature and, under pressure, a coolant boiling point of about 270 degrees F.

Modern cooling systems have a coolant reservoir tank, which stores additional coolant and allows for expansion and contraction of the coolant as temperature increases and decreases. These tanks have marks indicating the proper coolant level. Coolant is added to this tank, rather than to the radiator itself.

Cooling systems require both maintenance and occasional repair. Coolant itself must be replaced, though manufacturers are now recommending service intervals of as long as 5 years or 150,000 miles. Thermostats and water pumps can wear out and require replacement.

Radiator hoses don't last forever, either. Unfortunately, hoses often fail from the inside out, without the slightest change in outward appearance until large clouds of steam begin to escape from under the hood. Even when a hose doesn't burst, deterioration inside the hose can cause it to collapse during heavy coolant flow, creating an obstruction in the cooling system leading to overheating. More on diagnosis of overheating is in Sidebar: "Engine Overheating."

One way to check the internal condition of a radiator hose is to squeeze it at its ends and in the middle. If the ends feel softer and more pliable than the middle, the hose should be replaced. This is a sign of electrochemical degradation (ECD) inside the hose. ECD is a chemical reaction in which the hoses, coolant, and engine form a galvanic cell, a battery really, that creates a chemical reaction that attacks the interior of the hose.

Dex-Cool, G-05 and the Green Stuff

There are four categories of antifreeze on the market: green ethylene glycol or propylene antifreezes, Dex-Cool antifreeze, G-05 antifreeze, manufacturer-specific antifreezes, and so-called "universal" antifreezes. These are the differences among them.

The old style green antifreeze is still an acceptable choice for older vehicles: those made before the mid-1990s. These antifreezes contain silicates as their anti-corrosion mechanism. Essentially, the silicates form a protective coating over the internal cooling system parts. But that protection depletes as well, so these antifreezes are only good for a couple of years before the corrosion protection capability is depleted.

Dex-Cool is ethylene glycol antifreeze developed by General Motors in the mid-1990s and currently manufactured by all of the leading antifreeze producers. It has been used for over a decade as the original equipment antifreeze in General Motors vehicles and was used by Chrysler for a number of years, as well. Dex-Cool is an "organic additive technology" (OAT) antifreeze: instead of coating the parts with silicates introduced by the antifreeze, Dex-Cool contains ingredients that promote the natural tendency of both aluminum and iron to form their own protective coatings.

Dex-Cool is orange. It can be mixed with green anti-freeze, but it would be senseless to do so. Dex-Cool has a recommended change interval of 5 years or 150,000 miles. If mixed with green antifreeze, it must be changed after 2 years.

G-05 is a "hybrid OAT" antifreeze, meaning that it's a lot like Dex-Cool with some silicate added. It was developed in Germany, originally used by Mercedes-Benz and adopted by Chrysler as its factory-fill antifreeze in 2001. Ford began using it in 2003. The service life for G-05 is the same as for Dex-Cool. To complicate matters, all G-05 antifreezes are not the same color: Mercedes is light yellow; Chrysler, Dodge, and Jeep are orange; and, Ford is yellow.

Japanese and European manufacturers often use antifreezes that are unique to the individual brand. Toyota Long Life Antifreeze Coolant is a silicate-free formula that's pink in color. Honda, too, has its own silicate-free OAT antifreeze. BMW and Porsche have their own antifreezes, as well, the latter costing about $50.00 a gallon. Antifreezes in European cars will be phosphate-free, as the use of phosphates in antifreeze is not permitted in European countries. U.S. antifreeze manufacturers offer their own products to suit these vehicles, though these products do not have the vehicle manufacturer's approval.

Then there are the "universal" long-life antifreezes, which claim to be compatible with any type of anti-freeze, including Dex-Cool and G-05, and to offer the same 5 year, 150,000 mile corrosion protection. The manufacturers of universal antifreezes claim that they can be used to top-off other antifreezes as well as replacing the original antifreeze. In order to be compatible with both Dex-Cool and G-05, universal antifreezes should not contain either silicates or phosphates. Even then, it's likely that use of these antifreezes may affect the service life of Dex-Cool, G-05, and other manufacturer-specific coolants. Unless your vehicle's recommended coolant is the ordinary "green stuff," it's probably wisest to avoid so called universal antifreezes.

The best rule is to stick with what came in the car from the factory. The old-style ethylene glycol antifreezes may be better for older cars with brass radiators, as these radiators usually have lead solder in them that may not be compatible with OAT antifreezes. If, however, the car came with Dex-Cool, then that is what should be used when it is time to add or replace antifreeze. The same is true of G-05.

It is very important to maintain the proper coolant level with OAT antifreezes and to avoid any additives. Dex-Cool, in particular, has been blamed for problems that were ultimately traced to the vehicle owner's failing to maintain proper coolant level, exposing the coolant to excessive amounts of oxygen, thereby eventually degrading it.

Additives are unnecessary with these products. They are specifically designed to be long-life coolants exactly as formulated.

It makes sense to replace radiator hoses before that happens. Because cooling systems are pressurized to prevent coolant from boiling and because heat in the system increases the pressure, hose failure usually occurs in the hottest weather. Whenever it occurs, failure of a radiator hose is never convenient.

Replacing radiator hoses is a relatively simple job, one that can be accomplished with simple tools and patience. Here's how to do it:

Parts for this job

Upper and Lower Radiator Hoses
Antifreeze of the type specified
  by the vehicle manufacturer
Distilled water
  (unless using premixed antifreeze)

Tools for this job

Hose clamp pliers or
  large Channellock-type pliers
Floor jack
Jack stands
Wheel chocks
Lift pads: commercially purchased
  or self-fabricated
Drain pan

Engine Overheating

Sometimes it's obvious that the engine is overheating. Other times, however, you are just concerned that it is running too hot.

Before concluding that there is a problem, check the owner's manual to determine the normal operating temperature range for the car. Modern automobile engines are designed to operate at higher temperatures because this promotes efficient combustion and reduces emissions.

If there is an overheating problem, there are a number of usual suspects:

Of course, a defective radiator hose is one potential cause of an overheating engine. Low coolant level, debris in the radiator fins or in the air intakes leading to the radiator can cause overheating, as can a loose serpentine drive belt (replacing the serpentine drive belt is covered in Chapter 8). If the fan shroud is severely broken or entirely missing, the radiator may not receive sufficient airflow, leading to overheating.

One of the most common causes of engine overheating, apart from defective radiator hoses, is the thermostat. A thermostat is essentially a valve controlled by a thermostatic spring that prevents the flow of coolant from the engine to the radiator when the coolant temperature is low (so the engine warms up faster) and then opens to allow full coolant flow when operating

Two thermostats, one new and one failed. The coiled spring contracts and expands with temperature, opening and closing the valve that allows coolant to flow from the engine to the radiator. The old thermostat was replaced because it stuck partially open. This type of thermostat is integral with the housing and cannot be replaced separately from it.

temperature is reached. If it stays closed, however, the engine will overheat. If the thermostat opens only partially, some coolant will flow through, but the flow will be restricted.

A defective thermostat may manifest itself only when you drive above certain speeds. If the thermostat is only partially closed, it may allow sufficient coolant flow at low speeds to maintain a normal engine temperature. But at higher speeds the restricted flow can no longer maintain normal engine temperature.

One way to check for a thermostat that has stuck in the closed position is to feel the radiator hoses as the car warms up. If the hose into which coolant flows through the thermostat to the radiator remains cool, the thermostat is stuck closed. Incidentally, if the engine overheats for another reason, replacing the thermostat is a good precaution. Overheating can damage the thermostatic spring.

Anything that lets air into the cooling system, including a leaking radiator or a coolant reservoir cap that doesn't seal properly, can cause overheating. Pressurization of the cooling system raises the boiling point of coolant. If that pressure is lost, the coolant will boil at a comparatively low temperature and will no longer be effective at absorbing and carrying away heat.

The fans can also cause overheating if they fail to turn on at the designed temperatures. Fans in most modern cars are electric, and are turned on by the powertrain control module when the coolant temperature sensor reports reaching a specified temperature (see Chapter 9). When there are two fans, one of them will be an auxiliary fan designed to activate at a higher coolant temperature than the other fan (usually, the auxiliary fan is also designed to activate whenever the air conditioning is turned on). If the coolant temperature sensor fails or reports a lower than actual temperature, one of the fans may not activate. Fan failure can also be caused by a blown fuse, an electrical short, worn or corroded wiring, or a defective electric motor.

Bucket with pouring spout
Funnel
Pliers (if applicable)

Time for this job

The length of time required for this job largely depends on the difficulty of accessing the hoses. If the hoses are accessible, this is a job you can easily perform in an afternoon, usually with time to spare. If the hoses are not accessible, this is a Saturday afternoon job—so that you have Sunday to finish it, if necessary.

Advance Planning

You should buy a gallon of the type of antifreeze used in your car. Spilling some antifreeze is inevitable when draining the radiator and replacing the hoses. Antifreeze is sold two ways: straight—you must mix it 50-50 with distilled water—and pre-mixed by the manufacturer.

Before making that decision, however, you should take a look at your antifreeze and also test its freeze point. If it appears dirty or contaminated or it's no longer providing adequate freeze protection, you should simply flush the old anti-freeze out and replace all of it. That's covered in Sidebar: "Flushing the Cooling System."

Also, of course, you'll need to buy the replacement radiator hoses. You should purchase original equipment or OE equivalent replacement hoses. Cheap hoses usually have less strength than OE quality hoses. Also, they often don't fit as precisely, which makes them harder to install.

There are two other hoses that you may want to replace at the same time, if you're truly ambitious: the heater hoses. They are much smaller in diameter than a radiator hose, and route from the engine (often near the water pump) to the heater core, usually located on the firewall in the engine compartment. These hoses, like radiator hoses, can deteriorate over time. Of course, if one breaks, coolant escapes from the entire system, just as it does when a radiator hose breaks. On some cars, the hoses are molded to specific shapes, in the same manner as radiator hoses, and must be purchased as a specific replacement part. Other cars use a standard flexible heater hose sold at auto parts stores by the foot. As long as you're going to the trouble of draining the coolant and replacing the radiator hoses, you should inspect the heater hoses, as well, and replace them if there is any question of their condition.

Hazard Warning

NEVER REMOVE THE CAP FROM THE COOLANT RESERVOIR OR THE RADIATOR WHILE THE COOLANT IS HOT. Work on the cooling system only when the engine is cold. If the coolant reservoir cap or radiator cap is removed when coolant is hot, the sudden release of pressure will instantly drop the boiling point of the coolant, creating a scalding geyser of coolant. Anyway, there's no reason to remove the cap while the engine is hot: adding coolant when the engine is hot can create "thermal shock" by exposing hot metal to much cooler liquid,

resulting in a cracked engine block.

Antifreeze is poisonous to dogs and other pets (as it is to humans), yet they seem to love to drink it. A very small amount of ethylene glycol antifreeze can cause kidney failure and be fatal. If you have pets, do not leave antifreeze in any uncovered container, do not allow spilled antifreeze to remain on the garage floor or driveway, and keep the pets inside while you're doing this job.

If an animal does drink antifreeze, immediate action is required. Symptoms do not appear until after the kidney damage has occurred. Induce vomiting, if possible, by giving the animal one teaspoon of 3% hydrogen peroxide per five pounds of weight—which should cause vomiting in 10 minutes—and then immediately get the animal to a veterinarian. The window of time to commence treatment with antidotes is six to eight hours.

Let's do it

Before doing anything else, compare the new hoses to the old ones, side-by-side. The time to find out that they're different is before you start the job, not after you've removed the old hoses.

Draining coolant from an engine sufficiently to replace the upper and lower radiator hoses usually requires draining only the radiator. In most cars, draining the radiator will not remove all of the coolant from the engine. However, draining the radiator will lower the coolant level sufficiently to prevent coolant loss when the radiator hoses are removed.

To drain the radiator, it will be necessary to open a drain valve or petcock located near on the bottom of the radiator. On some radiators, the coolant drains through the petcock. On others, it is merely a valve and the coolant drains through a nozzle located nearby.

Exercise some restraint when opening the drain valve. The radiator is likely made of soft aluminum; if not, it's made of brass, which is even softer. It is not unusual for a drain valve to resist turning, but it should not take excessive force to open it. These valves ordinarily open

The drain valve will be located on the bottom of the radiator, often on the passenger's side.

counter-clockwise. The drain valve may also operate much like a radiator cap: that is, it may be necessary to push it down as it is turned until it passes a detent and can then be turned freely.

Once the drain pan is positioned and the drain valve is opened, loosen the cooling system pressure cap, but do not remove it. Leave the cap sitting on the cooling system filler neck to prevent dirt or objects from getting into the system. This cap likely won't be on the radiator, but will be on the coolant reservoir or surge tank. This is a pressure cap, so you have to push down on it, firmly, in order to turn it counter-clockwise past the first detent, after which it will unscrew easily. Drain out the coolant, until the flow subsides.

There is no reason that you cannot reuse the coolant you drain out in order to replace a radiator hose, provided that it is clean and appears to be uncontaminated. If the coolant does appear dirty or contaminated, you should take this opportunity to flush the cooling system and refill it with fresh coolant.

To reach the drain valve and the lower radiator hose, it may be necessary to raise the front of the car and put it on jack stands. Obviously, raising the front of the car also raises the radiator in relation to the hoses, so the hoses and engine block may retain antifreeze that would otherwise have drained out through the radiator. To fully drain the hoses, after opening the drain valve you may need to lower the front of the car over the drain pan until the car is as level as possible, then raise it again after the

The coolant may drain through a separate nozzle located under the valve.

Be sure to have the drain pan positioned before opening the drain valve, and be sure the drain pan is clean if you intend to reuse the coolant.

Adjust the jaws so that they are close to parallel when grasping the ends of the hose clamp.

To drain, loosen the valve. It may have a detent that must be overcome before it will turn freely.

Once the drain valve is open, loosen the cooling system pressure cap to allow air into the system, but do not remove it. That keeps dirt out.

Once the valve is opened, coolant flow from the valve will be immediate.

If you do not have hose clamp pliers, a pair of Channellock-type pliers will work. You can wrap the jaws with electrical tape if you want to avoid marring the hose clamp's surface finish.

radiator and hoses have completely drained, in order to remove the lower radiator hose. Once the radiator has finished draining, close the drain valve.

Now release the hose clamps. Hose clamps come in two basic varieties: screw and spring. The screw-type tightens or loosens the hose clamp with a screw at the side of the clamp. The spring-type is basically a very strong circular spring. The ends can be squeezed together to make it larger in diameter. When released, it clamps around the hose.

Screw-type hose clamps are inexpensive. If the ones you are removing don't appear pristine, use new ones to install the new hoses.

To open a spring-type hose clamp, just squeeze the ends together. A special hose clamp pliers is made for this task. However, if don't have one of those, a pair of very large Channellock-type pliers can be used instead. If you want to protect the appearance of the clamps against scratches, wrap the jaws of the pliers in electrical tape. Spring-type hose clamps can be reused if in good condition.

Slide the clamps toward the center of the hose. This takes pressure off the hose ends, so that you can remove them.

Removing an old radiator hose is simple, in theory: just twist it side-to-side until it breaks loose, then remove it. The key to removing a stuck radiator hose is breaking the bond between the hose and the fitting to which it is attached.

Often it is not that easy. The hose slides onto a metal pipe or fitting. The heat of that fitting on the rubber of the hose creates a very tight seal.

If the hose is reluctant to release, be patient. Keep twisting it gently, using moderate pressure. Usually, that will be enough to remove it.

If not, there are a couple of approaches: use a tool, or cut it off. But, both of these can be an expensive mistake if done improperly.

The metal pipe or fitting onto which the radiator-end of the hose slides is made of either brass or aluminum. Either way, it's very easily bent. Once bent, it will require a radiator shop's attention to restore it. Even if the

This is the theromostat/water pump end of the upper radiator hose. To remove it, squeeze the tabs on the hose clamp toward each other.

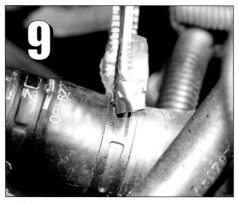

With the tabs compressed, move the clamp toward the center of the hose, off of the flange to which the hose itself is attached.

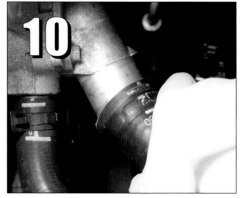

Gently twist the hose to remove it. If it doesn't want to twist, try to get a finger under an edge and pull on it—not to remove it, but to break the heat bond between the hose and the flange to which it is attached. This is the engine end of the lower radiator hose.

This lower radiator hose connection with the water pump inlet on this car also houses the thermostat. If the thermostat were to be replaced, it would be a matter of removing only two bolts.

This is a view upward from underneath the car. Remove the radiator end of the hose. There isn't a lot of room around this lower radiator hose, but there is enough. When reinstalling the hose clamp, be sure that it is angled in a way that will allow you to grasp it should you ever need to remove the hose again.

Removing the lower hose at the radiator involves the same process: compress the clamp and park it away from the radiator.

fitting isn't bent, scratching it creates a route for a leak. Cooling systems operate under very high pressure, so anything that can leak, will leak.

If you are removing a hose for replacement, you can use a sharp utility knife to cut through it, outboard of the fitting. Then put a small cut into the remaining piece of the hose, perpendicular to the fitting, and peel the hose off with your fingers. Do not cut the hose against the fitting because that will gouge a deep scratch and create a future leak site.

Especially if you need to preserve the hose, you can also remove it if you use your smallest flat-bladed screwdriver to break the bond between the hose and its fitting. Wrap the tip of the screwdriver blade in a layer of electrical tape and very carefully slide it between the hose and the fitting. This is a bit tricky, because

you don't want to damage the inside of the hose or scratch the fitting, but the electrical tape will offer some protection against causing damage. As the screwdriver lifts the hose, it will release the bond holding it to the fitting.

Once you have loosened the hose at one end, repeat the process at the other end.

Then remove the hose.

Repeat the process with the other radiator hose.

Another view upward from underneath the car, at the radiator end. Once the clamp is removed, it is merely a matter of pulling off the hose. Be prepared for a bit of an antifreeze shower, because there is probably some coolant retained in the hose even though the drain valve has been opened. As long as you're down there, close the drain valve now, so that you don't forget to do it later.

Remove the hose from the vehicle. Before pulling it out, take a close look at how it is routed, so that you can put the new one in the same way.

Everything that was on the old hose must be transferred to the new hose. This hose has a plastic sleeve that is intended to insulate it from the air conditioning piping that passes directly beside it.

The upper radiator hose is removed in the same manner as the lower hose. It was necessary to remove the radiator shroud, however, to gain effective access to the hose clamp.

As before, park the hose clamp away from the end of the radiator hose.

Removing the upper hose is relatively easy, because it is an easy reach.

Once the hoses have been removed, clean off the fittings. If any bits of rubber from the old hose remain on the fittings, the new hoses may leak. If you need to scrub it, you can use a Scotch-brite pad dipped in a little antifreeze. It is now time to install the new hoses.

Put the hose clamps onto the new hoses, sliding them away from the ends.

Install the ends of the hose onto the fittings. Start with the end of the hose partially over the fitting and twist it on, taking care to not tear the inner surface of the hose in the process. Slide the hose fully onto the fitting. When both ends are on, make sure the hose is properly aligned and is not twisted.

Then move the hose clamps onto the ends of the hose. Wait until both ends of the hose have been installed before moving either hose clamp into place, so that you can easily realign the hose, if necessary, during installation.

The fitting onto which the hose slides has a lip at its outer edge. The hose clamp should be positioned halfway between that fitting and the end of the hose.

Spring-type hose clamps are self-adjusting, so they need only be properly located. Screw-type hose clamps, however, must be tightened to the proper tension. Over-tightening a hose clamp can damage the rubber of the hose, another source of an eventual leak. A screw-type hose clamp is properly tightened when the surface of the clamp is flush with the surface of the hose itself.

It is now time to refill the cooling system, assuming that you've not decided to flush it. Make sure you did, in fact, close the drain valve.

With the car lowered back to the ground, pour the anti-freeze back into the coolant reservoir or surge tank, using a large funnel. You have to allow air to escape as the antifreeze is poured in, so pour slowly.

Many coolant reservoir tanks have an "X" in the filler neck that makes it difficult to get the funnel to stand straight. You can modify a large plastic funnel to make refilling an easier task. Eyeball the length of the funnel neck and the distance from the top of the tank neck's threads to the "X." Cut off the neck of the funnel to about that distance with a hacksaw. Use sandpaper to eliminate any scraps of plastic hanging from the cut.

Not only will this funnel stand straight during the filling process, but also you will be able to look through the neck of the funnel into the reservoir tank to see the coolant level. You won't have to remove the funnel every time you need to check whether there's room for more coolant.

When the antifreeze is filled to the top of the radiator, you may still have some that hasn't yet made its way back into the engine. Air is still trapped in the cooling system. Start the engine and, with the engine at idle, continue the process of pouring until you have poured back all of the antifreeze into the cooling system.

For some vehicles, there are specific procedures for getting air out of the cooling system when replacing or adding antifreeze. It is extremely important that these procedures be followed because air in the cooling system can create an "air lock" that blocks coolant flow and causes overheating. The factory shop manual contains the specific procedures for refilling the cooling system, which may include operating the engine at specific RPM for specified time intervals during the refilling process.

Once all of the antifreeze has been returned to the system, double-check that there are no leaks.

Then top off the cooling system with fresh antifreeze of the proper type, filling to the "full cold" mark on the coolant tank. This mark is usually molded into the plastic of the tank.

Replace the cooling system pressure cap and you're done.

Don't be alarmed if there is some steam from the engine when it is first warmed up after replacing the hoses. Sure, go ahead and check that everything is alright. But you likely did spill some antifreeze in the process of doing the job and, even though you wiped up all that you could see, there will be some that got into places you couldn't see. Those spills will steam as the engine warms up.

Slide the new hose into place. Push it all the way on with a gentle twisting motion to ease it on. If you need help sliding it on, put a little antifreeze on the inside of the hose where it will contact the hose flange.

The technique for installing the hose without damaging the interior rubber is to slide it on at an angle first, then rotate it on the rest of the way. Take care not to tear the interior, as that will lead to a premature hose failure.

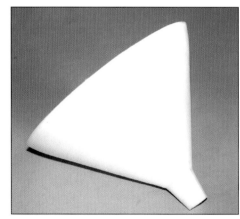

Modifying a plastic funnel by amputating part of the nozzle makes it sit straight and allows you to see through the nozzle to check the coolant level without removing the funnel.

Fill the system with coolant. Using a bucket with a pour spout makes it imuch easier. Be sure to follow the vehicle manufacturer's instructions for refilling to avoid an air lock in the system.

Flushing the Cooling System

Flushing a cooling system is very much like filling a cooling system, but using water without antifreeze. One tip: if you're going to replace all of the coolant in the car, don't buy the pre-mixed antifreeze.

Modern cars have aluminum radiators and, more likely than not, an aluminum cylinder block and aluminum cylinder heads. Modern antifreezes are formulated to provide corrosion protection for five years. Flushing the cooling system today is less about removing accumulated corrosion than it is about getting all of the old coolant out when replacing antifreeze in the entire system.

The flush procedure involves repeatedly flushing the cooling system with water until it runs clear from the radiator drain valve. Draining the radiator won't drain much of the engine block, which will retain coolant. There also are drain plugs located in the engine block itself, but they are almost impossible to access with the engine in the car.

Because the engine retains coolant, when refilling the cooling system, it is likely that the engine will be retaining some of the flush water. That means that adding a 50-50 mix of distilled water and antifreeze will not result in a 50-50 solution in the cooling system. It also means that some of the water will be tap water containing chemicals unless you used distilled water in the flushing process, or at least the ending phases of that process.

Here's the drill: Look up the drain and fill process in the factory shop manual. There may be special procedures specified which are designed to prevent trapping air in coolant passages.

However, here are the basics: Starting with a cold engine, drain the system through the drain valve at the bottom of the radiator. Then refill the system with water through the coolant reservoir or surge tank. Then warm the engine until the thermostat opens. Thermostats normally begin opening at about 180 degrees F, and are fully open by 200 degrees F. A thermostat will close at a lower temperature than that at which it opens, so it may remain open even though the coolant temperature has dropped to 140 degrees F.

You should be able to ascertain when the thermostat has opened by cautiously feeling the radiator hose near where it attaches to the thermostat housing. When the hose warms, the thermostat has opened.

Also turn the heater full on. The heater core is a small radiator and also contains coolant. Once the thermostat is open, turn off the engine.

Let the engine cool, and then drain out as much of the coolant as possible. Refill the system with water, and repeat the process. Make sure to allow the engine to cool before refilling the system, because running cold water into a hot engine's cooling passages can crack a cylinder block. Repeat the process until the fluid draining out is nothing but clear water.

On some vehicles, it may be possible to expedite this process by removing the thermostat temporarily. If the thermostat is an independent unit, retained in a housing that bolts to the engine block, it can be removed during flushing. A new gasket should be used when reassembling the thermostat housing. Also, when removing the thermostat, take a very close look at it before taking it out of the engine so that you know which way it should be facing when you reinstall it. It is easy to get a thermostat reversed when installing it. Many thermostats have markings stamped onto the thermostat's edges to indicate the proper installation. On other vehicles, the thermostat is a unit with its housing and cannot be removed independently of the housing itself.

It is a good idea to use distilled water in at least the last stages of the flushing process. Because the engine will retain some of the coolant in the cylinder block, some of the water used in the flushing process will also be retained in the engine's cooling passages. If you use tap water, that's what's going to be inside the engine when you add new coolant. Using distilled water avoids that problem.

Once the coolant runs clear, close the drain valve. Then calculate how much antifreeze to mix with distilled water to reach a 50-50 mix.

Here's a trick for doing that: On the last draining of the system, be sure to start with an empty drain pan. Then measure the volume of the drained fluid by pouring of the contents of the drain pan into a container of known volume, such as a one-gallon milk jug. Check the cooling system capacity in the owner's manual. The difference between that capacity and what's drained out is the amount of water still inside the engine. The water retained in the engine must be included in the calculations if you are to achieve a real 50-50 mixture.

This is why premixed antifreeze is not a good idea when flushing and refilling the cooling system with new coolant. You may need to add a mix with proportionally more than 50% antifreeze to achieve an actual 50-50 mix in the car.

Once the system has been refilled, start the engine, let it run for a while, and recheck the coolant level, adding a 50-50 mix of coolant and antifreeze as necessary to bring coolant level to the mark molded into the side of the coolant reservoir/surge tank. This will warm up the coolant, so the proper level will be above that mark, somewhere between the "hot" and "cold" marks. If the only mark is for "cold" coolant, fill with warm coolant to about 0.5 inch above the "cold" mark. Local regulations may or may not address disposing of old antifreeze. It should not be dumped into a storm sewer because it is poisonous to animals. In many communities, the recommended disposal is to the sanitary sewer system, i.e., pouring it down the toilet, because the chemicals in the waste treatment process will biodegrade old antifreeze.

CHAPTER 8

SERPENTINE AND "V" BELTS
MAINTAINING, DIAGNOSING,
AND REPLACING DRIVE BELTS

Every car has at least one "accessory drive belt." Some have three. Drive belts are what turn the alternator, water pump, air conditioning compressor, and power steering pump. There are two types of drive belts: "serpentine" drive belts and "V" belts.

Serpentine belts get the name because one belt snakes around a number of accessory drive pulleys. Serpentine belts have multiple parallel ribs running the length of the belt, which fit into matching grooves in the drive pulleys. For that reason, they are sometimes called "ribbed v belts" or "poly v belts." Typically, one serpentine drive belt turns all of the engine accessories.

Most serpentine belts have only one ribbed surface; but, some are ribbed on both sides. Typically, serpentine drive belts have six ribs and are 13/16-inch wide. But there are also four, five, seven, and eight rib serpentine drive belts. There are even serpentine belts that are 13/32-inch wide and have only three ribs.

A "V" belt gets its name from the cross-sectional shape of the belt: it looks like a "V" with a flat bottom. V belts drive only one or two engine accessories, so typically two, three, or even as many as five V belts will be used in a single vehicle.

The purpose of the serpentine belt tensioner is to apply constant tension to the drive belt, so that the belt is retained in the tracks on all of the pulleys it operates.

Serpentine systems normally include at least one "tensioner" and at least one "idler." The idler is a free-spinning pulley used to locate the belt between accessory pulleys. The tensioner is a free-spinning pulley on a spring-loaded arm. The tensioner applies constant pressure against

the belt to keep it tight on the pulleys. The pulley on an idler or tensioner may either be grooved to match the belt or smooth if it contacts the back of the belt. These tensioners are sometimes called "automatic" tensioners because the spring-loaded mechanism automatically takes up any slack in the belt created by stretching as the belt wears.

Tension on a V belt is almost always adjusted manually, usually by loosening a pivot bolt and a tension bolt on a driven engine accessory, repositioning the accessory, and then retightening the bolts (see Sidebar: "Inspecting, Adjusting, and Replacing a 'V' Belt."

Whether it is a serpentine system or a V belt arrangement, drive belts are a way of transferring crankshaft rotation to the accessory drives. In either system, the drive belts are moved by a pulley or pulleys on the front of the crankshaft.

There are a variety of belt arrangements. Though most serpentine belt systems use a single belt, some cars drive most accessories with a serpentine belt but use a V belt to drive an isolated accessory. Some cars with transverse engines use two serpentine belts, one at each end of the engine.

There is often a certain redundancy built into V-belt systems. For example, a

Inspecting, Adjusting, and Replacing a "V" Belt

V belts do not last as long as serpentine belts. Here are signs that a V belt needs replacement:

Squealing belt

Fraying at the edges of the belt

Glazed belt sides

Bottom of belt glazed

Deep cracks in bottom of belt

Many small cracks in bottom of belt

Separation of the belt's layers

Belt turns over on the pulleys

Belt comes off the pulleys

The V-belt tension is set by manual adjustment, so as a V belt wears and stretches, it will become looser than it was when the tension originally was set. If tension is not periodically checked and readjusted as necessary—at least every 10,000 miles—tension on the belt will become progressively lighter, until eventually the belt may begin to squeal. When a belt squeals, adjusting belt tension may eliminate the noise for a time. But, it will probably start squealing again fairly soon. Don't use belt dressing: it may eliminate the noise for a short time, but the noise will come back. Worse, the dressing will attract dirt and grit that cause extra wear to the pulleys.

The contact between a V belt and the pulley is entirely at the sides of the belt. The bottom of the belt should not touch the pulley. When a belt slips, friction heats the sides of the belt and eventually glazes them, a telltale sign of belt slippage even without belt noise. When a V belt squeals, it indicates that this process is fairly advanced. So, even after adjusting tension, the belt's ability to grip the pulley is diminished.

When a V belt is glazed at the bottom, it means something more: either the belt is too small or a pulley is damaged. The bottom of a V belt should not contact the pulley. If it does, it means the cross-section of the belt is too small for the pulley or that the sides of the pulley are worn or damaged. Pulleys do wear over time. If the inner sides of a pulley are "dished"— eroded into a concave curve by wear—to the extent of 1/32 inch, the belt will sit too low in the pulley and only the upper part of the belt sides will contact with the pulley. That leads to slipping and separation between the layers of the belt.

Just as with a serpentine belt, chirping or fraying at the side of a V belt indicates pulley misalignment, either parallel or angular. Pulley alignment is checked the same way, too: by laying a straightedge against the faces of the pulleys. If a V belt twists to be upside down in the pulley, it indicates either insufficient belt tension or severe pulley misalignment.

There are a few rules that should be followed when replacing V belts. Obviously, you need the correct length and width. Parts stores stock belts by the belt manufacturer's part number, so usually you should be able to buy or order a belt simply by the make, model, and engine of your vehicle and, sometimes, whether it has air conditioning or certain emissions control equipment.

Should you need to know the size of a belt, though, it is determined by measuring the width of the belt at the top and its outside circumference. The easiest way to measure outside circumference is to put a chalk mark or piece of tape at one spot on the belt, then roll the belt on a flat surface and measure the distance it travels in a single revolution. To measure the pulleys to determine the necessary belt length, use a tape measure around the tops of the pulleys.

There is also a recognized system for categorizing V belt sizes, though some manufacturers don't use it. Most automotive belts are either 3/8- or 1/2-inch (9.5- or 12-mm) wide. These widths are "3L" and "4L," respectively. This is followed by a second number specifying the length of the belt in tenths of an inch. So a 4L460 belt is 1/2-inch wide and 46-inches in circumference. Typically, automotive V belts have a 40-degree side angle inward from top to bottom. There are also V belts that have notches in the bottom of the belt. These, however, are designed for pulleys with unusually small diameters and shouldn't be used unless the vehicle manufacturer recommends them.

Here's where that really big screwdriver comes in handy. It is perfect for tensioning "V" belts. After the "pivot bolt" and "tension bolt" are loosened, seat the screwdriver on a solid part of the engine and pry the accessory against the belt.

Inspecting, Adjusting, and Replacing a "V" Belt CONTINUED

As a general rule, all engine V belts should be replaced at the same time and with the same belt brand. Partly, this is because all of the belts will probably wear out at about the same time. But in one situation, it is crucial: if two belts drive the same accessory, both belts must be replaced at the same time with the same manufacturer's belts. There will be slight variations in length and cross-sectional width and shape between belts of the same size made by different manufacturers. If a new belt and old belt, or two belts of different brand, are used to drive the same accessory, one will be shorter than the other and the shorter one will carry almost all the load.

Metric belts should never be used on standard pulleys and standard belts should never be used on metric pulleys, even if the belts are ostensibly interchangeable. The cross sections of these belts are often different, as are the shape and width of pulley grooves.

Typically, initial adjustment of a V belt is accomplished by moving the driven accessory. The accessory will have two bolts, one the "pivot bolt" and the other "the tension bolt." The tension bolt holds the accessory against the belt and permits a range of adjustment. Loosen the two bolts. Then find a solid point on the engine that you can pry against with your really large screwdriver. Pry the accessory away from the engine to tension the belt. Then tighten the tension bolt, then the pivot bolt. Check the belt tension and readjust until it is satisfactory.

The ideal way to check belt tension is with a tension gauge, but these cost about $150. The more practical way to check belt tension is by deflection. Find the mid-point of the longest distance between the belt's pulleys. Push down on the top of the belt with your finger. If the belt distance between the two pulleys (measured from where the belt first touches the pulley)

is 7 inches to 11 inches, the belt should deflect 1/4 inch. If the distance is 12 inches to 16 inches it should deflect 1/2-inch. If the distance is more than 16 inches, belt deflection should be increased proportionally.

It is as important that a belt not be too tight as it is that it not be too loose. A belt that is overly tight will apply extra pressure to the bearings of driven accessories. That will wear the bearings prematurely. Bearing wear causes pulley misalignment—eventually you have to replace the accessory. Alternators are particularly susceptible to damage from an overly tight belt because the pressure on the shaft damages the bushings inside the alternator (see the sidebar in Chapter 6 titled, "How an Alternator Works").

Once all of the V belts are tensioned satisfactorily, start the engine and let it idle for at least fifteen minutes with all accessories operating. This seats the belts in the pulleys and pulls out any initial stretch in the belts. Having the accessories operating puts as much load on the belts as possible.

Then shut off the engine and check the tension for all of the belts, and readjust as necessary. According to belt manufacturers, a new V belt loses 60% of its tension in the first several hours of operation, so belt tension should again be checked after five to ten hours of driving.

V belts can fail even when they do not appear worn. The cords inside the belt can break without visible damage to the exterior of the belt. This makes it important to follow the vehicle manufacturer's recommended belt replacement schedule, if any, and replace belts when age or mileage suggest it is time to do so.

Holding the tension with the screwdriver, tighten the tension bolt. You can then release the screwdriver and check belt tension before tightening the pivot bolt.

Belt tension is measured at the middle of the greatest distance between two of the belt's pulleys. It should not be overtightened. A loose belt will slip. An overtight belt can damage the bearings in the alternator and other belt-driven accessories.

system with three belts may be arranged so that all of them are rotated by the crankshaft and all of them rotate the water pump before routing to another accessory. There may also be two belts turning the same accessory. That way, a single belt breaking will not disable the water pump, and a single belt breaking may not disable any of the driven accessories.

Serpentine belts have largely supplanted V belts in most automotive applications because they require less space in the engine compartment, are easier to install and adjust, wear longer (because the thinner cross-section allows them to dissipate heat more quickly), and are less likely to slip. The drawback to serpentine systems is that if the belt breaks or comes off, all engine accessories stop. That leaves you stranded.

Regardless of which type of belt is used, the key to preventing belt failure is inspecting the belt and replacing it when its appearance, age, or mileage suggests that it is time to put on a new one. Most auto manufacturers do not prescribe a specific serpentine belt replacement interval, instead simply recommending periodic inspection. Belt manufacturers, however, suggest replacing serpentine belts at least every five years (or 60,000 miles) and V belts every four years (or 50,000 miles).

Here's how to inspect and, if necessary, replace a serpentine drive belt.

Parts for this job

Serpentine drive belt

Tools for this job

1/2-inch drive breaker bar, correct size socket (most vehicles), or Serpentine drive belt tool
Any other tools necessary to remove parts needed to access belt, pulleys, and tensioner

Time for this job

Replacing a serpentine drive belt is not time consuming, in and of itself. It could take as little as five minutes or so. Unfortunately, on some vehicles it may be necessary to lift the front of the car to remove and install the belt on the crankshaft pulley and it may be necessary to remove other parts to remove and install the belt. On some cars, it is even necessary to support the engine and remove a motor mount to replace a serpentine belt. Ultimately, how long the job will take primarily depends upon access to the belt. Review the removal and installation procedures in the shop manual. If it looks like disassembly of other components will be required, allow ample time: an afternoon without evening commitments, for example.

Advance Planning

Before beginning to remove a serpentine belt, it is essential to have a picture or diagram of the belt's routing on the pulleys. Most cars have a label in the engine compartment that shows this routing and, of course, it's also in the factory shop manual. If you do not have a diagram, make one before you begin to remove the belt. You may think this is silly and that you'll remember where it goes. But, you might not. Why chance it?

When replacing a serpentine belt, you will need a new belt of the correct ribbing, width, and length. Length is critical. Economy belts may be listed as fitting several slightly different applications. However, precise fit of a serpentine drive belt is crucial to its performance. If a serpentine drive belt is not exactly the correct length, it will wear prematurely and either be prone to slipping or impose higher loads on bearings in driven accessories. That can lead to premature failure of those parts. To insure that a replacement serpentine belt meets all vehicle manufacturer specifications, either buy an original equipment belt or a quality OE equivalent belt, such as one made by Goodyear or Gates. Verify the belt's width, length, and number of ribs against the specifications in the factory shop manual.

You may need an assistant for this job. Usually, removing and installing a serpentine belt is a one-person job. However, on some vehicles it may be necessary to have one person hold the tensioner against its spring while another person routes the belt over the pulleys.

Finally, you should determine if you will need a special "serpentine belt tool." On some vehicles, clearance around the belt tensioner is too narrow to accommodate a breaker bar and socket. All auto parts stores carry specially designed serpentine belt tools, which are long, narrow wrenches designed to fit tight spaces around tensioners. They usually cost between $20 and $50. But, make sure the tool will work on your specific vehicle. Some engines require a belt tool made for that specific application, particularly certain Ford engines (3.8- and 4.2-liter V-6, 4.6- and 5.4 liter V-8).

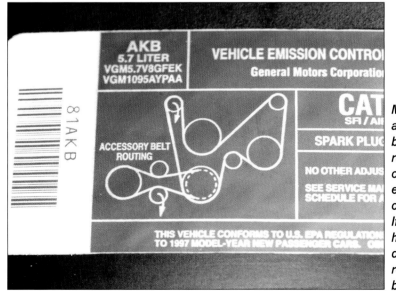

Most cars with a serpentine belt put a routing diagram on a label in the engine compartment. If you don't have a diagram, draw one before removing the belt.

Hazard Warning

The serpentine drive belt runs near a number of engine components that will be hot if the vehicle has recently been running. Wait to do this job until the engine has cooled off.

The serpentine belt tensioner contains a powerful spring. Removal and installation of the serpentine belt requires using a wrench to push against this spring. If the wrench should slip, the tensioner will spring back with significant force.

Never attempt to remove the tensioner arm from the spring case. This can suddenly release the spring, causing severe personal injury.

It may be necessary to lift the car to remove the serpentine belt from the crankshaft pulley and some of the drive pulleys. If so, be sure to use jack stands and secondary supports.

There are certain cars in which the electric fan(s) can turn on even when the ignition is off. It is prudent to disconnect the negative battery cable before starting this job because you will be working near the fan(s). You may wish to use a computer memory saver (see Chapter 4) to preserve radio presets and other memory settings.

Let's do it

The tensioner consists of two parts: the arm, to which the pulley mounts, and the housing or "spring case" that contains most of the spring that supplies the tension. The spring case bolts to the engine or to a mounting bracket.

To inspect the serpentine drive belt, first check the wear indicators on the tensioner spring case and tensioner arm. These are marks cast into the parts themselves. Individual marks or a raised area are cast into the spring case. These marks indicate the permissible range of tensioner self-adjustment. A mark cast into the tensioner arm indicates the present adjustment. If that indicator mark is beyond the maximum mark on the tensioner case, the serpentine belt must be replaced. A new belt should put the indicator mark toward the minimum end of the maximum and minimum range.

The tensioner has two parts: one part, the housing, is solidly mounted to a support bracket; the other, the tensioner arm, is mounted on a spring-loaded shaft. At the end of that shaft is the pulley on which the belt runs.

Marks that are cast into the tensioner housing and tensioner arm indicate whether the tensioner is properly adjusted or should be replaced.

Between normal-wear cracks in a belt and those cracks that obviously require replacing the belt, are cracks like these: small, but plentiful. The belt rubber has lost resiliency and the belt should be replaced.

Using a breaker bar and socket, simply push the tensioner away from the belt.

Holding the tensioner away from the belt with the breaker bar, simply lift the belt off the tensioner pulley with your fingers.

On some tensioners, such as the one illustrated here, there are three marks on the spring case. The outermost lines indicate the permissible range of self-adjustment and the center line indicates the position of the tensioner with a new belt.

Assuming the belt passes at the tensioner, the next step is to inspect it for cracks. A normal serpentine drive belt is expected to have occasional light cracks across some of the ribs. Light cracks perpendicular to the length of the belt are ordinary wear and are not cause for belt replacement. However, if there are a lot of cracks and they are close together on all or most of the ribs, the belt is worn out and should be replaced.

If the belt has cracks that run deeper than the bottom of the ribs, if chunks of rubber are missing from the ribs, or if there are cracks on the belt running parallel to its length, the belt should be replaced. The belt should also be replaced if an edge is fraying, the edges are glazed, or the ribbed surface of the belt is glazed. If there is oil or grease on the belt, it must be replaced, as well. If a serpentine belt is squealing or has been slipping, it should be replaced—even if it otherwise looks fine. Slipping polishes the belt surface; once it has started, it can only get worse.

Other than cracks merely indicating wear, all of these conditions indicate an underlying problem, which should be addressed before replacing the serpentine belt.

Once you have gained access to it, removal of the old serpentine drive belt is straightforward.

Assuming you've located the serpentine belt routing diagram in the engine compartment or made your own sketch of it, to remove the serpentine belt simply put the breaker bar and socket on the bolt holding the tensioner pulley to the tensioner arm. By exerting leverage on the bolt, push the pulley and arm toward the engine, away from the belt, removing tension from the belt. While maintaining this pressure on the arm, slide the belt off the pulley and then gradually release the pressure on the arm.

Once the belt is off the tensioner pulley, you can remove it from the other pulleys over which it runs, such as the alternator pulley.

The old belt must be removed from the crankshaft pulley, as well as an idler pulley and other accessory drive pulleys. After that, the pulleys should be checked for rubber residue and cleaned, as needed.

After the belt has been removed from the tensioner pulley, it is then simply a matter of removing the belt from the remaining accessory drive pulleys, and from the car.

Some tensioners are designed to accept a 1/2-inch breaker bar without a socket. On these, simply insert the socket end of the breaker bar directly into the matching square hole in the tensioner arm.

There are a very few tensioners that require a different method. One is used on the Volkswagen VR6 engine: to remove belt tension, a long metric M8 bolt with 1.25 pitch must be threaded through a hole in the tensioner spring case to push the tensioner arm away from the belt. Certain Chrysler and Jeep 4- and 6-cylinder engines do not use an automatic tensioner, but instead set a fixed tension with a manually adjustable idler.

After removing the old belt, double-check the length of the new belt by comparing it side-by-side with the old one. They should be almost exactly the same length, allowing only for a little stretching of the old one. Also verify that they are the same width with the same grooves.

Before installing the new belt, inspect and test the tensioner, tensioner pulley, and idler pulley(s). These pulleys should spin freely, smoothly, and without clicking or grinding noises. The pulley should not have any wobble or end play on its shaft. The tensioner should move freely throughout its range of travel.

Some professional mechanics recommend replacing the tensioner whenever the serpentine belt is replaced. The underlying theory is that the tensioner may outlast one belt, but not two. Professional mechanics have learned by bitter experience that they will be blamed if anything goes wrong with a system they've serviced, even though the problem has nothing to do with their work. So, they naturally want to replace anything that might become a problem. But, replacing the tensioner triples the cost of the job and should not be routinely necessary.

The new belt must be routed over the crankshaft pulley first, routing it up from there toward the tensioner.

The last step of installation is slipping the new belt over the tensioner pulley. Take the time to double check that the belt is correctly seated on every pulley.

Many tensioners only show the range of acceptable movement of the arm, but some— including this one—also show the proper tension for a new belt. This one is at that mark.

Also inspect the pulleys, including the accessory drive pulleys and crankshaft pulley. They must all be clean, free of rubber residue, oil, grease, or dirt. Brake cleaner and twine or cotton swabs can be used to clean these pulleys. Use a towel to catch the dirt and drips. Keep brake cleaner off of rubber parts, including drive belts. Brake cleaner can damage rubber and plastic parts. For this job, a non-chlorinated brake cleaner (it specifies on the can) is probably preferable because it is not flammable and does not leave any petroleum residue. You can also use a Scotch-Brite pad to clean these grooves, but do not scrape them with a screwdriver or use a wire brush to clean them. Scratches in the pulley surfaces can abrade the rubber of the serpentine belt. See Chapter 12: Disc Brakes, for more about brake cleaners.

Next check the alignment of the various accessory drive pulleys, the tensioner pulley and the idler pulley. These must all align in the same plane. Check alignment by placing a straightedge across two or more of the faces of the pulleys to see whether the straightedge lies flat across their surfaces. If not, there is a misaligned pulley. A misaligned pulley in one of the accessories, such as the alternator, may be the result of bearing wear or an improperly aligned pressed-on pulley.

If all of the pulleys are properly aligned, installation of the new serpentine belt is the reverse of removal: slide the belt over the various accessory drive pulleys and idler, in accordance with the serpentine belt diagram, and then move the tensioner toward the engine and slip the belt over the tensioner pulley.

Be sure that the serpentine belt has seated into all of the pulley grooves on all of the pulleys. Particularly if it is hard to see, it is very easy to install a serpentine belt with a groove projecting over the side of a pulley. Check the tensioner to verify that that the tensioner arm indicator mark lines up properly with the adjustment range marks on the spring case before starting the engine.

CHAPTER 9

ELECTRONIC ENGINE MANAGEMENT

THE BASICS

The oxygen sensor is but one of the many sensors that your car's computer relies upon to manage the engine, though one of the most important.

Before the development of electronic engine management, every function in an engine was the result of designed-in compromises between economy and performance. Fuel flow was determined by your foot, a mechanical pump, and a complex series of air venturis and gasoline jets known as a carburetor. Spark timing was set by a bolt on the distributor shaft and advanced by vacuum or centrifugal force, or both. Cold starts were handled by a spring designed to coil or uncoil according to temperature, called an automatic choke. This was technology evolved directly from the first internal combustion engines. It used the same basic engine management methods as the Model T.

Electronic engine management was a revolution. It changed the way everything in the engine operated, except the valves and the pistons. In the early 1980s, automobile manufacturers began to use computerized engine controls, which also allowed the computer to monitor systems it controlled. However, there was no standardization in the systems, either in what was monitored or how the data could be retrieved.

Starting with the 1988 model year, California required a basic on-board diagnostics capability to monitor emissions-related engine functions. This created an element of standardization among manufacturers, though there were still significant differences between the on-board diagnostic systems of each manufacturer. Today, these are commonly referred to as "OBD-I" systems.

Beginning with the 1996 model year, federal law required that every new automobile and light truck be equipped with a system monitoring all components that could cause excessive emissions. The law also required that motor vehicle manufacturers use a uniform system of codes to identify emissions-causing malfunctions. Finally, the law also required that these codes be retrievable through a standardized data port located inside the passenger compartment. The result was On-Board Diagnostics Generation Two, or "OBD-II."

Emissions are, as a general proposition, the result of inefficient combustion. Inefficient combustion occurs because something isn't working optimally, and results in poor gas mileage, poor engine performance, engine overheating, as well as increased emissions.

If you were to install electronic sensors to monitor every system in the engine that could degrade combustion efficiency away from the "optimum," then a problem could be spotted as soon as it happened, even before it was noticeable to the driver.

But, you could do more. You could collect information from all of the sensors and feed it to a computer that would integrate it. The computer could be given a set of rules to use in deciding what priorities to give to each piece of information it collected and when to change those priorities. With that information, the computer could automatically readjust the engine systems to regain optimal combustion. You could even use different definitions of what is "optimum" to suit different driving situations.

You could also eliminate a lot of moving parts and the maintenance they require. The computer could take over the functions of the carburetor and distributor, determining how much fuel should go to each cylinder and when the spark plug should fire in that cylinder. That, basically, *is* electronic engine management.

Here's how electronic engine management works in cars with OBD-II systems. (OBD-I systems may be similar, but have fewer monitored systems and fewer decisions allocated to the engine computer.)

The computer is the "powertrain control module" (PCM), sometimes called the "engine control module" (ECM) or "engine control unit" (ECU). It receives data from sensors, stores that data, learns from that data, and makes choices and issues commands based on that data, guided by its past experience. It is the PCM that decides how much fuel to inject into a cylinder and when to fire that cylinder's spark plug.

The PCM's overall goal is to run the engine at a fuel/air ratio of 1 to 14.7, which is known as the "stoichiometric" ratio. In theory, this proportion provides the most efficient combustion because the amount of air is exactly sufficient to burn all of the fuel. In reality, the fuel/air mixture isn't always kept at this ratio, for a variety of reasons, including engine load. But, as a working hypothesis, the PCM assumes it should be hitting that ratio. When the amount of air in the mixture is less than 14.7 units to one unit of fuel, the mix is called "rich." When there is more than 14.7 units of air for one unit of fuel, the mix is "lean."

The PCM is programmed with a set of rules that it follows in deciding whether or not it should make the fuel/air mixture richer or leaner. These rules even dictate priorities. For example, when the throttle is wide open, the computer's priority will be creating power. When the throttle the throttle is only partially open and the vehicle is at a steady cruising speed, the computer puts fuel economy first. The PCM is constantly adjusting the fuel/air mixture and spark timing in a never-ending effort to achieve optimum engine performance.

To understand electronic engine management (PCMs), it helps to first understand sensors.

Many sensors operate by measuring voltage. Some sensors measure current against resistance. Measuring the amount of current provides the data. There are even sensors that actually create voltage (literally out of the air) by chemical action. The amount of voltage created yields the data.

Information from each sensor is fed to a "controller." A controller is a device that operates a function. In this instance, the PCM is the controller and the function is mixing fuel and air and determining when to ignite that mixture.

This is the part that your car really depends upon: the quick connect electrical connector. Airtight and waterproof, vibration and shockproof, they're plastic, so they're also light and durable. This one connects to the left bank coils.

This is a "coil near plug" ignition system. Each cylinder has its own ignition coil.

The long cylindrical, stick-like tube paralleling the intake manifold (up about a third of the picture from the bottom) is the "fuel rail," the device that transports fuel at a specific pressure to the fuel injectors and positions the injectors.

When you start a car with a cold engine, the PCM knows the engine is cold because the "coolant temperature sensor" (CTS) reports that information. The CTS is a "thermistor." That is, its electrical resistance varies according to temperature. The PCM's rules tell it that a cold start requires more fuel, so it reacts to this data by richening the fuel/air mixture. It also advances the spark; that is, it fires the spark plug earlier in relation to the piston's travel to the top of its cylinder than it would were the engine warm. A piston at the top of its travel in the cylinder is at "top dead center" (TDC).

As the engine warms, the PCM changes priorities. It now tries to achieve the stoichiometric fuel/air ratio. To do this, at first it makes an educated guess based on stored data about how much less fuel to supply and how much closer to TDC the spark plug should fire.

However, it shortly gets information about the quality of its guess and adjusts the fuel/air mix accordingly. That information comes from the heated oxygen sensors (HO$_2$S) located in the exhaust manifold or the exhaust pipe near the manifold. Many vehicles have multiple

This is the left bank number one oxygen sensor, which is located in the exhaust manifold. It reports the extent to which fuel or oxygen has not been consumed in the combustion process.

oxygen sensors, one "upstream" in the exhaust manifold and another "downstream," before or after the catalytic converter. The HO$_2$ sensors create voltage through a chemical reaction caused by the difference in the amount of oxygen in the exhaust and that in the atmosphere. Measuring the voltage tells the PCM how much oxygen is in the exhaust. From that data, the PCM can determine whether the fuel/air mix is lean or rich: the presence of oxygen means the fuel was expended but oxygen remained, i.e., lean mix; the absence of oxygen means there wasn't enough oxygen to burn all of the fuel, i.e., rich mix. The PCM uses that information to increase or decrease the length of time the fuel injectors are open.

This is "closed loop" operation; the PCM's output, i.e., its directions to the fuel injectors, are being measured by the HO$_2$ sensors, which feed that data back to the PCM. The PCM then adjusts the fuel injector duration accordingly, and the data loop begins anew.

"Closed loop" operation is critical to electronic engine management because the automatic self-correcting character of the system is the key to achieving combustion efficiency. When an engine is in "open loop," i.e., not relying on feedback data to decide output, it can't self-adjust. That may occur because the PCM has chosen to ignore the feedback at that moment based on other priorities, such as sudden wide open throttle (WOT), that require quickly richening the fuel/air mix for maximum power. But if the engine stays in open loop in normal driving, something is wrong.

Of course, the PCM must consider the other part of the ratio: the air. Sensors measure the rate of flow, temperature, and density of air drawn into the engine. Air flow is measured with a "mass airflow sensor" (MAF). Temperature is monitored by the "intake air temperature" sensor (IAT). Density is measured by the "manifold absolute pressure sensor" (MAP). Some cars use MAP without MAF, because MAP is essentially a measure of vacuum; from that, airflow can be calculated. This is called a "speed density" system.

An oxygen sensor is one of the most clever components in your car, not so much because of what it does as because of the way it does it. An oxygen sensor signals the presence or absence of oxygen in the exhaust by actually creating voltage from air.

Outside air is about 21% oxygen. An engine's exhaust, however, contains only about 1% to 2% oxygen; the exact percentage depends on the efficiency of the engine's combustion. The typical oxygen sensor is constructed of a metal bulb in which two porous platinum electrodes sandwich a zirconia ceramic electrolyte between them: think of a big "U" with a smaller "u" inside it. The "U" structures are the platinum electrodes, and the zirconia electrolyte fills the space between them.

The oxygen sensor screws into the exhaust manifold or exhaust pipe so that the bulb-part of the sensor protrudes into the exhaust stream. This exposes the exterior "U" to the exhaust flow. The top of the "U," however, remains outside the exhaust manifold or pipe, so that oxygen can get inside the smaller, interior "u." The difference in the oxygen levels between the two platinum electrodes (the "U" and the "u") causes a flow of ions through the zirconia electrolyte that separates them.

Ions are atoms in which there are an unequal number of positively charged protons and negatively charged electrons (see Chapter 6). That, in turn, creates voltage. The greater the disparity between the oxygen content of the outside air and that of the exhaust, the greater the voltage. Because the amount of oxygen in the exhaust reflects the deviation of actual combustion from the stoichiometric ideal, that voltage tells the PCM if the fuel/air ratio is lean

How an Oxygen Sensor Works

or rich. If there is a lot of oxygen in the exhaust, that indicates there hasn't been enough fuel to combust the remaining oxygen, so the mixture is lean.

In a healthy oxygen sensor, voltage output will range from a low of about 0.2 volt to a high of about 0.9 volt. As the PCM continually compensates for the most recently received information from the sensor, the ion flow changes and the voltage fluctuates above and below the mid-point of 0.45 volts, signaling lean or rich to the PCM. This happens about five to seven times per second. This switching process is sometimes referred to as a "cross-count," for the number of times the voltage crosses 0.45 volts.

This type of oxygen sensor is sometimes called a "narrow range oxygen sensor" because the sensor reacts drastically to very slight changes in oxygen content. That is, a slight change in oxygen content will cause an almost complete change in voltage, from low to high or the reverse. Functionally, this type of sensor is much like a switch, all on or all off. If you were trying to light a room the way an oxygen sensor operates, you'd attempt to get the correct amount of illumination by constantly switching the lights on and off.

The metals used in an oxygen sensor create voltage only when the sensor is extremely hot, at least 600 degrees F. As originally developed, oxygen sensors would simply stop creating voltage whenever they dropped below that threshold temperature, such as during cold starts and periods of idling. In that situation, the PCM would go into "open loop" and rely on "long term fuel trim" (LTFT) to set the fuel/air mix.

To make oxygen sensors more quickly operational upon start-up and keep them operating thereafter, engineers simply installed a heated wire down into the "U"s of the sensor. Think of an upside-down ice cream bar: the stick is the heater. A heated oxygen sensor should become operational within about half a minute of a cold start.

Early oxygen sensors actually exposed the platinum electrodes to the outside air by incorporating a small hole. That, however, made the sensor vulnerable to dirt. Today, oxygen sensors vent to the outside air through the sensor's wires.

Unheated oxygen sensors have one or two wires, depending on whether connection to the electrical ground is through the screw threads into the exhaust system or through a wire. Heated oxygen sensors add two wires for the heater circuit, so oxygen sensors in OBD-II vehicles have either three or four wires.

An OBD-II vehicle may have as many as four oxygen sensors. Oxygen sensors are not only used to monitor the oxygen content of exhaust as it comes from the engine, but also to monitor the efficiency of the catalytic converter. For that reason, one oxygen sensor may be located "upstream," in or near the exhaust manifold, and another may be is located "downstream," in the exhaust pipe after the catalytic converter. In a car with a V-6, V-8, V-10, or V-12 engine, there will be an oxygen sensor for each cylinder bank. With dual exhausts, there may be a downstream sensor in each exhaust, as well. In some cars that have V configuration engines that route the exhaust through a single catalytic converter, an "upstream pre-catalyst" oxygen sensor may be positioned shortly before the converter and a downstream sensor shortly after it.

A second type of oxygen sensor has come into limited use recently: the "air/fuel ratio sensor," sometimes called a "wide range" or "wideband" oxygen sensor to distinguish it from the more common narrow range sensor just described. Though made similarly to a typical oxygen sensor, an air/fuel ratio sensor uses electrical resistance to measure oxygen content. This allows it to measure resistance in proportion to oxygen content, which allows the PCM to precisely determine the adjustments necessary to the air/fuel mix as the resistance changes. High-performance tuners use the wideband sensor's greater degree of accuracy to provide the information necessary to properly tune modified engines.

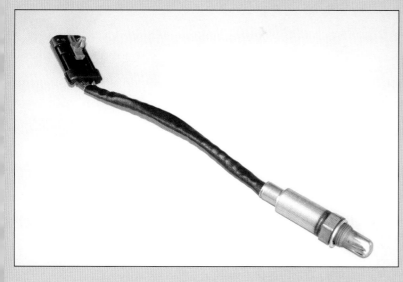

A new heated oxygen sensor: the sensor at one end is complete with the correct anti-seize compound on its threads and just bolts into the exhaust manifold or exhaust pipe. The quick connector at the other end plugs in to send signals to the engine computer.

The intake air temperature sensor, in combination with sensors reporting barometric pressure and air density, provides information used by the engine computer to determine the amount of oxygen in the air.

This is the mass airflow sensor, about which more is said in Chapter 10.

The mass airflow sensor uses current flow that heats wires exposed to intake air to calculate the rate of airflow.

In addition, the PCM considers throttle position and engine speed. The former is monitored by the throttle position sensor (TPS). The later is reported by the "engine speed sensor" (ESS), sometimes referred to as the "crankshaft position sensor" (CKP) because it also reports the crankshaft's rotational position.

In short, there are six factors that determine fuel/air ratio and spark advance: engine load (measured by the various air sensors), engine speed, engine coolant temperature (the CTS), throttle position, intake air temperature (IAT), and exhaust oxygen (HO_2S). The PCM decides the relative importance of each of these factors in determining how much fuel to supply and when to fire the spark plug.

There are, of course, many more sensors that can affect the PCM's decisions about engine operation. There is a "camshaft position sensor" (CMP or CPS), an "engine knock sensor" (KS), a "vehicle speed sensor" (VSS), a sensor for barometric pressure (BARO), as well as input from the "transmission control module" (TCM).

So what happens when something goes wrong? Because there are so many sensors in a modern engine, it is easy to assume any problem with the engine is caused by one of them. But, the basic job of any sensor is to report information. Engines still operate on the same principles as they did before silicon was formed into wafers, and engine problems are still caused by some of the same things that affected engines with carburetors and distributors: vacuum leaks, bad gaskets, electrical shorts, oil control problems, fuel contamination, and so on.

Nonetheless, an electronic engine management system is integrated. That means that the solution to a malfunction, whether mechanical or electronic, usually lies in understanding how the systems affect one another.

For example, a slight leak at the intake manifold gasket will add air to the airflow. But, that added air that won't be monitored by either the MAF or MAP sensors because the leak is downstream from them. Because it doesn't know about the air, the PCM cannot take it into account in setting the fuel/air mix. But the extra air will be spotted by the HO$_2$ sensors because it will create extra oxygen in the oxygen. The PCM will see the HO$_2$S data as indicating a lean fuel/air mixture and add fuel to compensate. As the leak gets worse, the amount of air added may exceed the ability of the PCM to compensate, and it will illuminate the instrument panel malfunction indicator light telling you to "check engine" or "service engine soon."

Another example is a dirty MAF, a current resistance sensor discussed in Chapter 5: Induction. A dirty MAF will underreport air flow to the PCM. Dirt on the wire acts as an insulator, retaining heat and reducing the cooling effect of the air flow, so it takes less current than it should to maintain the wire's temperature. The PCM reads this lower current as reduced air flow and, accordingly, supplies less fuel. But, as with the intake leak, the HO$_2$ sensors will report the lean condition to the PCM, which will add fuel to compen-

sate. As the condition worsens, the PCM will turn on the "malfunction indicator light" (MIL).

Of course, all of these sensors have another purpose: reporting a problem. If the PCM cannot compensate for a problem, it tells you to get the problem fixed. It sets a diagnostic trouble code (DTC), stores data generated by various sensors at the moment the fault occurred as a "freeze frame," and illuminates the MIL, telling you to "check engine" or "service engine soon." This is addressed in the next chapter.

The throttle position sensor tells the engine computer the throttle's position within the throttle body: how far open or closed.

The manifold absolute pressure sensor: the gold object in the center, buried under the alternator in this car. Counting the MAF, IAT, BARO, and TPS, this is the fifth sensor reporting about the air before air enters a cylinder.

The throttle position motor: this is a true "drive by wire" system, in which the accelerator pedal sends a signal to this motor, which controls movement of the throttle. There is no mechanical linkage.

The air check valve, a part of the emissions system. Air is injected into the exhaust to promote complete burning and reduce emissions. This valve prevents exhaust from flowing backwards into the air injection system.

CHAPTER 10

DIAGNOSIS USING OBD-II TROUBLE CODES

Your car cannot tell you what's wrong with it. But it can describe symptoms.

The PCM is programmed to recognize when data received from the various system sensors is outside prescribed parameters, makes no sense, or isn't being received at all. It sets a diagnostic trouble code when any of those things happens.

A "diagnostic trouble code" (DTC) is a combination of a letter and number that identifies the system in which a problem has been detected and, further, identifies the fault that has been detected in that system. This code is stored in the PCM the instant the problem occurs.

You can retrieve a DTC by connecting a code reader or scan tool to the "data link connector" (DLC) in your car and downloading the code.

There's more. When the code sets, the PCM also stores a "freeze frame" of data about what other systems in the car were doing at the instant the fault occurred. That data, too, can be accessed by a code reader or scan tool.

Freeze frame data is a further step in the diagnostic process. Because electronic engine management involves a number of interdependent systems—if something happens in system A, in response the PCM adjusts system B, and then system C also has to be adjusted—knowing what was happening in other systems when the trouble code was set can help narrow down the possible causes.

Parts for this job

None

Tools for this job

Code reader or scan tool

Time for this job

Downloading DTCs and freeze frame data takes only a minute or two. Diagnosis from that data can take longer, of course.

Advance Planning

If your code reader or scan tool provides a code number but does not display a description of the code, you'll need to locate a list of trouble codes for your vehicle. This will be in the factory shop manual and may also be available on the Internet.

Hazard Warning

None

Let's do it

Before plugging in the code reader or scan tool, it may help to know a bit more about the data that you are about to receive.

There are two types of codes: "generic," and "enhanced." Further, there are "P" codes, "B" codes, "C" codes, and "U" codes. Also, there are Type A and Type B codes. Each of these can be an "active" code or a "history" code. All you have to do is memorize them.

Just kidding...about the memorization, that is. There really are that many different kinds of codes. Here goes:

"Generic" and "Enhanced" Diagnostic Trouble Codes

As mentioned in the previous chapter, federal law requires OBD-II codes for certain emissions-related functions. Also, the law requires that the codes be uniform: that is, the same code number will have the same meaning regardless of vehicle manufacturer.

These are "generic" codes. The actual numbering system is established by the Society of Automotive Engineers (SAE).

However, automobile manufacturers are also allowed to create their own proprietary OBD-II codes to provide additional monitoring of both emissions-related systems and other systems. These codes are unique to the individual manufacturer and are not shared with other manufacturers, even if both use the same letter and number for the code. Indeed, these codes can be unique to a particular model produced by a single manufacturer. These proprietary codes are called "enhanced" codes.

Both types of codes, generic and enhanced, begin with a letter: B, C, P, or U. The letter indicates the code category: B for body (lighting, climate control, power accessories); C for chassis (traction control, variable assist power steering, load leveling); P for powertrain; and, U for network (system communication).

Following the letter, a diagnostic trouble code has four digits. The first is usually either a "0" or a "1." A zero indicates that this is a generic code. A "1" means it's an enhanced code. So, a DTC that begins "P0 - - -" is a generic powertrain code.

The next number in the code, whether generic or enhanced, indicates the system monitored: 1 is fuel and air metering; 2 is fuel injector; 3 is ignition system or misfire; 4 is emission control; 5 is vehicle speed or idle control; 6 is computer output; 7 and 8 are transmission; 9 is control modules and input and output signals.

The last two numbers in the code indicate the specific fault. So, for example, "P0201" is a generic powertrain code pertaining to the fuel injection system. Referring to the more specific description of the code displayed by the code tool, found in the factory shop manual or on the Internet, it is a fault in the control circuit for the number 1 injector.

Additional code categories have been created by the SAE for future use and are beginning to be implemented. For example; P2 and P3 for additional generic codes; B2 and C2 for new enhanced codes; and, B3 and C3 (currently unassigned).

"Active" Codes, "History" Codes, and Code Types

Any diagnostic trouble code, generic or enhanced, will be either an "active" or a "history" code. A history code is one stored in the PCM, along with the freeze frame data, at the moment the fault occurred. An active code is one occurring at the moment the engine is being monitored with a scan tool.

Trouble codes are also classified as Types A, B, C, or D. Type A codes indicate faults causing a substantial increase of emissions. Type B codes indicate faults causing a less serious emissions increase, such as a misfire. Type C and D codes are not emissions-related.

When a fault triggers a Type A code, it immediately illuminates the "malfunction indicator light" (MIL) on the instrument panel telling the driver to "check engine" or "service engine soon." Simultaneously, the PCM sets both a history code and a freeze frame of the OBD-II data for later retrieval.

When a fault triggers a Type B code, the computer waits to see if it happens again. If that same fault reoccurs in the next "drive cycle," the code will be set and freeze frame stored in the PCM, and the MIL will be illuminated. If it doesn't reoccur, the "pending" code is erased. A "drive cycle" is the set of driving circumstances that causes all of the OBD-II sensors to be transmitting data to the PCM, allowing the PCM to verify that all sensors are functioning properly; this verification is a "self-test." What constitutes a drive cycle varies from one manufacturer to another. However, it always includes a cold start and warming up to operating temperature, i.e., a "warm-up cycle," and then driving at certain speeds for specified durations of time.

Once a code is set, it can go away. If the system completes three successive self-tests without that fault recurring, the MIL will be extinguished. However, the history code will continue to be stored in the PCM, and typically will only be erased if the vehicle completes 40 warm-up cycles without recurrence of the fault.

Trouble codes are stored in "nonvolatile memory," which means the PCM remembers the code and freeze frame data even if the PCM doesn't have power. So, disconnecting the battery will not clear a trouble code.

There are four important things to remember about DTCs:

First, your car can be sick without setting a code. Much as a human being can have a temperature even though he or she doesn't yet have chills, a car may be malfunctioning before the problem crosses the threshold that sets a code.

Second, when a code is set, the cause may not be in the system that set the code; the system that set the code may be the one affected by fault, rather than the system in which the fault has occurred.

Third, the cause may be mechanical. Just because the sensors are electronic, it doesn't mean that the malfunction is electrical.

Fourth, even if a sensor is the cause, the responsible sensor may not be the one that set the code.

Diagnosis Using Diagnostic Trouble Codes and Freeze Frame Data

So, what's next? Retrieve the DTC and freeze frame data.

For most cars, it will be necessary to use either a "code reader" or a "scan tool" to retrieve DTCs and freeze frame data. There are a very few vehicles that can display DTCs on the instrument

The data link connector is located inside the passenger compartment, usually under the dash on the driver's side. It may have a cover.

Buying a Code Tool

To retrieve OBD-II diagnostic trouble codes and other OBD-II data, you will need a special instrument: either a "code reader," or a "scan tool."

A code reader can retrieve diagnostic trouble codes and turn off the MIL. Some code readers will also display the trouble code's description and can display freeze frame data, i.e., the engine parameters existing when the code was set (RPM, temperature, throttle position, etc.) Some are multilingual, providing information in English, Spanish, or French. Among the most widely available brands of code readers and scan tools are those manufactured by Equus/Innova, Actron, Autoxray, and CarMD. A basic code reader can be purchased for as little as $50. To get one with additional functions, such as the Equus 3110 pictured in the photos in this chapter, expect to pay between $100 and $200.

Scan tools do everything code readers do, but also read and record real time data. The least expensive scan tool will cost about $200. That's still a bargain compared to professional scan tools, such as the Tech II used by GM dealers, which cost about ten times that amount. The number of systems monitored and the way the data can be parsed and displayed become more sophisticated and complicated as the price of the instrument goes up. The most sophisticated scan tools can also run diagnostic tests on monitored systems.

Terms like "scan" or "scanner" are often used in the product names of code readers, even though the product is not, in fact, a scan tool. If it doesn't say it's a "scan tool" in those words, it probably isn't. That doesn't mean code readers aren't good tools; they are good. It means that you should evaluate a code tool on its capabilities and specifications, not its model name.

An alternative to a scan tool is software, such as ProScan, AutoTap Diagnostic, EASE, AutoEnginuity, and Digimoto, which can be downloaded to a laptop computer or personal digital assistant (PDA) to enable it to function as a scan tool when connected to the car by a cable that comes with the software.

Here is a list of features that you should look for in when buying a code reader, scan tool, or scanning software for a laptop or PDA:

1. The ability to retrieve "enhanced" codes. Many code readers and scan tools will only display generic codes. Some will read enhanced codes only for specific vehicle makes. Manufacturers create enhanced codes to refine the diagnostic process. If you are unable to retrieve them, you won't know if the information you are retrieving is complete.

2. The ability to display "freeze frame" data. Think of freeze frame data as the context in which a code is set. This can be very helpful because it provides additional information about what else was happening when the fault occurred.

3. The ability to be updated, usually online by linking the instrument to your computer, with new codes. Manufacturers develop additional enhanced codes as they develop new platforms and systems. If it can't be updated, the code tool will become outdated.

4. The ability to read the "CAN" protocol. The "protocol" is the way the vehicle's electronic system communicates within itself. CAN, which stands for "computer area network" is the single protocol that all automobile manufacturers are required to use beginning with the 2008 models. Many manufacturers began implementing CAN several years before that. If a code tool can't read CAN, it's obsolete already.

5. The ability to read trouble code categories set aside for future use: P2, P3, B2, B3, C2, and C3 codes.

panel digital display. These include Chrysler products with a digital odometer, C5 Corvettes, and the Cadillac DeVille/DTS. Even for those vehicles, however, a code reader or scan tool is necessary to retrieve freeze frame data. Do a Google search for "retrieve diagnostic trouble code," and your car's brand, and you should find the procedure, provided your car has that capability.

The code tool, whether a code reader or scan tool, is connected to the vehicle by a cable that slides into the OBD-II "data link connector" (DLC). This is a port inside the passenger compartment

of the vehicle. It is usually, but not always, located under the instrument panel on the driver's side (it may be under a plastic dust cover).

If the DLC is not under the driver's side instrument panel, look for it in or near the console, behind the front ashtray or under a cup holder. Depending on the make and model, look: close to the console on the passenger's side (some Acura, Honda, Volvo, BMW, Porsche 911,

This is what the DLC looks like without the cover, and the covers are often omitted or lost.

This code reader activates automatically when the ignition key is turned to the "on" position without starting the engine. Unlike code readers, scan tools can provide real time data with the engine running.

All data link connectors have the same configuration: they're all 16 pin connectors of the same shape. There are, however, differences between various manufacturers (and even the same manufacturers in different years) in which pins are used.

The code reader or scan tool simply plugs into the DLC. This is a reasonably priced code reader with freeze frame capability readily available online or at many auto parts stores.

and Land Rover models); behind an interior trim panel (some BMWs); behind a flip-up panel cover (Mercedes-Benz); behind the fuse panel cover (some Lexus); near the rear seat console ashtray (many Audis); in the passenger's foot well (Lotus Esprit); or, in the glove box (some Rolls-Royce and Bentley models—don't you wish).

Though you will, of course, follow the instructions for the particular code reader or scan tool that you are using, usually all that is required is to plug the tool into the DLC, turn the ignition key to the "on" position, and switch on the tool. It may also be necessary to answer some questions posed by the tool, such as identifying the manufacturer of the

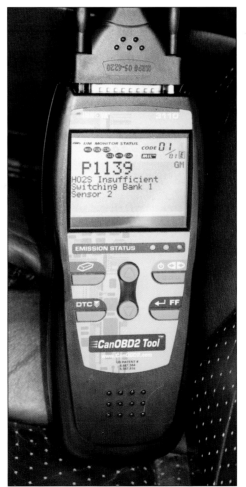

P1139 is the trouble code for "Insufficient Switching, Bank 1, Sensor 2." This code reader also tells you that it is an enhanced code (the "E") and the only code stored in the engine computer.

vehicle. At that point, the code reader or scan tool should download the data automatically.

Here's an illustration of how this works, using an Innova CanOBD2 3110 (also sold under the Equus name) which is a code reader that also displays the code and its description, captures and displays freeze frame data, and can be updated on-line. The vehicle is a V-8 with dual exhausts.

It's this simple: plug the tool into the DLC, turn the ignition key to "on," and the code reader activates automatically. In response to a prompt, identify the vehicle manufacturer as "GM." The code reader does the rest. In a few seconds it downloads "P1119," which it identifies as "HO$_2$S Insufficient Switching Bank 1 Sensor 2."

It also shows that this is the only code currently set and that it is an enhanced code. Because this is a code reader, not a scan tool, it does not give us "real time" data. Hence, all codes it displays are history codes.

By pushing a button, the freeze frame data can be displayed:

At the moment the code was set, both cylinder banks of the V-8 engine were operating in closed loop, the coolant was at 197 degrees F, calculated load was 8.2%, and RPM was 1773.

Additionally: vehicle speed was 32 mph, throttle position was 7.4%, the mass airflow sensor was reporting flow of 2.75 lb per minute, intake manifold pressure was 11.5 in.Hg.

Last but not least, the fuel trim data: STFT Bank 1: 0.7%, LTFT Bank 1: 13.2%; STFT Bank 2: -3.9%, LTFT Bank 2: 9.3%.

This data tells you that the code was set at a time when the engine was under a light cruising load and at normal operating temperature. The throttle was barely open, the car traveling about 30 mph, with low air flow into the intake. The later is indicated both by the MAF reading and, as well, the intake manifold pressure, which is another way of measuring vacuum. "in. Hg" is an abbreviation for "inches of mercury," a common measure of vacuum. Engine vacuum is highest when the throttle is closed because the

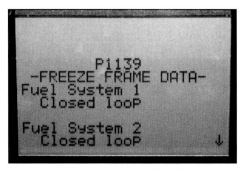

Pushing a button switches the display to freeze frame data. This is a snapshot of what the engine was doing at the moment the code set. At the time the code set, both banks of this V-8 engine were in "closed loop," meaning the engine computer was relying on sensor data rather than memory to set the air/fuel ratio.

It's called "manifold absolute pressure" because absolute pressure is the total of atmospheric pressure and any additional pressure being created. So, the measurement remains accurate even when atmospheric pressure changes.

engine is trying to draw air in through a restricted opening, which creates vacuum. When the throttle is fully open, engine vacuum will be near zero because there is no restriction of air flow into the engine.

The data also shows that the PCM has added fuel to the bank 1 fuel injectors, with LTFT at +13.2%, indicating an overall lean fuel/air mixture. However, by this increase in long term fuel trim, the PCM has adequately compensated for the condition, as STFT for bank 1 is only +0.7%. Overall, though, the PCM is adding more fuel to bank 1 than it is to bank 2. In fact, at the moment the code was set bank 2 STFT was actually -3.9%, meaning the PCM was subtracting fuel from the LTFT base.

Replacing an Oxygen Sensor

The theory of replacing an oxygen sensor is simple enough: it is, in essence, a bolt. You unbolt the old one and screw in the new one.

The problem is that it is also likely to be a bolt that is difficult to access because it is located somewhere on the exhaust manifold or exhaust system. To access the sensor, it may be necessary to disassemble other components. It is not unusual to have to remove or lower portions of the exhaust system to access some oxygen sensors. If it is in the exhaust system, it also may be necessary to remove a cover designed to protect the sensor and its wiring from road debris.

Oxygen sensors are not all the same, and you will need to obtain the correct replacement if you are performing that repair.

An oxygen sensor should be warm when it is removed; not hot, but warm. That expands the metal into which it is installed and makes removal easier.

Oxygen sensors require a special anti-seize compound, which will not affect the electronic grounding of the sensor through its housing to the exhaust manifold or system, and cannot contaminate the sensor itself. You'll need that compound, too, if you are replacing a sensor.

If replacing an oxygen sensor, you will also need to know the correct torque value for the sensor at the specific location at which it will be installed.

Oxygen sensors are extremely delicate. To quote from the Corvette factory shop manual, "[a] dropped oxygen sensor is a bad oxygen sensor." Also, it is important that the sensor end be kept free of dirt or any contaminants.

The first step is figuring out where the oxygen sensor is located. If it is a "Sensor 1" sensor, it will be located in the exhaust manifold. If it is not a Sensor 1, then it is located somewhere in the exhaust. Though "Sensor 2" may be the sensor located after the catalytic converter, you cannot automatically assume it is so. In some cars, including certain Hondas and Toyotas, there are sensors both before and after the catalytic converter.

The exhaust manifold or exhaust pipe into which the sensor is installed should be warm when attempting to remove the sensor: warm, but not hot. A temperature of about 120 degrees F is ideal. Do not try to remove an oxygen sensor from a cold engine. The force required to do so can damage the threads into which it is bolted.

To remove an oxygen sensor, a special socket is required. The oxygen sensor has a "pigtail" of wires coming out of it. An oxygen sensor socket has a slit up its side through which these wires can be routed, so that the socket can fit over the sensor without damage to the wiring.

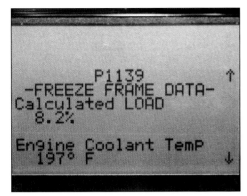

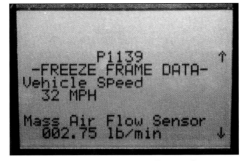

Calculated load and coolant temperature tell you how hard the engine was working at the time and whether it was at operating temperature. Calculated load is a measure of how much of the engine's power generating capability is being used.

The intake air sensor data interrelates. When the throttle is opened, airflow should increase as vacuum decreases, thereby increasing manifold pressure. When sensor data does not integrate in the expected manner and the deviation exceeds permitted variation, a diagnostic trouble code is set.

This car was loafing when the code set: the throttle barely open, little load, low RPM, low vehicle speed, low airflow, and low pressure.

The first step in removal of the oxygen sensor is disconnecting the wiring at the connector. Due to the hot environment in which an oxygen sensor operates, the wiring connector is always about a foot distant from the sensor itself.

Once the wiring is disconnected, use the oxygen sensor socket and an appropriate breaker bar or ratchet to unbolt the sensor itself. Apply force evenly. Oxygen sensors are installed with anti-seize compound, so it will come out.

Installing the new sensor is the reverse of removal, with the addition of anti-seize compound. New sensors are usually precoated with the correct anti-seize compound, so nothing more needs be added. However, if you should ever reinstall an oxygen sensor that has been previously removed, it will be necessary to coat the threads of the sensor with anti-seize compound that states on the packaging that it is safe for oxygen sensors.

Once the sensor is installed, complete the tightening with a torque wrench, to the factory specification. This is one of those rare instances in which the

factory-specified torque value will assume the use of an anti-seize compound, so you do not need to adjust the torque value downward to compensate for its use.

Connect the pigtail at the connector, and the job is completed.

The electrical end of the sensor must be disconnected first, so that the sensor may be unscrewed from the manifold or exhaust pipe.

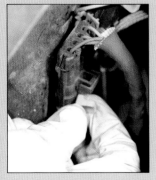

This connector has a security latch (a pin through a slot) that must be removed to open the connector.

The sensor unbolts with a special socket that has a slot down one side to allow the wiring to protrude. Access to oxygen sensors is often very restricted. Look for an avenue long enough to get the socket through with adequate leverage, whether from above or below the car.

Lastly, you have the code and its description: "insufficient switching" in a heated oxygen sensor for Bank 1. Referring to the factory manual, this is listed as an enhanced code, and Sensor 2 is a precatalyst sensor.

An oxygen sensor of the type used in this car (and most cars) creates voltage from the disparity in the amount of oxygen present in the exhaust and that present in the ambient air (see Chapter 9 Sidebar: How an Oxygen Sensor Works). The greater the disparity, i.e., the lower the oxygen content of the exhaust, the greater the amount of voltage created. Comparing the voltage received from the sensor to a mid-point reference voltage allows the PCM to decide whether the fuel/air mix is lean or rich and add or

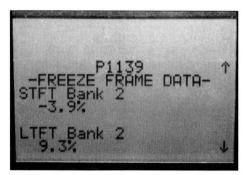

But fuel trim tells a different story. The code set for bank 1. This is what bank 2 was doing at the time: subtracting short term fuel trim, leaning the air/fuel mixture. That's what you'd expect under the conditions in which the car was operating.

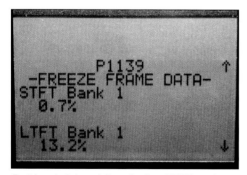

But bank 2 is adding fuel to STFT and LTFT, compared to bank 1. For some reason, the engine computer believes that bank 2 is operating leaner than bank 1. That is consistent with a sluggish oxygen sensor.

subtract fuel in an effort to hit the stoichiometric ratio. If the oxygen content of the exhaust is low, the PCM sees this as a rich fuel/air mix, on the theory that there wasn't enough oxygen to completely combust the fuel. Conversely, if there is high oxygen content, the PCM reasons that some oxygen remained after the fuel was completely combusted, which means lean.

When functioning properly, an oxygen sensor should be switching back and forth across this reference voltage as the PCM alternatively adds and then subtracts fuel in its never-ending quest for the perfect ratio these are called "cross-counts"). A healthy heated oxygen sensor in a vehicle with port fuel injection (fuel is directly injected into intake ports in the cylinder head) should switch from lean to rich and back again five to seven times per second when the engine is operating at 2,500 rpm.

When a sensor becomes sluggish, it usually is because contamination has affected the sensor's ability to create voltage. It is the disparity between the oxygen in the exhaust and that in the air that creates the voltage sent to the PCM indicating whether the fuel mixture is lean or rich. A large disparity creates more voltage because there is less oxygen in the exhaust indicating a rich mixture: one proportionally lower in oxygen.

An overall reduction in an oxygen sensor's ability to create voltage, consequently, will falsely bias it to the lean side. To compensate, the PCM will add fuel by having the fuel injectors stay open a bit longer.

In this case, both LTFT and STFT are higher on bank 1 than on bank 2. This is consistent with contamination of the sensor over time, to the point that the switching performance of the sensor degraded enough that it didn't meet the PCM's minimum switching parameters.

But, even with all of this data, reviewing the diagnostic protocol in the factory shop manual can be invaluable. Particularly with enhanced codes, there may be several reasons that a specific code may set, some obvious merely from the code's definition, some not so obvi-

ous. For example, the factory manual for this car indicates that this is a Type B code that is set when the sensor's cross-counts drop below 30 in each direction (lean to rich and rich to lean) within 100 seconds. As a Type B code, of course, this must occur in two consecutive driving cycles to illuminate the MIL. However, the manual also indicates that this code may be set when the heater circuit in the HO_2 sensor fails, when defective wiring shorts the sensor to ground, or when corrosion at the wiring terminals interferes with conductivity. In the latter instances, there may be nothing wrong with the sensor itself and a wiring repair might solve the problem. It also points out that the problem may be contamination of the sensor, caused by fuel contamination or excess oil consumption.

In the end, you'll have to lift the car, inspect the sensor and its wiring, and probably remove and replace it. But the DTC told you where to look and the freeze frame data has given you data that confirms a diagnosis of a defective sensor. The shop manual gives you the information necessary to determine if there is an underlying problem that caused that, or if the sensor has simply worn out from old age.

In the present case, the odometer of the car shows 140,000 miles, so old age is a good bet. Once you've fixed the problem, get out the code reader again: a code reader or scan tool also erases codes.

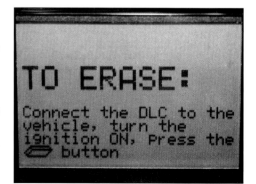

This data doesn't tell you what's wrong; you still need that factory manual. It gives several reasons that P1139 will set, and not all of them are a defective oxygen sensor. It also gives the diagnostic protocol for further nailing down the diagnosis and fixing the problem.

MAINTAINING AND SERVICING THE AUTOMATIC TRANSMISSION

When you first drive your car after finishing this job, you'll kick yourself for not doing it sooner. The smoothness of the transmission's shifts will remind you of how it felt when new. Particularly if you've put on a lot of miles without changing the fluid, you'll be amazed at what you've accomplished.

Changing automatic transmission fluid (ATF) is usually fairly easy, a job that's not much more complicated than changing engine oil. At the same time, however, you should also replace the transmission fluid filter(s), clean out the inside of the sump pan (the pan at the bottom of the transmission that holds the fluid), and clean off the magnet in the bottom of the sump that attracts and retains metal particles that get into the fluid. This job is unbelievably messy.

Parts for this job

Automatic transmission fluid
in required quantity
Automatic transmission filter or
filters (if applicable, see text)
Sump gasket
(if not reusable, see text)

Tools for this job

Very, *very* large drain pan—
at least 8-qt capacity

Socket ratchet, appropriately sized
socket, and any necessary
short extension
Torque wrench
(may need to be in-lbs)
Lint-free rags
Transmission fluid funnel or
equivalent, i.e., a funnel with a
narrow spout that will fit into ATF
dipstick/fill tube or opening
One funnel with a large mouth
Nitrile gloves
Two empty one-gallon milk jugs (or
equivalent: you need to be able to
see through the sides)
Lots of old newspapers
ScotchBrite pad (if needed)
NOTE: Inexpensive pumps, such as the hand-operated Mityvac 07249 Fluid Transfer Pump at about $25, can be used (in some instances) to suction ATF from the transmission through the dipstick/fill tube or opening. Using a pump is not a substitute for draining ATF by removing the sump pan. The sump pan must be removed to service the transmission filters, sump magnets and the pan itself. However, once these services have been performed and fluid changed, using a hand pump can make it possible, over time, to withdraw enough transmission fluid to allow replacement of the fluid that had been contained in the torque converter at the time fluid was changed. A

hand transfer pump may also be necessary when adding ATF to a vehicle that does not have a dipstick.

Time for this job

Apart from time spent lifting the car, changing transmission fluid is normally not a lengthy process (though draining the torque converter, can easily double the necessary time). But, there can always be a bolt that is difficult to access or a sump gasket that doesn't want to be loosened. Figure about three to four hours for the job, but allow extra time the first time.

Advance Planning

You need an adequate quantity of the correct automatic transmission fluid. Using the wrong fluid can damage the transmission.

The transmission's full fluid capacity is listed in the owner's manual and the factory shop manual. But, in most instances, you will not need that much ATF for this job. Because the torque converter—see Sidebar: "How an Automatic Transmission Works"—will retain about 1/3 to 1/2 of the total amount of fluid in the transmission even after the sump pan has been drained, what you will actually replace is the total fluid capacity

How an Automatic Transmission Works

An automatic transmission is a hydraulic device, which means that the automatic transmission's fluid is used to transmit force, not merely as lubrication. Though the automatic transmission was first introduced in 1940 by Oldsmobile, its basic form was firmly established in 1948 by the Buick Dynaflow, the first automatic to use a "torque converter." The same concept is still the basis for today's latest automatics, which have six, seven, or even eight forward speeds.

To understand how a torque converter works, visualize two ordinary table fans facing each other, one turned on and the other turned off. The air blowing from the operating fan will turn the blades of the other fan, even though that fan is off. But, if you were to reach out and grab the blades on the non-operating fan and stop them, the blades on the operating fan would not be affected.

In a torque converter, the operating fan is called the "impeller" or "pump." The non-operating fan is the "turbine." The impeller is connected directly to the engine crankshaft. The turbine connects to the transmission input shaft through a splined coupling, i.e., a long gear on which it can slide forward and backward. Both the impeller and the turbine are surrounded by a housing or "cover" filled with automatic transmission fluid. There is, however, no direct connection between the impeller and the turbine.

In the fan example, the speed of the fan that's turned off will depend on the speed of the operating fan. But if you were to put a third set of fan blades between the two fans and make the pitch (angle) of those blades variable, then you could alter the direction and force of airflow from the operating fan to the other fan. By doing that, you could control the speed of the second fan independently.

That, basically, is how a torque converter works. The fan in the middle with the variable pitch blades is the "stator." The pitch of the stator blades can be changed as vehicle speed changes, to decrease torque and increase turbine speed. Eventually, the impeller and turbine will rotate at essentially the same speed. But, even then, there is some slip in the fluid coupling, from 2% to 8%.

When the impeller turns, it creates pressure in the transmission fluid. That's why the impeller is also called the "pump." The faster the impeller moves, the more pressure it creates. By routing that pressurized fluid through passages that include spring-loaded valves that open only at specific pressures, the transmission fluid can be used to shift gears—real gears in mesh with each other—in addition to powering the turbine. That means the pitch range of the stator can be used in each of several forward gears.

The "lock-up" feature on modern torque converters is an illustration of how fluid pressure can control the mechanical aspects of the transmission. To eliminate the pumping loss from the fluid coupling, the pressure from the impeller can be used to push fluid through a narrow passage, opening a valve, and push a piston outward to physically lock together the crankshaft and input shaft.

Instead of using spring-loaded valves to control the flow of fluid through the body of the transmission, modern transmissions open and close those valves electronically. This makes for a much smarter transmission, because the powertrain control module (PCM) or transmission control module (TCM) can take factors beyond the fluid pressure into account in deciding which valves to open and when to open them. But the basic operating principle is still the same.

The same process can be used to lock or freewheel gears in a "planetary gearset." Planetary gears are nothing new in automobiles. Henry Ford used planetary gears in the transmission of the Model T. But, the planetary gearset in an automatic transmission is a much more sophisticated application of the principle.

A planetary gearset consists of a "ring" outer gear, with teeth facing only inward, a "sun" inner gear in the center, and gears running between the two, which are the "planet gears." The planet gears are equally distributed around the perimeter of the sun gear by a "planet carrier," essentially a bracket in the shape of a circular disk of almost the same diameter as the ring gear. By changing which of the gears in the set are allowed to rotate and also changing which gears are used as the input and output gears, you can change the "gear ratio."

The planetary gearset in an automatic transmission makes a few improvements. It is called a "compound planetary gearset" because it is basically two planetary gearsets with one common planet gear.

Visualize it this way: put two sun gears side-by-side on a common shaft, but make the second smaller in diameter than the first. Because the second sun gear is smaller, ordinarily it would require larger planet gears to engage the ring gear. Instead, make the ring gear and the planet gear as long as the two sun gears and add a second set of planet gears between the smaller sun gear and the ring gear.

Whichever of these gears is allowed to turn controls the output speed of the transmission. The ring gear is the output gear and one or the other of the sun gears will be the input gear. You get different speeds depending on which sun gear is used and which planet gears are allowed to rotate. If you connect both sun gears together so that they rotate at the same speed, you get a 1:1 ratio because the planet gears, as they rotate in opposite directions, will lock the ring gear to the sun gears.

Engagement of these gears, i.e., which is allowed to rotate and which are not, is controlled by bands and clutches. A band is a steel strap that wraps around the planet gear carrier or sun gear to hold it in place. Clutches are alternating layers of steel and friction material. The steel layers have splines on the outer circumference that fit into slots cut into the end of the ring gear. The friction layers are splined on the inside, where the splines engage one of the other gears. Pushing them together physically connects the gears. The clutches are spring loaded to release when the pressure is removed.

More speeds equal more complexity and more clutches. Clutches are the weakest link in an automatic transmission and their life expectancy is directly linked to the condition of the transmission fluid.

minus the fluid retained by the torque converter. So, you will probably only need enough fluid to equal about 2/3 of total capacity—plus a spare quart, just to be on the safe side.

You also will need to obtain a replacement transmission filter (or filters). Most domestic and European auto manufacturers employ at least one filter in the automatic transmission sump. Some use two filters. There is also a rubber gasket that fits around the neck of the filter to seal it to the transmission. That should be included with the replacement filter.

Transmission filters are designed primarily to remove metal particles, and other loose material created by clutch wear, without impeding fluid flow. They're usually very simple in design, and relatively light. The filters are not expensive and should be replaced whenever the ATF is changed. Some older Asian import models, including Nissans and Toyotas, have no transmission filters.

You may need a new sump gasket. Then again, you may not. Many of them are "reusable."

Reusable sump gaskets have metal rings around the bolt holes to prevent over tightening the pan bolts, are made of rubber designed to remain resilient, and are thicker than ordinary gaskets. Over the past decade, this type of gasket has become very popular. They are used as original equipment by many auto manufacturers and are available on the aftermarket for retrofit to older vehicles.

Don't be afraid to reuse a reusable gasket. If the gasket is in good condition when inspected after removing the pan, there is no reason not to reinstall it. Should it ever become necessary to replace a reusable gasket, make sure the new gasket is also reusable. Because reusable gaskets are thicker than ordinary gaskets made of neoprene or rubber and cork, substituting an ordinary gasket may not create a good seal.

The shop manual will specify whether the sump gasket is reusable. An alert parts-store counterman should be able to tell you, as well. If your vehicle does not have a reusable gasket, but one is available on the aftermarket, consider upgrading. While reusable gaskets are more expensive, the cost evens out the first time it's reused and it will make the job easier next time.

Some vehicles use "formed rubber" sump gaskets. These are made with formed rubber edges that are designed to fit over a lip at the edge of the sump pan. These are common on Audi, BMW, Mercedes-Benz, and Volkswagen models using ZF automatic transmissions. Any replacement gasket must be identical to the original equipment gasket to insure a proper seal.

Sump gaskets and transmission filters are often sold together as a "transmission kit." Don't buy a kit unless, first, you know you'll need the gasket and, second, the kit contains an OE equivalent gasket. The same basic automatic transmission that is in your vehicle was used in a number of different models and for many years. It's easy to produce one gasket and claim it fits all of those vehicles (because it will), even though the OE gasket was better quality or of a different type.

The bolts holding the sump to the transmission case must be tightened in the proper sequence and to the correct torque specification. So you will need to check the factory manual for that information, as well as the torque values for the drain bolt, if any.

Most domestic vehicles do not have drain plugs in the automatic transmission sump. Fluid is drained by letting it flow over the edges of the sump pan as it is loosened, so you need a big drain pan that can hold a lot of fluid. A large aluminum-foil roasting pan from the grocery store will do the job, but be sure its sides are tall enough to hold about 8 quarts.

Finally, location: If possible, do this in the garage. You are going to expose the interior of the transmission to open air, so it's important that there isn't dust or dirt in the air. If you must do this job outside, find a spot that's sheltered from the wind.

Hazard Warning

As discussed in Chapter 2, never get under a car that is not properly supported by jack stands *and* by secondary supports. Also, be sure you have enough light to see what you're doing.

If you drain transmission fluid while it is warm, there will be exhaust and engine components near the transmission that are much hotter than the transmission fluid and can burn you.

Transmission fluid level is always checked with the engine idling and you may have to reach over engine components to remove the ATF dipstick. Be careful that you don't get loose clothing or fingers caught in a moving drive belt.

Let's do it

The basics of changing automatic transmission fluid are: lift the car; drain the fluid and remove the sump pan; remove and replace the filters; clean the sump pan and magnet; replace the sump pan; and, refill with the same amount of ATF as you drained.

It really is that simple. But, as mentioned before, it's very messy. Transmission fluid spilling onto the floor is inevitable. So spread newspapers around a large area under the vehicle and have a stack of extra papers handy. When fluid drips onto the newspaper, just put another one on top. That way, you don't have to clean up until you're finished.

The vehicle should be level to ensure that the transmission drains as fully as possible. Once the vehicle has been placed on four jack stands, the first step is cleaning away any dirt or accumulated debris around the transmission sump and sump pan. Before opening up the transmission, it is important to make the environment as clean as possible.

There are two types of automatic transmission sump pans: those with a drain plug bolt, and those without a drain bolt. Most American-built domestic cars fit into the latter category; no drain bolt. Many European and Japanese brands have drain bolts.

How Often Should You Change Automatic Transmission Fluid?

Replacing automatic transmission fluid at an interval of 30,000 to 50,000 miles—unless a shorter interval is specified by the vehicle manufacturer—is an inexpensive way to protect the transmission and keep it shifting smoothly. Sure, lots of automobile manufacturers claim their ATF is good for the "lifetime" of the car. But, the transmission warranty is of a decidedly shorter duration, isn't it?

Automatic transmission fluid (ATF) is made from petroleum distillates or the synthetic equivalent. ATF does not degrade nearly as rapidly as engine oil. Partly, this is because an automatic transmission is not exposed to the extreme temperatures generated by combustion; partly, it is because ATF is not exposed to combustion by-products that contaminate engine oil. But, primarily, this is due to a very sophisticated additive package that includes friction modifiers, oxidation inhibitors, anti-foaming agents, corrosion resisting agents, viscosity stabilizers, and anti-wear agents.

Still, automatic transmission fluid doesn't last forever. Its chief enemy is oxidation. Oxidation is a chemical reaction in which oxygen molecules combine with other molecules, in this case lubricant and additive molecules. When that happens, the original molecules break apart and reform into new molecules, some containing oxygen and some not, but none of them the same as the original molecules. Because they are not the same, these new molecules do not have the same properties as the original molecules.

While oxidation affects the lubricating properties of ATF, it's most severe impact, at least initially, is on the additives, especially the friction modifiers. Friction modifiers are designed to work with the internal transmission clutches to provide smooth, positive shifts. When they're oxidized, i.e., destroyed, the shifts can become rough or jerky and there may be shuddering when shifting.

Of course, oxidation also increases the fluid's viscosity and decreases its lubricant capacity. Eventually, the fluid turns a darker color and takes on the "burnt toast" smell commonly associated with worn-out ATF. But, long before the aroma is noticeable, the additives have lost a great deal of their capability. Though the loss of lubricating capability certainly adds to transmission wear, it is the damage to the friction modifiers and other additives that has the most direct impact on clutch wear and, consequently, transmission life.

Heat accelerates oxidation. Normal operating temperature for an automatic transmission is 175 degrees F. That's the temperature on which claims of 100,000-mile oil life are based. The rule, however, is that for every 20 degrees F of increase in operating temperature above normal, fluid life is cut in half.

There are many circumstances when transmission operating temperatures will exceed 175 degrees F: towing, driving in hot weather (i.e., 90 degrees F or above), stop-and-go driving, driving in mountainous or hilly terrain or with a heavy load, and driving that maximizes the vehicle's accelerative capabilities (such as over, say, a quarter of a mile).

As a starting point, consider following the vehicle manufacturer's recommended change interval for "severe use." Depending on your driving environment, you may elect to change even sooner. But, the severe use change interval usually should be a safe one for what most people would consider normal driving. If you really are giving the vehicle "severe use," such as towing or racing, change fluid much more frequently: at half the manufacturer's recommended "severe use" interval or 25,000 miles, whichever is less.

Here's a quick test you can use to determine the condition of your transmission fluid: first, look at the fluid to see if it has become discolored. It is acceptable if it is the original color or has darkened some. But if it is dark brown, it's time for a change.

Next, sniff. If it has the pungent aroma of "burnt toast," it has oxidized to the point that it should be changed. Both color change and foul smell are common signs of oxidation.

Finally, drip a couple of drops of the fluid on a clean white paper towel. After about half-a-minute, the drops should have soaked into the towel and spread out to more than twice original diameter. If the fluid spreads that far, it's still good. If it doesn't spread at all, it is overdue for replacement. Spreading to less than twice original diameter indicates fluid that is partially oxidized.

Clues to the condition of transmission fluid are its smell, it's color, and how much it disperses on a paper towel.

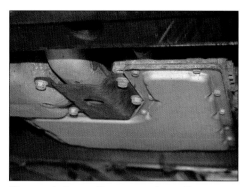

On most domestic cars, automatic transmission fluid is drained by removing the transmission sump pan: there is no drain plug. Transmission drain plugs are more common on foreign-made vehicles.

If the transmission sump has a drain bolt, remove it and let as much fluid drain out as possible. Once the fluid has stopped flowing, it is time to remove the sump pan.

If the transmission does not have a drain bolt, fluid is drained from the sump pan by unbolting it and letting fluid pour over the edge of the pan. This is why you need a very large drain pan. There is a technique for doing this.

Loosen all of the pan bolts one turn, then remove alternate bolts all the way around the pan. Determine which side of the pan you will let the fluid pour from. Remove all of the bolts holding that side of the pan to the transmission case. Now, loosen—but do not remove—the bolts at the opposite side of the pan.

The objective is to loosen the bolts on the opposite side enough to permit the pan to be lowered on the pour side to about a 30-degree angle, but without bending the lip of the pan. Loosening the bolts by three turns is probably about right to accomplish that.

While supporting the pan with one hand, remove all but one of the bolts on the remaining sides. Leave the bolt closest to the pour side in place, but loosen it by about three turns. Attempt to lower the pour side of the pan. If it doesn't come free, you can pull on it with your fingers. The bolts in place will prevent it from suddenly dropping, even if you end up having to use both hands.

Do not insert a screwdriver or putty knife between the lip of the sump pan and the transmission case to pry the sump pan loose, even if you don't care about preserving the gasket. These surfaces must be kept absolutely smooth. If you put a scratch in either surface, you create a path for fluid to leak. Prying on the pan also stands a good chance of bending the lip, in which case it won't seal properly.

With the pan loose, and still supporting the pan with one hand, remove the remaining two bolts and gently lower the pan to pour out the old transmission fluid. Loosen the remaining bolts as necessary to allow the pour side of the pan to drop down, but continue supporting the pan as fluid drains, so that you aren't putting stress on the lip that's still bolted to the transmission.

When most of the fluid has drained, remove the remaining bolts, remove the pan and pour off the fluid remaining in the pan, and set the pan aside on a workbench or other clean surface.

If the transmission has a sump drain bolt, the process is basically the same: loosen the bolts slightly, so that you can break the pan loose from the transmission case. Then, remove most of the bolts, but leave enough in place to fully support the pan. While supporting the pan with one hand, remove the remaining bolts with the other hand and remove the sump pan from the vehicle.

The bottom of the transmission itself is now exposed, including the filter or filters. The transmission will continue to drip fluid for a while, so this is a good time for measuring the drained fluid, cleaning the sump pan and magnet and, if it's not reusable, removing the old gasket.

It is important to know how much fluid you drained out. Otherwise, you cannot know how much new fluid to put in. An automatic transmission can be damaged by overfilling it with ATF. It can

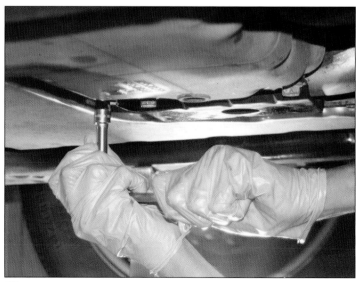

When removing the drain pan, loosen all of the bolts and then support the pan with one hand while you remove them.

Leave loosened bolts in one end of the pan to serve as a hinge when you lower the other end to initially drain the old fluid. Make sure that these bolts are loose enough that the pan lip does not bend when the other side is lowered.

After you've drained fluid out of the pan, you can remove the remaining bolts while supporting the pan. The pan will not be empty, so remove the pan carefully to avoid spilling what remains in the pan.

It is important to measure the amount of fluid that is drained from the transmission, so don't just discard it. You have not fully drained the transmission because as much as half the fluid is retained in the torque converter. To avoid overfilling it, you need to know how much you drained from the transmission.

Pouring off the old fluid into gallon milk jugs makes it easy to estimate how much was drained: they are a known capacity and you can see into them. This looks to be a little over 6 quarts.

also be damaged if it is underfilled. So, measure how much you drained out.

The easiest way to do this is with empty gallon-size milk jugs. Using a wide-mouthed funnel, pour the old transmission fluid from the drain pan into the milk jugs. You can see how much fluid is in each jug (four quarts to the gallon), which makes it easy to calculate how much was drained out. Since ATF comes in quart containers, it's easy to figure out how much you'll need to put in.

If you are replacing the gasket and pieces of it remain stuck to the sump pan lip, try to remove the fragments with a solvent (such as penetrating oil) and a shop towel. If that doesn't work, try solvent and a ScotchBrite pad. If that doesn't work, you can use a single-edge razor blade, with solvent as a lubricant, to scrape it off. You can also use a gasket scraper for this job, but do not use a screwdriver. A gasket scraper looks like a screwdriver with a broad chisel-shaped tip. The tip is wide so that the edges don't come in contact with the surface being scraped.

Now clean the sump pan and magnet. The magnet is removable, but you can clean it in place. Either way, clean it completely with a shop towel, getting into all grooves and around the edges. Wipe out the interior of the sump pan, as well, until all accumulated residue is gone. It probably won't be necessary to

do more than wiping it clean, but if you need a cleaning agent, use brake cleaner.

It's now time to get back under the car. With a clean lint-free shop towel, carefully dab and wipe away the drops of transmission fluid clinging to the bottom of the transmission. Also wipe off the edge of the transmission case to which the sump pan bolts. Remove any gasket

Clean the sump pan with a lint-free rag. This is a reusable sump gasket, so the old fluid is carefully cleaned from it, too. The gasket is inspected, but otherwise left in place.

There is a magnet in the sump to attract metal particles. The magnet is there because it is expected that the friction surfaces of the transmission clutches will create debris.

So don't panic, but do clean the magnet, either in place or by removing it. If you remove it, put it back where you found it.

The end result should be a clean sump pan, free of residue, and a clean magnet.

residue stuck to the machined edge of the transmission case. It is ultra-important that this surface not be scratched.

The transmission filter or filters should be very visible at the bottom of the transmission. Generally, these filters have a tube that simply pushes into an opening of 1 inch or so in diameter in the bottom of the transmission. Gently pull the filter downward to remove it, twisting a little if necessary.

There is a rubber gasket around the tube that fits into the transmission. These sometimes stay in the hole, rather than coming out with the filter. So, look to make sure it came out. If it didn't, pull it out with your finger. Compare the old filter with the new one to be sure that they're the same.

As indicated previously, some older Asian vehicles do not use transmission filters and instead use a fine mesh screen. If yours is one of them, unbolt, remove, clean, and reinstall that screen.

On most vehicles, this is all that needs to be done before installing the new filters and reinstalling the sump pan. On some vehicles, however, there is more to do. Some BMW models, for example, have two sumps. Both must be drained. The process for each is the same as that just described.

General Motors 4T60-E or 4T80-E automatic transmissions retain fluid in a side cover. The 4T60-E uses a thermostatic valve that closes when fluid is hot, so fluid should be cold when draining a 4T60-E to drain the side cover. The 4T80-E version used with the Northstar V-8 (front wheel drive Cadillacs), always stores fluid in the side cover. There is a separate hexagonal drain bolt for this fluid, accessible only after removing one of the filters. Consult the factory shop manual to determine if there are any similar special procedures applicable to your vehicle.

Carefully wipe the remaining droplets of old fluid from the bottom of the transmission and from the transmission housing, using a lint-free rag. Just carefully dab the drops away, so they're not dripping on you as you remove and replace the filter(s).

This is one of the filters, in place. This transmission, a GM automatic, uses two filters in this transaxle application.

The filter is simply pulled out with your fingers. This is typical. However, if you're not sure exactly how the old filter removes, look at the new part and you should be able to figure it out.

There is a rubber ring around the neck of the filter. Check to be sure that the ring did not come off and stay in the transmission. If it did, it will prevent proper installation of the new filter. The location from which the other filter was removed can be seen at the right side of this picture.

It is now time to install the new transmission filter(s). Usually, these just press into the receptacle in the transmission. Make sure the rubber sealing gasket is in place on the new filter and then push it gently into the hole until it seats.

With the filter(s) installed, it is time to reinstall the sump pan. Make sure the magnet has been returned to the pan (if it was removed). Verify that there is no dirt or lint in the pan. If you are replacing the gasket, install the new one. If you are reusing the gasket, wipe off the surface of the old gasket so that it is clean and dry.

You should not use gasket sealers on sump pan gaskets. First, it's not neces-sary, absent specific instructions in the factory shop manual. Sump gaskets are designed to seal when properly installed. Using sealer can actually make it more likely that the gasket will leak. Second, there is a risk that some of the sealer will get into the sump and clog passages or valves inside the transmission.

When installing a new gasket, posi-tion it on the pan by using a few of the pan bolts. With many gaskets, the bolt holes are just enough smaller than the bolt diameter and will hold the bolts in place. Otherwise, hold the gasket in place with one bolt as you lift the pan into place, install the bolt a few turns, and

The pan is then reinstalled. Once the bolts are installed finger-tight, they should be further tightened in a pattern specified in the factory shop manual to ensure that the gasket seals evenly.

This transmission has a side cover that stores fluid, in addition to the fluid in the sump pan, which drains through this bolt next to the receptacle into which the second filter fits. This illustrates the value of having a factory shop manual for your car. Even though this same basic GM automatic is used on tens of thousands of GM vehicles, there are variations among them according to the specific vehicle.

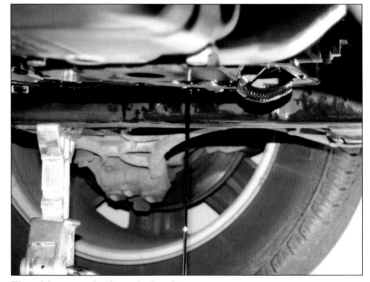

The side cover is then drained.

Before installing the new filter, carefully wipe away old fluid with a lint-free rag, so that it is installed into a clean receptacle.

Then new filter simply pushes into place.

then install another bolt opposite it, also only a few turns. Check to make sure that the gasket is located properly. Install the remaining bolts a few turns each, and then check the gasket to make sure that it is flat against the pan lip all the way around. You may need to push it down around the bolts. Then, finger tighten the bolts.

If you are reusing a reusable gasket, you have an easier job because the gasket holds itself in place on the pan. Position the pan on the transmission case and, while supporting it with one hand, install a few bolts finger tight. Then install the remaining bolts, also finger tight.

The factory shop manual will specify the sequence in which the pan bolts should be tightened and the torque value for those bolts. It is important that the bolts be tightened in the correct sequence and that they not be over-tightened. Using the wrong sequence or overtightening can distort the gasket, causing leaks. In the absence of a speci-fied sequence, the Filter Manufacturer's Council recommends that the bolts be tightened in a criss-cross pattern.

Using the proper sequence, tighten the bolts gently with a socket and

Tightening should be completed with a torque wrench. Overtightening will distort the gasket and create leaks.

ratchet. Do not tighten them much beyond the point that you begin to feel resistance. The rest of the tightening is done with a torque wrench.

Precise tightening of sump pan bolts is important to insuring proper sealing. It is important that these bolts not be over-tightened. This means using a torque wrench. Though many vehicles

specify the torque value in ft-lbs, some express it in in-lbs. The vehicle manu-facturer may also specify that the tight-ening be done in stages, to a specific in-lbs value at each stage.

If the sump uses a drain bolt, clean it off and reinstall it. Tighten the bolt to the manufacturer's specified torque value.

Lower the car to the ground, unless it is one on which the transmission is

This is a typical automatic transmission dipstick/fill hole cap. However, a number of automobile manufacturers are omitting this feature, in which instance special procedures must be followed to refill the transmission from under the car.

Remove the cap.

Refill the transmission with a little less new fluid than you drained. Then start the car and shift the transmission through each gear and check the fluid level.

filled from the side of the transmission case.

Remove the dipstick and, using a transmission fluid funnel or another fun-nel with a narrow enough body and spout to fit into the dipstick-tube/fill-hole, slowly pour new ATF into the trans-mission. Add only as much as you drained. Otherwise, you will be overfill-ing the transmission because there is still old ATF in the torque converter.

After you have added an amount equal to that drained, replace the dip-stick and start the engine. As it idles, with your foot on the brake, move the gearshift lever through the gears, letting the transmission engage in each. Do this several times.

Then check the fluid level with the dipstick. With the transmission in "park" and the engine idling, pull the ATF dip-stick, wipe it off, reinsert it (making sure it seats fully) and remove it again.

There will be two marks on the dip-stick, one for fluid level when "cold" and the other for fluid level when "hot." These marks indicate the full level at those fluid temperatures. If the fluid level on the dipstick indicates that fluid should be added, shut off the engine, remove the dipstick and add ATF as needed to bring the level to the mark. But, add it in stages, checking fluid level each time, to avoid overfilling the trans-mission

Note: On certain Chrysler rear wheel drive vehicles, the fluid level is checked with the engine idling, parking brake engaged, and transmission in neutral.

Once the fluid level is at the correct level, replace the dipstick and you're done. Except, of course, for clean up and recycling.

Most communities recycle transmis-sion fluid in the same manner as motor oil. Many parts stores will also accept transmission fluid for recycling. Wash any dirty shop towels as soon as possi-ble—and not with anything else—and dispose of the fluid soaked newspapers in the trash. Remember that these are both fire hazards.

After a few days driving, recheck the fluid level.

Manual Transmission Fluid Change

It is actually easier to replace fluid in a manual transmission than in an automatic transmission. Again, the owner's manual or the factory shop manual will provide the recommended interval for fluid replacement, as well as specifying the correct fluid. Beware of any claim that the fluid is "lifetime." For the same reasons that ATF should be regularly replaced, so should manual transmission fluid (MTF).

Different manual transmissions use different types of fluids, including specific gear oils, automatic transmission fluid, and multiple viscosity engine oils. It is important to use the fluid specified by the vehicle manufacturer, especially while the transmission is under the powertrain warranty (which may be longer than other elements of the warranty). For many foreign-nameplate vehicles, that's an MTF sold under that manufacturer's brand name.

For manual transmissions that use gear oils, there are two American Petroleum Institute service designations: GL-4 and GL-5. Each of these service designations is available as a multi-viscosity oil, such as 75W-90, established according to Society of Automotive Engineers (SAE) standards.

Though GL-5 is newer and generally has superior attributes, it does not supersede GL-4 and should not be used when GL-4 is specified. GL-5 fluids (including synthetic versions) often contain sulphur and phosphorous additives. These can be detrimental to bronze, copper, and brass parts, which may have been used in manual transmissions requiring GL-4 gear oil. So, if your transmission specifies GL-4, stay with it. On the other hand, don't use GL-4 in a transmission that specifies GL-5. GL-5 has much higher shear strength properties than GL-4, as well as anti-oxidants and other additives.

Some manual transmissions specify the use of motor oil or automatic transmission fluids. Though this may seem strange, motor oil is designed to operate in a much more hostile environment than a transmission and ATF operates in a very similar environment. What the transmissions that use these fluids have in common is close tolerances. Hence, they need fluids of lower viscosity than gear oil.

But, manual transmissions sustain much more sudden shear loads than do automatic transmissions. That is, you can drop the clutch at 2,500 rpm and that sudden load hits the transmission gears full force. The fluid that keeps the moving parts separated in a manual transmission has to be able to handle that sudden shearing load.

This leads into two observations: First, as in just about any lubricant situation, synthetic manual transmission fluids are superior to conventional equivalent fluids, provided the synthetic fluid is of the same viscosity as the specified conventional fluid.

Second, when ATF is specified as a manual transmission fluid, a synthetic successor ATF—such as Dexron VI to Dexron III, or Mercon LV to Mercon—will be lower in viscosity than the specified conventional ATF. Because manual transmissions that use ATF already use a low viscosity fluid, it should not be further reduced. Unless the vehicle manufacturer approves, these synthetic successor ATFs should not be used in a manual transmission. In fact, General Motors specifically states that Dexron VI is not suitable for use in manual transmissions for which Dexron III was originally specified. If you wish to use a synthetic ATF in place of a conventional ATF in a manual transmission, use one that retains the viscosity of the original equipment fluid.

Now, for the actual fluid replacement: Particularly if the vehicle uses gear oil, the manual transmission should be drained with the fluid warmed up. So, drive the car enough to do that, and then put it on four jack stands. It must be level to properly drain and refill the transmission because the fill hole is the fluid "full" mark.

REMOVE THE FILL PLUG BOLT FIRST. Why? Because both the fill plug and drain plug bolts can be very difficult to loosen. If it turns out to be impossible to remove the fill plug bolt, it is better to discover that situation before draining the fluid from the transmission. If either bolt is stubborn, use penetrating oil and give it time to work.

It may be necessary to remove other parts to access the fill and drain plug bolts. For example, on certain front-wheel-drive Asian brands, the right front fender inner liner must come out. On certain BMW models, there are two heat shields that must be removed. Consult the factory shop manual for the specifics. Also, be sure to clean off any transmission fluid that spills on rubber parts, such as constant velocity joint boots.

Now, drain the fluid. Some fluid may trickle out when you remove the fill plug, so have the drain pan ready. Then remove the drain plug and drain out the remainder of the fluid. Keep the drain and fill plugs separate, as the drain plug may be magnetic and will need to be replaced in the drain hole. If a magnetic drain plug has a coating of fine metal particles when removed, that should be considered normal wear.

Clean the drain plug and the drain hole and reinstall the drain plug. If the drain plug used a "crush" washer, one designed to deform inward as the bolt is tightened, it should be replaced with a new one and not reused. With a torque wrench, tighten the drain plug bolt to the manufacturer's recommended torque specification.

It may be possible to refill the transmission through a funnel and length of flexible hose. If there is not sufficient space to do this, it will be necessary to use a hand-operated fluid transfer pump to refill the transmission. However, the typical fluid transfer pump does not work well with the heavier viscosity of most gear oils. For gear oil, the best bet is a hand-operated "gear oil pump" (used to pump gear oil into the transmission on outboard motors), which can be purchased at any marina for about $10.

Fill the transmission to the bottom of the fill hole, until a bit of fluid streams out. Then install the fill plug bolt, again replacing any crush-type washer with a new one and tightening the bolt with a torque wrench to the torque value specified in the factory manual.

CHAPTER 12

DISC BRAKES
SERVICE AND REPLACEMENT OF PADS, ROTORS AND CALIPERS

Many people who work on their own cars don't do brakes. There's a sense that it's alright to replace spark plugs yourself because the worst that can happen is the car won't start. But when the worst that can happen is that the car won't stop, some people leave it to a professional mechanic to do the job.

In fact, servicing disc brakes is not complicated and is easily within the competence of the home mechanic. You may need a few specialized tools, but nothing that's very expensive.

Disc brakes have three basic components: the rotor, the caliper, and the pads. The rotor is the metal disc that attaches to the axle and rotates with the wheel. The caliper is a big metal clamp mounted over the rotor. The typical caliper can move sideways in relation to the rotor (i.e., laterally) on smooth bolts or "pins," which is why this type of disc brake is called "floating" or "sliding." The pads are made of a friction material and are positioned in the caliper on each side of the rotor. Inside the caliper, behind the inner brake pad, there is a small piston within a cylinder. When the brake pedal is depressed, brake fluid is forced from the master cylinder, located in the engine compartment, through

This is a typical front disc brake. The slots in the rotor are for cooling. This is a "floating caliper" disc brake.

brake lines (metal tubes and reinforced rubber hoses) that lead to each brake caliper.

The brake fluid, in turn, forces the caliper piston to move outward in its cylinder, toward the brake rotor. This pushes the inner brake pad into contact with the rotor. The cylinder, however, is part of the brake caliper. Because that caliper can slide laterally, the same force that pushes the piston outward also pushes the caliper body in the opposite direction. That pulls the other brake pad, the outer pad, into contact with the

This is a typical rear disc brake. Rear disc brakes bear less of a vehicle's weight during braking, so they are smaller and lighter than front brakes. This, too, is a floating caliper disc brake.

other side of the rotor. Thus, the action of the single piston applies the brake pads to both sides of the brake rotor, and the car stops. The friction created converts the kinetic energy of the car's motion into heat energy stored by the metal of the rotor, which is then dissipated as the rotor cools.

NOTE: For the sake of completeness, "fixed" caliper brakes have pistons on both sides of the caliper. The caliper does not itself move, but is "fixed" in relation to the rotor. Fixed caliper brakes are a high-performance system, much more expensive to manufacture and service than "floating" or "sliding" caliper brakes. If you have a C6 Corvette Z06 or a new Porsche 911 Carrera S, you have fixed caliper disc brakes. Otherwise, you probably don't.

Replacing brake pads is routine maintenance. Some higher-priced vehicles have electronic sensors to indicate when pads should be replaced. Most cars simply have a "wear indicator" on the pad itself: a soft metal tab that makes a metallic squeal during braking when pads need replacement.

Replacing rotors is one of those "not if, but when" things. Disc brakes function by creating friction between the pads and the rotor. Just as brake pads wear down, so do rotors, just not as fast. It may take a lot of miles, but eventually the rotors wear out.

Replacing a brake caliper is not routine, but it is to be expected Calipers operate in a very dirty environment. Yet, a little dirt in the wrong place, such as the bore in which the caliper piston moves, can seize the caliper. It's something of a marvel that they don't fail more often.

Brake pads and rotors must always be replaced in wheel pairs, i.e., both front brakes at the same time, both rear brakes at the same time. Calipers can be replaced individually. When performing the work, do one side at a time. That way, you always have the other side to refer to if there is a question about how something is put together.

When servicing the brakes, be sure to check the condition of the brake fluid. If it is old, dirty, or appears contaminated, it may be time to replace it. More about that is found in Sidebar: "Brake Fluid." How to replace the fluid is covered in Sidebar: "Bleeding the Brakes."

Parts for these jobs

Replacing Pads
Brake pads
  (set, four pads total per axle)
Brake cleaner (aerosol)
Unopened can of brake fluid
  (DOT3 or DOT4, as specified by
  vehicle manufacturer)

High temperature silicone
  brake lubricant
Anti-squeal compound
Anti-squeal shims (if applicable)

Replacing Rotors
Everything required for replacing
  pads, except the anti-squeal pads
  and shims, plus:
New rotors, in axle pairs
New caliper bracket mounting bolts
  (if factory manual specifies
  replacement rather than reuse)

Replacing a Caliper
Everything required for replacing
  pads, except the anti-squeal pads
  and shims, plus:
New caliper, loaded or semi-loaded

Tools for these jobs

Replacing Brake Pads
Wrench—type varies (see text)
Breaker bar
Socket and any necessary adapter
  (again, see text)
Torque wrench
C-clamp—eight inch or greater
  opening (if applicable)
Disc brake caliper piston tool or
  needle nose pliers (if applicable)
Wire coat hanger, zip tie, or
  equivalent
Turkey baster or syringe
Old newspapers
Mechanic's nitrile rubber gloves
Fender cover

Replacing Brake Rotors
Everything required for replacing
  pads, plus:
Penetrating Oil
Impact screwdriver
  (foreign made vehicles only)

Replacing a Brake Caliper
Everything required for replacing
  pads, plus:
Brake bleeder hose or bleeder kit
Box-end wrench
  (fitting brake hose bolt at caliper)
Socket sized to fit brake hose bolt
  (for torque wrench)

Parking brake cable tool or open-end
  wrench (if applicable, for parking
  brake cable; see text)
Drip pan
A short length of narrow hose to
  plug the "banjo fitting" (see text)
A 2 x 4-inch piece of wood about
  18 inches long

Time for these jobs

It takes about an hour to an hour and a half to change disc brake pads on both sides of one axle, not counting the time spent lifting the car.

Replacing a rotor is an extra 15 minutes, if it comes right off. If rust has frozen the rotor to the axle stub, it will take much longer.

Preparing a new caliper for installation takes some time, and bleeding the caliper once it is installed requires an assistant, but the entire process can be done in an hour.

However, these times assume everything goes smoothly. When you're doing something on the car for the first time, everything will *not* go smoothly if you're feeling rushed. So, allow at least an afternoon for any of these jobs and be sure to plan ahead by applying penetrating oil, as suggested below, the night before.

Advance Planning

Replacing Brake Pads
You will, of course, need new brake pads. Brake pads are sold in sets of pads for both brakes on the same axle. Normally, the pads come with the additional hardware required to do the job, such as anti-rattle clips and shims.

There are many different types and brands of disc brake pads on the market. They differ, as well, in composition, performance, characteristics, noise level, and durability. For more information, check Sidebar: "Choosing the Right Brake Pads."

You need to know the proper torque value for the vehicle lug nuts and for the caliper mounting bolts/guide pins. This information probably won't be in the owner's manual. Consult the factory shop manual. If you don't have a factory shop manual, you really should get one. In the meantime, your friendly neighborhood library may have a reference that contains this information. You should not guess about these torque values or try to tighten these bolts by feel. Depending on make, the proper torque value for caliper mounting bolts can be anywhere between 20 and 90 ft-lbs.

You also need to know the type of piston used in the brake calipers. On many cars, the rear brake caliper pistons must be screwed into the caliper; they cannot be compressed in with a C-clamp and attempting to do so will damage the caliper piston seals. This information will be in the factory shop manual or other reference, but not in the owner's manual.

There are certain tools you may need, depending on the specifics of the brakes installed on the vehicle. Some disc brake caliper mounting bolts are ordinary hex head bolts. Others, however, use large recessed-head Allen bolts or Torx bolts. You will need the proper socket or socket head to remove these bolts.

A special "disc brake piston tool" is available to use on disc brakes that require screwing the piston into the caliper. Though it may be possible to use the ends of a pair of needle-nose pliers instead, the special tool makes the job much easier and only costs about $10 at an auto parts store. The tool is pictured on page 123.

The C-clamp used when the caliper piston is to be compressed into its bore is a *big* C-clamp. For most brakes, a C-clamp with at least an 8-inch opening is needed.

Replacing Brake Rotors

You will need to do all the advance planning required for replacing pads, plus you will need a pair of new rotors, unless you are planning on resurfacing the old ones. There is a vast selection of new rotors on the market, ranging from economy rotors to more expensive high-performance rotors, as well as OE and OE-equivalent rotors.

In addition to the torque specifications for the caliper mounting bolts, you will need the manufacturer's torque specification for the caliper bracket mounting bolts that bolt the caliper bracket to the suspension assembly. This is in the factory shop manual.

NOTE: On some vehicles, caliper bracket mounting bolts may not be reused and must be replaced with new bolts. Bolts of that type are designed to be tightened to very high torque values and stretch slightly as they are tightened, applying tension to the joined parts. Once used, these bolts are "stretched out" and weakened. If the specified torque value for the caliper mounting-bracket bolts approaches or exceeds 100 ft-lbs, check the factory manual to determine whether the bolts may be reused.

Rotors frequently rust where big hole in the center of the rotor fits over the axle stub. Ideally, the night before you're planning on doing the job, you should lift the end of the car you'll be working on, remove the wheels, and inspect the rotor. If the rotor doesn't appear lose on the axle stub, soak that seam with penetrating oil. On foreign makes, there will probably be a screw, usually a Phillips, installed through the rotor into the axle stub. That, too, should be soaked with penetrating oil. Avoid, however, getting any penetrating oil on the wheel lugs because that will affect the torque value when the wheels are reinstalled.

Replacing a Brake Caliper

Buying a new brake caliper isn't just a matter of going to the parts store and asking for one. You may need to know some specifications for your car. Plus, do you want one that's "loaded" or "semi-loaded?" How much is the "core charge" going to cost? Should it be new or rebuilt? Answers to all of these questions are in Sidebar: "Buying a New Brake Caliper," found on Cartechbooks.com.

In addition to the torque specifications for the caliper mounting bolts, you will need the manufacturer's torque specification for the brake hose bolt at the caliper.

You also will need a brake bleeder hose or kit. This doesn't have to be fancy or expensive. The one in the pictures accompanying this chapter cost five dollars. Any parts store can supply one. Be sure the hose is clear so that you can see any air bubble in the fluid flowing out of the caliper.

Next, find or buy a short length of narrow rubber or neoprene hose, such as fuel line hose, at a parts store or hardware store. This isn't for bleeding the brakes. It's for plugging the "banjo fitting" in the brake hose. You'll only need about 2 inches of hose, but you may need to tailor the hose by removing a lengthwise slit.

Last, ask someone to help you when it comes time to bleed the brakes. Even if you buy a "one man" brake bleeder, to do the job properly, you still need an assistant to push on the brake pedal while you watch the bleeder hose.

Hazard Warning

Brake dust should not be inhaled. Even though asbestos has not been used in most disc brake pads for the last decade, there remain concerns that brake dust can be cancer-causing. At the very least, inhaling it is not good for your lungs. Do not brush away brake dust and don't blow it away with compressed air. Use only special brake cleaners designed for that purpose, as described in the text.

After working on the brakes, you will have a low brake pedal for the first few brake applications. The car will not stop normally until you've applied the brakes a few times.

Anytime you disconnect a brake line, you will admit air into the brake system. Whenever a brake line is disconnected, that line must be "bled" to purge all air from the line.

Always use fresh brake fluid from an unopened can. Brake fluid is hygroscopic, which means it absorbs water. Brake fluid can, and will, absorb moisture from atmospheric air. It is designed that way so that any moisture in the lines doesn't create pockets of boiling water. But moisture in the brake fluid lowers the overall boiling point of the fluid. Boiling fluid results in a spongy, ineffective brake pedal.

Choosing the Right Brake Pads

There are four types of disc brake pad: semi-metallic, non-asbestos organic (NAO), low-metallic NAO, and ceramic. Semi-metallic pads are primarily metal (30% to 65% by weight), which is usually some combination of steel and copper fibers, iron powder, and graphite held together with an organic compound. Semi-metallic pads dissipate heat well, but wear rotors more rapidly than other types of pads and can be noisy. Non-asbestos organic (NAO) pads combine organic materials such as glass, rubber, carbon, and aramid fibers (such as Kevlar and Twaron), with high temperature resins to create the friction material. NAO pads are softer than semi-metallic pads, so they don't wear the rotors as rapidly. But they do create more brake dust and wear out more quickly than semi-metallic pads. Low-metallic NAO pads are a compromise between these two, made by adding steel and copper fibers (less than 30% by weight) to organic pad material. The added metal provides better heat transfer than NAO pads, but low-metallic pads still create more brake dust than semi-metallic pads.

Ceramic pads use ceramic materials in conjunction with other materials, often including copper fibers, as the friction material. Ceramic pads have become popular as both original equipment (OE) and aftermarket replacement pads because they have the virtues of other types of pads without the vices. They're less abrasive than semi-metallic pads, so they last longer and rotor wear is reduced. Ceramic pads can handle

high temperatures before the friction material begins to turn to carbon, so they are fade-resistant. This also means they generate less brake dust, because brake dust is carbonized friction material. What dust ceramic pads do generate is lighter in color than the black dust generated by steel fiber pads, so it's also less visible on the wheels. Also, ceramic pads are less likely to squeal because their natural sound frequencies are outside the range of human hearing.

The term "ceramic" encompasses myriad materials, ranging from clay to potassium titanate fiber. Though all ceramic pads include some combination of ceramic materials, the term itself discloses neither the type of ceramic materials used nor the proportion of those materials to non-ceramic materials. Not only do formulations differ between pads made by different manufacturers, but also among pads made by a specific manufacturer for different applications.

This is because brake pads, no matter what friction material is used, are "application specific," which means that brake pads are manufactured to meet the requirements of a specific vehicle employing a composition of friction materials designed specifically for that vehicle after taking into consideration its characteristics and the demands likely to be placed on its brakes.

Original equipment brake pads in automobiles manufactured in 2001 or later (or trucks in 2003 or later) must meet a federal braking efficiency standard, Federal Motor Vehicle Safety Standard 135. Though FMVSS 135 is directly applicable only to OE brake pads, federal law prohibits automobile dealers and repair shops from installing aftermarket brake pads that degrade brake performance below OE levels. For that reason, aftermarket pads manufactured for vehicles to which FMVSS 135 applies should meet that standard, as well. Additionally, all pads manufactured by members of the Brake Manufacturer's Council (BMC) meet FMSSS 135. Members of the BMC include: ABS Friction Corp. (Ceramicool), Affinia Group (Raybestos), Akebono, Delphi, Federal Mogul (Ferodo), Honeywell (Bendix), Morse, OE Quality Friction, Performance Friction, and TMD Friction (Pagid, Textar, Mintex).

Any way you look at it, though, brake pads are a bargain. Even the top-of-the line seldom costs more than $100 for a set and aftermarket OE-equivalent brake pads are often about half that price at the parts store or online.

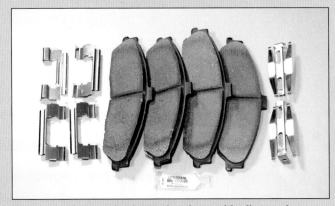

These are the new brake pads, along with clips and lubricant. This is everything that ordinarily comes when you go to the parts store and buy new pads.

BRAKE FLUID EATS CAR PAINT—INSTANTLY. Cover the fender before removing or adding brake fluid. If you get brake fluid on your hands, wash them with soap and water before touching the car.

As always, be sure the car is securely supported on jack stands before getting any part of you under it. Chapter 2 has complete information on lifting the car.

Let's do it

Removing Brake Pads

Though all disc brake systems are generically similar, there are myriad detail differences. While factory manuals are written for professional mechanics and may assume the reader has knowledge you don't, in fact, possess (which is the gap this book is designed to bridge), the factory manual will clue you into any unique procedure, as well as providing you with vital information, such as torque values, needed to properly perform the job.

NOTE: If you are replacing rear brake pads, be sure the parking brake is disengaged. Some parking brakes act through the brake caliper to push the piston and pad onto the rotor. If the parking brake is engaged, it will be impossible to remove the caliper to access the brake pads. If you are not replacing rear brakes, be sure the parking brake is engaged, so there's less risk of the car moving.

Before you start to work on the brake assembly, you should clean it with brake cleaner. Brake cleaner comes in an aerosol can and is available at any auto parts store. It is specifically designed to dissolve brake dust and brake pad residue without affecting the rotor's friction surfaces. The can usually includes a little

Before working on brakes, you should always clean them first with brake cleaner. Brake dust is toxic, so it is essential that you get rid of the dust. Use newspapers to protect the floor from the cleaner and crud that will drip from the brake assembly.

plastic tube that can be fitted into the nozzle so that you can direct the spray into narrow spaces.

There are two types of brake cleaner: chlorinated, and non-chlorinated. Usually, non-chlorinated is preferable. Chlorinated is flammable; non-chlorinated isn't. Chlorinated can damage rubber; non-chlorinated won't. Both effectively remove brake dust and both dry very rapidly, leaving a clean surface. Chlorinated brake cleaner is slightly better at removing grease.

Once the brakes are clean, the next step—for *front* brakes—is to depress the caliper piston into its bore. Because they are worn, the old brake pads are thinner than the new pads. The caliper piston must be pushed back into its bore to create the extra clearance required to fit the caliper fit back over the rotor once the new pads are installed. Depressing the piston is best accomplished while the old pads are still installed because the clamp can push on the backing plate of the old pad, rather than the piston itself. That protects the caliper piston seals.

Before depressing a caliper piston, always check the brake fluid level in the master cylinder reservoir. Depressing a caliper piston pushes fluid backward, so it will push some fluid back into the reservoir. Normally, the fluid level in the reservoir isn't so high that it can't

Brake cleaner dries very rapidly, without leaving a residue that would affect the brake's operation.

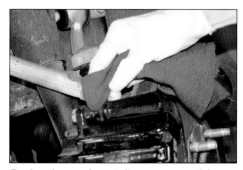

Brake cleaner is not, however, good for rubber. As much as possible, avoid getting it on rubber parts. If there is a rubber CV boot near the brake, for example, cover it before using brake cleaner. When getting cleaner on rubber parts, such as this boot covering a caliper slide, wipe it away as rapidly as possible.

accommodate the extra fluid. But if it appears that the reservoir could overflow, use a syringe or turkey baster to remove a little of the fluid before depressing the caliper piston. Put the cap back on the master cylinder reservoir, so that the fluid is not exposed unnecessarily to the air.

Because brake fluid absorbs moisture, even from the air, brake fluid that is removed should always be replaced with new fluid, either DOT3 or DOT4, as specified for the car on the master cylinder reservoir cap. "DOT3" and "DOT4" are U.S. Department of Transportation (DOT) minimum standards for brake fluids. A brake system is designed for one or the other, so stick with what the manufacturer specifies even though they're technically compatible. Never use silicone fluid, which is DOT5 (see Sidebar: "Brake Fluid").

Also, if the vehicle is equipped with an electronic brake-wear sensor—a wire leading to a plastic connector that is clipped into the brake caliper—it should be disconnected at the brake caliper before compressing the caliper piston to prevent damage to the connector and cable. This is *not* the anti-lock brake (ABS) sensor, which fits into the back of the hub assembly and does not need to be disturbed to change brake pads. Calipers on cars with ABS do not need to be treated differently, though there are

This is the fluid reservoir for the brake master cylinder, usually mounted near the firewall. It sits on top of the dual master cylinder—the aluminum color metal piece directly below it. The cap specifies the type of brake fluid to be used in the vehicle.

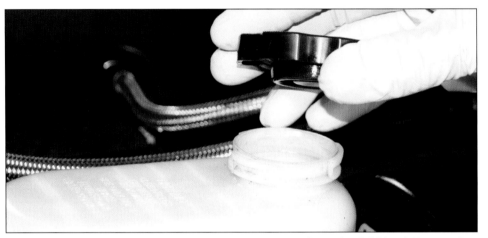

Remove the cap from the master cylinder reservoir and check the fluid level. Depressing caliper pistons—part of the process of replacing brake pads and rotors—can force fluid back into this reservoir, which could cause overflow if the fluid level is too high.

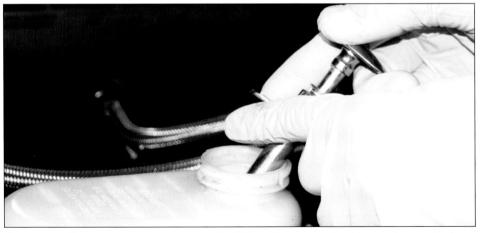

As a precaution, you can remove some fluid from the reservoir with a syringe or turkey baster. But don't let it get on the car's paint—brake fluid destroys paint instantly—and don't reuse fluid that's been removed: it can absorb water from the atmosphere.

some special considerations (see Sidebar: "Is ABS Special?").

To depress the caliper pistons in the *front* brake calipers, use a large C-clamp, one with an opening of about 8 inches. Position the screw portion of the C-clamp on the "backing plate" of the old outer brake pad, in the U-shaped opening in the caliper. The "backing plate" is the metal back of the pad to which the friction material is bonded. The top, or fixed, part of the C-clamp is positioned on the rear of the caliper. Usually, there is a flat surface that it can rest upon. Sometimes, the clamp must rest on the inlet fitting bolt, which attaches the brake hose to the caliper (the exact procedure will be specified in the factory shop manual). However, the C-clamp must always be positioned so that it is perpendicular to the brake pad and rotor. In other words, it must always be positioned so that it is pushing straight on the backing plate, not at an angle.

Holding the C-clamp in position with one hand, gradually tighten the clamp with the other hand to depress the caliper piston. You will feel resistance, but you should be able to smoothly depress the piston into the bore. Stop as soon as you can feel that it has bottomed. It is better to err on the side of not pushing the piston far enough into the bore than it is to risk forcing the piston into the bore. Forcing the piston into the bore could damage the rubber piston seals. If you did not initially depress the piston far enough to allow clearance with the new pads installed to slide the caliper into position over the rotor, you can depress the piston further during reassembly by putting one of the old brake pads over the piston and squeezing it in further with the C-clamp.

Some vehicles with floating or sliding calipers have two pistons in the front calipers. Because you're pushing with the brake pad that covers both pistons, this procedure will depress both pistons simultaneously. You may, however, have to alternate the C clamp between the two U-shaped openings in the caliper to depress the two pistons evenly.

Once the piston(s) is compressed into the caliper, remove the C-clamp.

Is ABS Special?

ABS wheel sensors and ABS wiring do not need to be disconnected or disturbed to replace brake pads, rotors or calipers.

Now for a little controversy: There is debate among professional mechanics over whether it is necessary to open the caliper bleed screw on a car equipped with anti-lock brakes (ABS, i.e., "anti-lock braking system") before compressing the caliper piston into its cylinder to change brake pads. The bleed screw is the fitting on the back of the caliper that can be opened to allow brake fluid to drain directly from the caliper (see Sidebar: "Bleeding the Brakes").

Some professional mechanics insist that the bleed screw must be opened before the caliper piston is compressed to prevent pushing any dirt in the brake line backward into the tiny valves in the expensive ABS control module. Other mechanics disagree, contending that opening a bleed screw is unnecessary, which is why it is not part of the factory-recommended procedure for changing brake pads.

If a bleed screw is opened, air will get into the brake line and it will be necessary to bleed that brake line. That means bleeding at least two brake lines when changing pads. All of that is avoided if the bleed screw is not opened.

So what should you do? The short answer is that you should look in the factory shop manual and follow the procedure it specifies. However, it appears most automobile manufacturers believe that there is not enough movement of brake fluid when a caliper piston is compressed to cause a problem with the ABS system.

If you do decide to open a bleed screw on an ABS-H equipped vehicle, there are two things to remember:

First, some ABS systems used in the early 1990s were "integral," meaning the master cylinder and the ABS controller, including the pump, accumulator, and control valves, were one unit. These systems keep the brake fluid under pressure even then the car is not running. Before opening a bleed screw in an integral system, the system must be depressurized by pumping the brake pedal 25 to 50 times with the engine off. You can determine if you have an integral ABS system by looking at the master cylinder. If the ABS modulator and the master cylinder are one unit, it is probably an integral system. If they are separate units, it is not an integral system.

Second, though individual brake lines can be bled in the described fashion, certain ABS systems (including Delco VI, Delphi 7, Bosch 5, and Teves Mark 20 ABS systems) retain fluid in the ABS control module at all times. If air gets into the brake lines at the master cylinder during caliper bleeding, it will require a proprietary scan tool to activate the module to fully bleed the entire system. So, it's doubly important to check the master cylinder reservoir fluid level frequently during bleeding.

For this same reason, you should consult the factory shop manual before bleeding the entire braking system on an ABS equipped vehicle, as some require use of a very expensive factory scan tool or special procedures to fully bleed the system, including the control module.

Now it is time to depress the caliper piston. This is done with a large "C" clamp or with a special tool that screws the piston back into the bore. Some cars use one method, others use the other, and some use a different method on the front and the back. Check the factory shop manual.

The screw-in portion of the clamp should be placed against the metal "backing plate" of the outer brake pad. There will be a location on the opposite side of the caliper where the clamp can be seated. Gradually push the piston into its bore by turning the clamp handle.

The method for depressing the caliper piston in rear brakes may be different, or it may be the same as the technique just described.

On some vehicles, such as the C5 Corvette pictured in this chapter, the rear caliper piston design is basically the same as it is for front brake calipers, though the calipers themselves are smaller. The caliper pistons are depressed in the same manner, using a C-clamp. Replacing the rear brake pads in such circumstances follows the same steps in the same sequence as described here for replacing front brake pads.

On other cars, however, the rear caliper pistons are designed to be compressed by screwing them into their bores. That's the case with the Cadillac DTS also pictured in this chapter. There are notches are cast into the top of the caliper piston that allow it to be turned like a very big screw, either with a large pair of needle nose pliers or a relatively inexpensive "disc brake piston tool" designed for that purpose. When caliper pistons are designed to screw inward, they usually turn clockwise. But it is not inevitably so: there are cars, including the 2005-and-later Ford 500, Ford Freestyle, and Mercury Montego, on which the caliper pistons turn in counter-clockwise.

If the brakes use the screw-in piston design, the caliper is removed before the piston is compressed (because you can't access the piston to turn it until the caliper has been removed).

Whether front or rear, the brake caliper is held in place by two bolts or caliper "pins" that must be removed to remove the caliper. The bolts can be the usual 6-sided hex head type, be of the TORX design, or be a recessed hex, i.e., Allen, bolt. On vehicles using Allen bolts, the bolt heads may be covered by plastic caps that must be removed to insert the wrench and/or protected by a rubber gasket through which the wrench is inserted into the bolt. Some Ford vehicles don't use bolts or guide pins; instead, they use "slide pins." "Slide pins" are V-shaped metal shafts with bumps cast into the each end that seat in a groove within in the caliper body. These slide pins are removed and installed with a hammer and a "drift." The drift can be a screwdriver or a special tool made for the task. Put the drift on the pin and hammer the pin into the caliper so it comes out on the inner side. Install it from the outside, tapping it in until it seats. A similar technique will remove the slide pins used in certain Volvo models.

It is usually necessary to remove both of the bolts or pins holding the caliper in place. However, sometimes only the lower one must be removed. On some calipers, the caliper simply slides on the top bolt and only the lower bolt keeps the caliper attached to the mounting bracket. On these calipers, removing the lower bolt allows you to rotate the caliper on the upper bolt or pin, exposing the pads without completely removing the caliper.

There is another pair of bolts on the back of the brake assembly: the caliper bracket mounting bolts. Don't remove these. The caliper bracket mounting bolts are the bigger bolts that hold the caliper bracket (what the caliper mounts to) onto the suspension.

When removing hex-headed caliper bolts, use a box-end wrench or 6-point socket to minimize the risk of rounding off the bolt head.

Remove the bottom caliper bolt/guide pin first, so that the caliper is still held in place by the top bolt. When loosening and removing the bolts, take care not to damage any rubber collar around the bolt. That collar is designed to keep dirt out, so that dirt does not contaminate the caliper slide. If it damaged, eventually the caliper bolt will corrode and the caliper will stick.

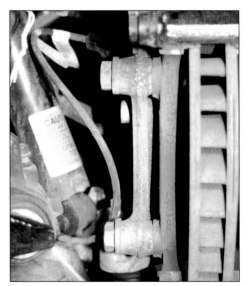

With the piston depressed, it is time to remove the caliper to access the brake pads. There are two pairs of bolts on the back of the caliper: the caliper bolts, and the caliper bracket mounting bolts. The caliper bolts are the ones that hold the caliper to the mounting bracket. The mounting bracket bolts hold the bracket to the suspension.

This is a caliper piston that is designed to be screwed into the bore to depress it. This piston cannot be pushed in with a C-clamp. Unfortunately, since you can't see the piston top until after you've depressed the piston and removed the brake pads, you need to know what type of piston is used before you start the job.

Before removing the upper caliper bolt/guide pin, you must be ready to support the caliper once the bolt is out. The caliper cannot be allowed to hang from the rubber brake hose. If allowed to hang free, the weight of the caliper will damage the hose where it joins the end fitting. Have a length of wire, bent coat hanger, or nylon zip-tie ready and then loosen the caliper bolt. Supporting the caliper with one hand, remove the

caliper bolt with the other hand. Use the wire or zip-tie to hang the caliper securely from the spring or upper suspension arm, keeping all tension off the brake hose.

If the caliper is of the design that pivots on the upper caliper bolt/pin, it is

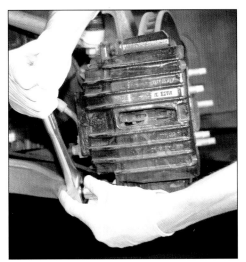

Remove the lower caliper bolt first. That way, gravity holds the caliper upright.

Then remove the top caliper bolt.

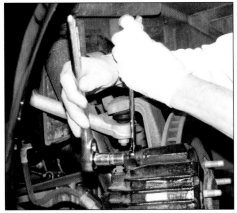

There are a variety of bolt configurations. This particular one uses a bolt that employs a locking nut that must be held in place while the caliper bolt is turned.

With the bottom bolt removed, support the caliper with one hand while removing the top bolt with your fingers. Do NOT let the caliper drop: that could damage the brake hose.

With the caliper removed, hang it from a suspension arm, spring, or something else sold with a strong piece of wire, bent coat hanger, or equivalent. It is important to secure the caliper so that it does not fall and damage the brake hose. The brake hose does not need to be disconnected to replace either pads or rotors.

This is the caliper after it has been removed. The pistons—this caliper has two of them—are in the circular objects with holes in the middle on the inner side of the caliper. The bottoms of the pistons— what you see here—push against the brake pad to push the pad onto the rotor.

These are the caliper mounting bolts. Often, caliper bolts are much longer than this and do double duty as the slide along which the caliper moves. These bolts merely hold the caliper in place on the slide. The red rings are factory-installed locking compound to prevent the bolts loosening with vibration.

not necessary to remove it to remove the old brake pads.

If you are removing a rear brake caliper of the screw-in piston design, once you have removed the caliper bolt/pin(s) bolts, the brake pads will still be in contact with the rotor and will tend to hold the caliper onto the rotor. You may need to use a large screwdriver to pry the caliper away from the rotor. If so, leave the upper caliper mounting bolt in place, though loosened. That way, the caliper cannot suddenly come off and fall, potentially damaging the brake hose and you. Pry only against the edge of the rotor, never against the rotor's braking surfaces. Also, be careful not to damage any "anti-rattle clips" installed in the caliper. These are thin wire or sheet metal clips, either attached to the side of the caliper or at the top and bottom of the pads, designed to dampen any vibration of the pads against the rotor or caliper during braking, preventing brake squeal. Unless the new pads came with new ones, these clips must be reused. These also can be purchased separately, usually as part of a "disc brake hardware kit." But, unless they are damaged, they should be reusable.

Remove the old brake pads. Brake pads often just stay in place as the caliper is removed. However, on some vehicles the inner brake pad clips into the caliper piston and will come away from the rotor with the caliper.

This is another kind of caliper mounting bolt. These are longer and do double duty as the slides. This is the rear brake pictured earlier. Note that this slide is showing corrosion nears the end by the bolt head. Corrosion can cause the caliper to stick and not slide.

When a caliper uses a piston that can be depressed only by screwing it into the bore, the brake pads may still be applying pressure to the rotor. If so, you can use a very large screwdriver to gently pry the caliper away from the rotor, resting the blade of the rotor on the frame surrounding the caliper that carries the brake pads.

The caliper mounting bracket serves as the fulcrum for prying the caliper up.

On some disc brakes, particularly the lighter rear brakes, it may not be necessary to remove the upper caliper bolt to change pads. The top caliper bolt may merely be a pin on which the caliper slides and the bottom bolt may be the only one actually holding the caliper to the bracket. If so, you can simply swing the caliper up and away from the rotor.

For rear brakes with the screw-in piston caliper design, after the caliper has been removed, it is time to depress the piston. Screw-in caliper pistons have two notches in the top of the piston. The "disc brake piston tool" fits onto a 3/8-inch ratchet with an extension and has multiple facets with different patterns to fit the different designs of various brake pistons. When the piston reaches the bottom of its bore, it will probably simply keep turning. So, you need to watch the level of the piston as you turn the wrench.

When the caliper piston has been fully depressed, make sure that the notches in the piston top will align with the tab cast into the backing plate of the new brake pad. The backing plate is the metal part to which the friction material is bonded. Usually, the notches in the piston should be aligned perpendicularly to an imaginary line drawn between the two holes through which the caliper bolts or pins are inserted.

Once the caliper has been removed, front or rear, the old brake pads can be removed.

Depending on the caliper design, both pads may be sitting in a cradle that straddles the rotor or the inner pad may be held on the caliper piston by a metal clip that slides into the top of the piston and the other pad may be clipped to the outer side of the caliper. Whatever the design, you should now be able to remove the old pads with just your fingers. Some disc brake designs also employ a thin metal sheet, called a "shim" or "anti-squeal plate," inserted between the pad backing plate and the caliper. This shim must also be removed.

Keep track of which of the old pads was the outer pad, which was the inner pad, and which pad has a wear indicator. The wear indicator is the little folded-over metal tab that runs part way down

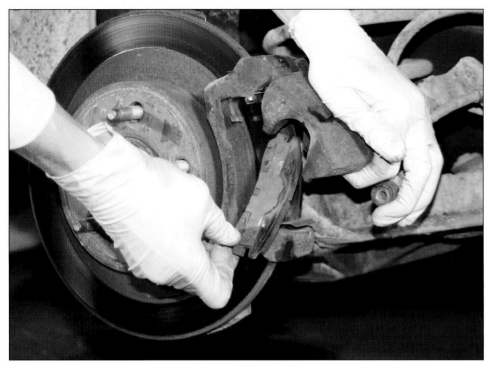

Then you can just pull the old pads out of the bracket with your fingers. Though there are clips that locate the calipers and serve to prevent them from being lose and rattling (which causes brake squeal), brake pads are essentially held in place by the clearance between the caliper and rotor, so they come out easily once the caliper is removed.

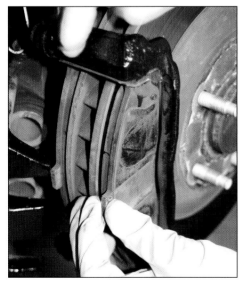

This is the front caliper mounting bracket, after the caliper has been removed. But, it's the same basic way to remove the pads: they just sit in the mounting bracket and can be removed with your fingers.

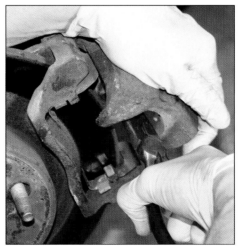

The rear caliper has a screw-in caliper piston. If you lack the correct tool, you can often use the tips of a pair of needle nose pliers to turn the piston in, by inserting the tips of the pliers into the depressions in the piston top and turning it with the pliers.

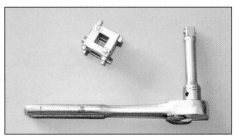

But it is always easier to use the proper tool. This handy "disc brake piston tool" fits onto a socket extension and has different pin configurations on each side, so that it fits a multitude of different brakes.

the side of the pad and squeals when the pad needs to be replaced.

Once the pads have been removed, visually inspect both the old pads and the rotor. Save the pads until you've done the other side of the car, so that you can compare all of the pads.

When pads on one side of the car are worn more than the pads on the other side, it indicates a sticking caliper on the more worn side. On the more worn side, if the inner pad is more worn than the outer pad, the problem is probably a sticking caliper piston. If the outer pad is more worn, the problem might only be corroded caliper bolts or slide pins. If the caliper bolt moves freely in its sleeve, even though corrosion is present, the problem is the caliper piston.

If there is a caliper problem, you should fix it now. The problem may not have been apparent with the old pads, but new pads will exacerbate it enough to cause caliper failure. Because the new pads are wider than the worn ones, installing new pads will force the piston further into its bore than did the old pads. New pads also will push the caliper further back on the caliper pin than did the old ones. This can force these moving parts into corroded areas they didn't reach with the old pads installed, which can result in a frozen caliper.

Brake rotors do not need to be resurfaced merely because they show some

Old pads on left vs. new pads on right. Note that one of the old pads is more worn than the other. That's an indication that either a caliper is sticking on its slides or that a caliper piston is sticking and not fully retracting. That problem should be solved before installing new pads.

scoring. Light scoring (1.2 mm or so) is normal. Though many professional repair shops routinely resurface brake rotors whenever replacing pads, most manufacturers strongly recommend against routinely resurfacing rotors. Resurfacing, sometimes called "turning the rotors," degrades the performance of the rotor because it removes layers of metal from it. Visually assess the depth of scoring. One millimeter is about twice the thickness of a postcard. More information can be found in Sidebar: "To Turn or Not to Turn: Should Rotors Be Resurfaced?"

Also inspect the rotor for any signs of hot spots or cracks. Rotors with heat discoloration in specific areas or cracks around the lug nut or axle hole areas should be replaced.

If the rotors and calipers are in good shape, you can skip ahead to "Installing Brake Pads." If not, read on.

Removing and Replacing Brake Rotors

Removing the brake rotors entails only a few steps beyond those required for replacing the brake pads. You merely add removing the caliper mounting bracket: the bracket to which the caliper attaches and which, itself, attaches to the vehicle's suspension, and then remove the rotor. Of course, as with changing pads, the caliper must be completely removed and secured out of the way in a manner that prevents any of the caliper's weight being placed on the brake hose. It should not be necessary to remove the brake hose from the caliper to remove or replace brake rotors. So, it should not be necessary to bleed the brakes, either.

Once the caliper is removed and secured, the next step is to remove the caliper mounting bracket. You can take out the brake pads first, or remove the bracket with the pads still in it. Just be sure to keep track of which pad was the inner pad and which was the outer pad, if you are reusing them.

In contrast to the caliper mounting bolts, which are usually (but not invariably) tightened to a relatively low torque specification, the bolts holding the

caliper mounting bracket to the suspension are normally very tight. As an example, the torque specification for the caliper mounting bracket bolts on the Cadillac DTS in the illustrations accompanying this chapter is 137 ft-lbs. This contrasts with the 63 ft-lb specification for the caliper mounting bolts/slide pins. Expect to exert some force to remove the caliper mounting bracket bolts, using the breaker bar and socket.

CAUTION: It is critical to consult the factory shop manual to determine whether the caliper mounting bracket

This illustrates a conventional single piston front caliper. The process for removing it, however, is essentially the same. Remove the bottom bolt, first.

Then remove the top bolt.

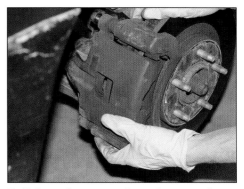

Pull the caliper away from the mounting bracket.

To remove the brake rotor after the caliper has been removed, the caliper mounting bracket must be removed. It is held on the suspension by two very large bolts.

The mounting bracket can be removed with the pads still in it, or you can take them out first.

bolts may be reused. Some vehicles use bolts designed to slightly stretch when tightened to keep the parts in constant tension. These bolts may not be reused. When such bolts are specified, use only original equipment replacements.

On American cars, brake rotors simply slide over the lug nuts onto the axle stub. They are not directly bolted to anything. Rather, they are held in place by the brake caliper, the wheels, and the lug nuts themselves. So, in theory, once the caliper and mounting bracket have been removed, the brake rotor should slide right off.

Often, it works exactly that way. But, sometimes it does not.

The clearance between the axle stub and the brake rotor where it slides over the stub can be quite tight. Because the entire assembly is exposed to the elements, rust can form at this seam. When it does, it can be very difficult to remove the brake rotor.

Unless the rotor is already loose on the axle stub when you remove the caliper mounting bolts, you should apply penetrating oil to this seam at the earliest practicable moment, if you didn't do it the night before. Penetrating oil takes time to work, so the longer it can soak into the rusted area, the better the chance you'll be able to remove the rotor without having to resort to extraordinary means.

On non-American vehicles, the brake rotor usually is directly connected to the axle stub. For reasons that are incompre-

hensible, these manufacturers usually put a screw, often with a Phillips head and sometimes with a "PoziDrive" head, through the brake rotor into the axle stub. A PoziDrive head looks very much like a Phillips, except that there are additional slot contact points at each of the interior corners of the "X" in the screw head.) This is the "rotor hold-down screw."

This screw, too, can rust solidly into place. It, too, should get an advance dose of penetrating oil.

The next step is to reinstall a couple of lug nuts onto the lugs to keep the rotor from suddenly pulling free when you try to remove it. Put them on backwards, so that the flat side faces the brake rotor. Leave some slack between the lug nuts and the rotor, so that there is room for the rotor to move outward, away from the car.

This is actually quite important. The first attempt at removing a reluctant brake rotor is simply pulling on it. Brake rotors are heavy. If it let's go suddenly, you have a heavy thing coming your way while you are falling backwards.

Of course, if you have a non-American car, you will need to remove that Phillips screw to remove the brake rotor. Sometimes, in life, you get only a single chance. This is one of those times.

It is a mistake to attempt to remove that Phillips screw with an ordinary screwdriver. Though it might work, the chances are good that it will not. If it

If the rotor is not loose, install a lug nut on one of the lugs to hold the rotor to the axle stub as you apply force to pull it away. That way, if it suddenly lets go, it won't hit you. The lug nut is reversed (flat side in) to put more surfaces on the rotor.

does not, it is also likely that you will damage the head of the screw in the process of failing to remove it. If that should that happen, the screw probably would have to be drilled out.

The way to remove that screw is with an "impact driver" or "impact screw-driver," which costs less than $25. This is not an air tool, of the type used in professional repair shops. It is something you hit with a hammer. The design of an impact driver transforms the sudden downward force into a sudden twisting force applied to the fastener. Simultaneously, of course, the downward motion of the hammer forces the driver's bit into the slot in the fastener, so it cannot readily slip. Impact drivers should not, however, be used with ordinary screw bits, but should be used only with those designed for impact tools. Usually, however, the price of the impact driver includes a selection of bits to be used with the tool.

The best tool to use when hitting an impact hammer is a "dead blow hammer," which is basically a hammer filled with shot. A dead blow hammer, as the name suggests, doesn't bounce upon impact, so its force is more concentrated.

Using an impact driver should allow you to readily remove the screw holding the rotor to the axle stub on vehicles that employ this method of attachment.

Perhaps to atone for using a Phillips screw to attach the rotor to the axle, most non-American manufacturers incorporate a simple mechanism for removing a rusted rotor into its design. Unlike American manufacturers, it is common for non-domestic vehicles to have a threaded open hole in the rotor.

This hole is there for a purpose: by tightening a bolt through that hole, the rotor is forced away from the axle hub and eventually pushed free of it. Look in the factory manual for the required bolt size. Be absolutely sure, however, that you have a couple of lug nuts on the lugs before tightening that bolt. When a rusted rotor comes free, it can pop off the axle stub with devastating force.

If, however, you are attempting to remove a rusted rotor from an American vehicle, you have no in-built mechanism by which to force it off. The best approach is to add patience to the penetrating oil, and give the penetrating oil time to work. You can tap on the rotor lightly with a hammer, in an effort to make the dispersal of the penetrating oil more effective.

If the rotor still won't come off, you can encourage it to come off with, first, a rubber mallet and, second, a dead blow hammer. However, do not strike on the braking surfaces of the rotor if you have any expectation of reinstalling the rotor. Hit directly on the outer rim of the rotor, i.e. the edge where you see the vent slots. Wear safety glasses or goggles when you do.

If, after all that, the rotor remains frozen to the axle stub, you'll have to use a "puller." How to get one and how to do it is covered in Sidebar: "Using a Puller to Remove a Rusted-On Brake Rotor" at this book's page on cartechbooks.com.

If your car has never had the brake rotors serviced or replaced, you may see small metal tabs that also appear to be retaining the rotor in place. These tabs are factory assembly aids that were simply left in place. They serve no useful purpose afterward, and can just be broken off and discarded.

Once the rotor has been loosened, remove the lug nuts and remove the rotor.

Now, the question is whether to do nothing to the rotors, have the rotors resurfaced, or replace them. The sidebar on the next page should help you decide those questions. Once you've executed that decision, there is one more step to take before beginning reassembly: clean the rust away.

Loose rust on the face of the axle stub where the rotor "hat" slides into

To help prevent the new rotor from rusting to the axle stub, apply a coating of anti-seize compound around the axle at those points where it comes in contact with the rotor.

This is the axle stub with the rotor removed. It is, of course, very rusty.

That rust should be cleaned away before mounting the new rotor. If the rust isn't removed, the rotor may not sit flat against the axle stub, which means the rotor will be crooked and create pulsing in the brake pedal.

To Turn or Not to Turn: Should Rotors be Resurfaced?

Some professional mechanics routinely "turn" rotors whenever replacing brake pads, a process that machines the friction surfaces of the rotors to remove any grooves or surface imperfections and make them smooth again. However, almost every automobile manufacturer recommends against routine resurfacing of brake rotors.

Resurfacing a brake rotor makes it thinner and thereby reduces its ability to absorb heat, which is basic to its function. Rotors do not need resurfacing if they merely show signs of normal wear, which is generally defined as scoring of 1.2 mm or less.

If, however, a rotor is severely scored, the rotor must be resurfaced or replaced. A rotor that is cracked must also, of course, be replaced. Whenever a rotor is replaced, the opposite side rotor must also be replaced.

Before a rotor may be resurfaced, it is necessary to determine its minimum allowable thickness. Rotors have a "discard" and/or a "machine to" specification cast into a non-friction surface of the rotor. A rotor that will be below either specification after resurfacing must be replaced (rotor thickness is measured with a micrometer at a minimum of eight to ten locations around the surface of the rotor). Machining a rotor can be done off the car on a lathe (a service offered by many auto parts stores) or on the car, which is how most auto dealers do it. Rotors must be resurfaced in axle sets to assure even braking. "Composite" rotors, such as the new rotors illustrated in this chapter, have a cast iron friction surface attached to a steel center and require special equipment to machine; ceramic rotors used on certain high performance Porsche and Mercedes-Benz models cannot be resurfaced.

Should the condition of the rotors make resurfacing necessary, consider replacing them instead. While machining rotors off the car may cost as little as $10 a rotor, it can't fix some common rotor problems. Resurfacing is unlikely to cure "warped" rotors, i.e., an unevenness of the rotor surface that causes pedal pulsation and tire judder. That problem is initially caused by the uneven transfer of pad material onto the rotor. Over time, these extra deposits of pad material become hot spots, transforming the cast iron surface underneath to cementite, which is a form of iron carbide. This isn't visibly different from the original cast iron material, so there is no way to inspect the rotor after machining to determine if all of the cementite has been removed. Cementite is harder than cast iron but absorbs less heat. If machining hasn't removed all of the cementite, as the rotor wears the process will start all over: the cementite will be hotter and will wear less than the surrounding cast iron, thereby "warping" the rotor again.

So, you waited a bit too long before replacing the pads and you do have severely scored rotors. Do you replace or resurface?

There is no single correct answer. As already mentioned, resurfacing rotors necessarily degrades their performance below that of equivalent new rotors. Rotors are designed to be resurfaced, howerver, which is why they have a minimum thickness specification. There is no reason that a resurfaced rotor should not perform adequately, provided that it is machined on proper equipment by a qualified operator.

On the other hand, replacing your old rotors with aftermarket OE-equivalent or better rotors can be an attractive option. Many auto parts stores and suppliers sell OE and OE-equivalent rotors at prices significantly less than list prices charged by dealers. As with pads, replacement brake rotors for vehicles manufactured for model year 2001 or later are required by federal law to maintain OE performance (see Sidebar: "Choosing the Right Brake Pads"). Moreover, the aftermarket offers many rotors with performance superior to those of OE rotors, especially when coupled with aftermarket performance brake pads. In other words, if you're going this far, why not live a little?

Next, it's time to install the new rotor.

It simply slides on over the axle stub.

place can create "radial runout." In other words, the rust acts as a wedge against the rotor, causing it to fit onto the axle slightly crookedly. Over time, this will overheat spots in the rotor, causing excessive amounts of pad material to adhere to the rotor and creating a "warped" rotor. Loose rust should be removed before reinstalling a rotor so that the rotor seats evenly against the face of the axle stub.

Installing a new rotor is merely a matter of sliding it into place and, if applicable, installing the Phillips or other screw retaining it to the axle stub. However, you can make life easier on

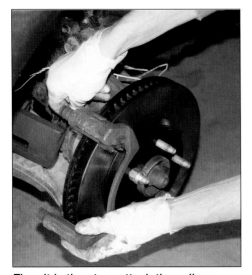

Then it is time to reattach the caliper mounting bracket. In this illustration, a lug nut has been installed to hold the rotor in place while the bracket is being installed.

yourself the next time. Coat the axle stub surface where it meets the rotor with anti-seize compound, so that there is a barrier against rust formation. Also use anti-seize on the screw retaining the rotor to the axle stub. Remember, however, that use of an anti-seize compound affects torque values. So, if the factory specified torque value for this fastener assumes a dry fastener (as it probably does), use of anti-seize requires reducing the torque value by approximately 30%.

You also need to clean the rotor. Some new rotors are delivered with a covering of Cosmoline, a rust-preventative protective coating that must be removed before the rotor is installed. It can be removed with brake cleaner. However, even if you don't have a protective coating on new or resurfaced rotors, cleaning them with brake cleaner once they're installed is a good idea. That removes any material remaining from the manufacturing or resurfacing process, as well as any of your own greasy fingerprints.

After replacing the brake rotor, reinstall the caliper mounting bracket.

The caliper mounting bracket must be tightened to the torque value specified in the factory manual (again, using new bolts if specified by the factory shop manual). Do not use anti-seize or thread locker compounds on these bolts unless directed to do so by the factory manual, as this will affect the torque values.

Repairing, Removing and Replacing a Brake Caliper

By this point, of course, you already have removed the caliper. (If you haven't, that's covered in the previous section on removing brake pads.)

If there are signs that a brake caliper is sticking or frozen—excessive wear on the pads on one side of the axle compared to the pads on the other side, or significantly greater wear on the inner or outer pad than the opposing pad—you need to diagnose the problem. Either the caliper pins/slide pins are sticking or the piston is sticking or frozen in the caliper bore.

To inspect the caliper pins, simply unbolt and remove them. These bolts slide inside a metal sleeve that is retained in the caliper by rubber dust boots through which the caliper bolt is inserted. This sleeve must be removed, as well, by carefully pulling the rubber dust out of the lip cast into the caliper into which it is seated. If you would like a picture of the part before you start disassembling, check the websites of auto parts suppliers that sell through the Internet. Often, their listings under "brakes—caliper bolt" include photographs of the parts. Caliper bolts and sleeves are always sold as an assembly, i.e., one part number. If you need to replace the rubber dust boots around the caliper bolts, those are available as part of the "disc brake hardware kit," which usually also includes other small parts

Tighten the caliper mounting bracket bolts initially with a ratchet.

Finish tightening with a torque wrench, to factory specifications.

required by the specific disc brake, such as new anti-rattle clips.

Once you've removed them, check the movement of the bolts through the sleeves. If either of the bolts does not move freely, replace it with a new one, including a new sleeve. The slide shank of the bolts must be lubricated with high temperature silicon brake grease before installation. Be careful, however, not to get any of that grease on the threads of the bolt, as that will make it impossible to determine when the proper torque is reached when tightening the bolt. Hand thread the bolt into place, and tighten it to specifications with a torque wrench.

Even if it's corroded, if a bolt moves freely in the sleeve, it isn't the problem. In that case, the problem is the caliper piston and that means replacing the caliper.

Replacing a brake caliper is actually pretty easy. If you can replace brake pads, you can replace a brake caliper.

To begin the caliper replacement, make sure the master cylinder reservoir is filled to the "full" mark with brake fluid. If not, add fluid from a new, unopened container. If you took out some fluid to replace the pads, now you have to put some in. Disconnecting the brake hose can allow some of the brake fluid to leak out and cause the level of fluid in the master cylinder to drop. If the level of brake fluid in the master cylinder drops below the openings to the brake lines you'll have to bleed the entire system. If your car is equipped with antilock brakes (ABS), letting air into the brake lines at the master

cylinder can result in trapping air inside the ABS controller. To fully bleed air from the controller (as opposed to bleeding a single caliper) an expensive scan tool is needed to activate the controller.

You will need to plug the brake hose, once it is removed, to keep fluid from leaking out. The fitting at the end of the brake hose where it bolts into the caliper is a unique type called a "banjo fitting." The name describes the way the fitting looks: a shank leading to a circle with a hole in the middle, sort of like a banjo.

To plug this fitting, stick a short length of hose through the hole in the banjo portion. You can unbolt the brake hose and look at banjo fitting to get an idea of the diameter you'll need and then bolt it back while you prepare the plug.

You probably don't have the perfect diameter hose on hand, but you can make a suitable plug by purchasing a short length of small diameter hose, such as fuel line hose, at an auto parts or hardware store. If the diameter is too large to insert into the banjo fitting, slit the hose lengthwise. Cut away some of the hose along the slit, so that the hose can be compressed to a smaller diameter. When you put it in the banjo fitting, locate the slit opposite to the hose end of the fitting.

Some mechanics pinch off the brake hose with a clamp to prevent fluid loss. Brake hoses are not designed to flex in that way. Though brake hoses are designed to be flexible over their length, the wall of the hose is designed to sustain high pressures. Crushing the sides of the hose with a clamp can damage the hose.

The idea is to fix the car, not damage it, so don't do that.

If your car has an "integral" ABS system, in which the ABS controller and pump are a single unit with the master cylinder reservoir, the ABS system must be depressurized before the brake hose is disconnected. This is explained in the Sidebar: "Is ABS Special?"

Place a drain pan below the disc brake assembly before loosening the banjo fitting to catch any brake fluid that does leak from the hose or caliper.

It is easier to loosen the brake hose bolt when the caliper is still firmly attached to the car, so disconnect the brake hose before removing the top caliper mounting bolt, guide pin, or slide pin. Note the position of the brake hose as installed, so that you can reinstall it in the same position. Then, using a box-end wrench, loosen and remove the bolt holding the brake hose.

I know, earlier a flare-nut wrench, a.k.a., line wrench, was described as the only tool for removing a brake line. The core concept, however, is to use a wrench that puts as many sides on the bolt as possible. With a true brake line fitting, the wrench must go around the metal line to hold the bolt. In this case, however, a box-end will fit. If you look at the other end of the brake hose, you'll see the situation in which a line wrench is indispensable.

The bolt holding the banjo fitting is reused. However, there are two washers on this bolt, one of which may remain sitting on the caliper when the bolt is removed. These washers should *not* be

These are caliper bolts—new on the left and old and corroded on the right. Caliper bolts that double as slides are sold as a unit with the sleeve in which they slide, so replacing a bolt also entails replacing the slide.

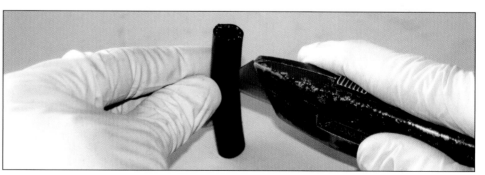

That means replacing the caliper, and replacing the caliper means removing the brake hose. That means plugging the brake hose "banjo fitting," the fitting at the hose end that goes into the caliper. To do that, you'll need to make a plug. Use a small length of hose, slit down the middle so that it can be squeezed into a smaller diameter hole.

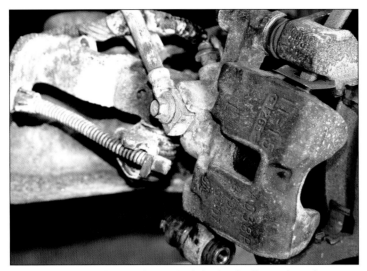

The "banjo fitting" is at the end of the brake line, where it attaches to the caliper.

The banjo fitting can be removed with an ordinary box end wrench.

reused. New ones should be included with the new caliper.

Plug the banjo fitting and tie it up out of the way with a baggie tie or equivalent.

Remove the caliper by removing the caliper bolts or pins or slide pins, just as you would to replace brake pads. Some calipers are designed to rotate on the upper bolt or pin after only the lower bolt is removed. While it is not necessary to remove the upper bolt to replace pads on these calipers, the method for fully removing the caliper entirely may not be self-evident. Calipers of this design will slide laterally off the upper bolt/pin once the lower bolt has been removed.

In addition to removing the caliper bolts/pins/slides, when replacing a rear brake caliper it also may be necessary to disconnect the parking brake cable to remove the caliper. Some parking brakes use the caliper piston and rotor as a parking brake and have a lever connected to the parking brake cable that moves the piston when the parking brake is engaged. The lever is part of the caliper assembly and the parking brake cable must be disconnected to remove the caliper from the car.

If disconnecting the parking brake cable is necessary, the parking brake must be released, the brake hose must already have been disconnected, and the caliper bolts or pins removed before attempting to disconnect the cable.

The parking brake cable will be held in place on the caliper assembly in two locations: at its end, and at a bracket several inches away from the cable end. A spring may run around the cable between the cable end and this bracket, to keep the cable automatically adjusted. In this arrangement, the cable must first be detached from the bracket and then detached at the cable end.

The cable may be held in the bracket by a unique type of collar clip in which splines flare outward, away from the cable at one end of the collar. In this arrangement, the cable cannot be pried out of the bracket. It slides out. To remove the cable, depress the splines. Then gently but

Once removed, plug the banjo fitting with the plug made from the small length of hose. Tie it out of the way.

firmly pull the caliper toward you so that bracket passes over the depressed splines. Slide the bracket off of the cable and the caliper can then be moved at an angle to release the cable end.

There is, of course, a special tool made to release parking brake cables of this design (Lisle tools, part number 40800, about $13; Snap-On, stock number BT22A, about $17). But, you can use an open-end wrench instead. Select a size that will just fit over the collar, below the splines, then slide the wrench onto the splines and rotate it to depress them. You can now remove the caliper.

Before beginning to install new caliper, compress the caliper piston into

This is the splined collar that holds the parking brake cable into a slot the barking brake cable bracket. It will be necessary to remove the parking brake cable from the caliper to remove the caliper, if the caliper is a rear brake caliper. There are specialized tools made to do this.

If you don't have a special tool, you may be able to make a box end wrench work. Slide it over the splines and rotate it to squeeze them together. This shows the parking brake cable after it has been removed, to better illustrate the nature of the retaining collar and how it may be released.

The parking brake cable fits through a slot in the bracket. When it is installed, the splines are on the side of the bracket facing the camera. They must be depressed so that the splined retainer can be pushed backward through the hole in the bracket. Once it has been pushed out, the cable itself is small enough in diameter to fit through the slot.

its bore using the same technique—a C-clamp or "disc brake caliper tool" or the jaws of a pair of needle nose pliers—that you used to remove the old caliper. Be very careful not to damage the rubber seals around the base of the caliper piston bore.

There is a little rubber plug pressed into or over the fitting on the caliper to which the brake hose attaches. Do not remove it until you are ready to attach the hose. It's there to keep dirt out.

The hardware that came with the caliper will include the caliper bolts/guide pins/slides. Some of the hardware may already be installed in the new caliper. By comparing with the old caliper, be sure

what needs to be installed in the new caliper is installed.

If the parking brake cable had to be detached, the next step is to reattach it, first at the end and then at the bracket. Once the cable is reattached, use a thin-bladed screwdriver to gently bend up the splines on the collar around the cable so that the cable can't pull loose when the parking brake is applied.

Lubricate the new caliper mounting bolts/pins/slides with the lubricant supplied with the caliper or with high-temperature silicone brake lubricant. Be careful not to get lubricant on the bolt threads.

Then install the caliper and tighten the caliper mounting bolts to factory specifications, exactly as you would

when replacing brake pads. Install any new parts, such as anti-rattle clips, that came with the new caliper.

It is now time to attach the brake hose to the caliper. There are two new washers included with the caliper. One of these goes on each side of the banjo

The first step to installing the new caliper is to thread the parking brake cable backward through the bracket. The bracket is part of the caliper assembly.

The parking brake cable in the new bracket, with the collar inserted but not quite seated. Pulling it another 1/4 inch will allow the splines to spring out and hold it in place.

This is the piston face on the new caliper. Actually, it's not new. It's a remanufactured caliper identical to the original equipment caliper. Brake calipers are commonly remanufactured.

The "disc brake caliper tool" has one facet that exactly fits the depressions on the caliper piston.

Apply high temperature silicone brake grease to the slide pin/caliper mounting bolts before installing them in the new caliper. The new caliper will come complete with all parts, including new hardware and the necessary silicone grease.

This is the same rear brake that was previously illustrated, in which the caliper pivoted on the upper mounting bolt. The caliper will actually slide over this bolt for installation, once the bolt has been properly installed.

fitting. Put one of these calipers next to the brake hose bolt head. Remove the plug from the banjo fitting, slide the banjo fitting onto the bolt and then slide the remaining washer onto the bolt. Remove the plug from the bolt hole in the caliper and hand tighten the brake hose bolt into the caliper.

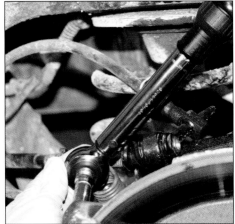

Properly installed means the bolt is tightened to the correct torque value.

The lower caliper mounting bolt is then installed and tightened to the correct torque value.

The new caliper includes a new bolt for the banjo fitting and the two new washers it requires. Banjo fitting washers should never be reused.

You should be able to feel the banjo fitting seat in the caliper. When it is properly seated, initially finger tighten the brake hose bolt then tighten it to the

The bolt goes through the banjo fitting, with a washer on each side of the fitting.

The banjo fitting is then inserted in the hole in the caliper and finger tightened.

Final tightening is done with a torque wrench.

manufacturer's torque specification with a torque wrench.

Now install the caliper on the caliper mounting bracket and install or reinstall the brake pads. That's covered a few paragraphs below, in the next section: "Installing the New Brake Pads."

Once the caliper and pads are installed, the next (and last) step is bleeding the new brake caliper.

NOTE: Bleeding is essential because there is air trapped in the new caliper and some air may have entered the brake line where it was removed from the old caliper. The bleeding procedure is explained in Sidebar: "Bleeding the Brakes."

One bleeding tip bears emphasizing: be sure to have a block of wood under the brake pedal when manually bleeding so that the pedal cannot go further toward the floor than its normal travel. With an empty caliper, the pedal could go all the way to the floor, well beyond its normal limit of travel. Were that to happen, it could damage the seals in the master cylinder.

Installing the New Brake Pads

If the calipers, mounting bolts, guide pins, or slides and rotors all pass inspection or have been replaced as necessary, it is time to install the new brake pads.

Anti-squeal compound is a defense against brake squeal caused by pads vibrating against the caliper or rotor during braking. This is the usual cause of brake squeal, not the friction of the pad on the rotor. Anti-squeal compound is available at any auto parts store as a gel in a squeeze bottle or tube or as an aerosol. Before installing the new pads in the caliper, apply a small amount of anti-squeal compound to the backing plate of each pad where it will contact the caliper or the caliper piston, and allow it to become tacky. If the brakes use metal shims, apply anti-squeal compound to them, too, unless the shims came with a proprietary compound.

Next, replace the anti-rattle clips and install the new pads into the caliper. Be

These are the new anti-rattle clips that come with new brake pads. The configuration of these clips varies, depending on the design of the caliper.

The new clips are installed on the caliper. This is the front caliper shown earlier.

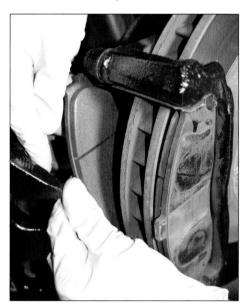

The brake pads slide in and are held in place by the clips.

This is the outside pad being seated.

This thin elbow of metal is the wear indicator. It is designed to contact the rotor without damaging it, and make a metallic squeal, when the pads are worn thin and should be replaced.

sure you have enough light to clearly see what you're doing as you install the new pads. It's easy to disturb anti-rattle clips and shims as you install the pads. So, you need to be able to see them to verify that they are properly seated.

At least one of the pads on each side of the car should have a wear indicator, the little metal tab that sticks partway down the side of the pad. Often both inner and outer brake pads have wear indicators, but if only one pad has an indicator it usually is installed as the inner pad. Pads with wear indicators should be installed so that the indicator is in the trailing position when the wheel is moving forward.

In anticipation of reinstalling the brake caliper, clean and lubricate any *unthreaded* slide portion of the caliper mounting bolts, guide pins, or slide pins.

Use a high-temperature silicone lubricant specifically made for brakes, available at any auto parts store.

Avoid getting any grease on the caliper bolt threads. In the absence of a specific recommendation to use anti-seize compounds or thread locking compounds, torque values specified in the factory shop manual are for dry fasteners. Anything that lubricates the fastener destroys the validity of the torque specification, because the actual tension placed on the tightened fastener will be much higher than the reading on the torque wrench. This caveat also applies

Continued on page 137

Bleeding the Brakes

Replacing a brake caliper allows air into the brake hydraulic system two ways: first, because the brake hose is detached from the old caliper; second, because there is air in the new caliper. To get that air out, it is necessary to "bleed" the brakes at that caliper. Fortunately, it should only necessary to bleed that caliper, not the entire system.

The simplest way to bleed a brake caliper is to use a hose, a container, and an assistant. It's also the most reliable method.

Though you can get by with a soda bottle and a hose that will fit over the bleeder nipple located on top of the brake caliper, it is better to buy a "brake bleeder hose" or "brake bleeder kit" at an auto parts store. These are inexpensive: the one in these pictures cost about $5. You also need a new and unopened container of brake fluid, either DOT3 or DOT4 as specified by the vehicle manufacturer in the label on the master cylinder reservoir cap. The bleeder hose should be clear so you can see into it as you're bleeding the brakes. If the kit doesn't include a container, you can use an empty clear plastic soda bottle.

You will need an assistant to push on the brake pedal while you handle the bleeding process at the brake caliper. Here's how to bleed the brakes using this method:

Place a 2 x 4-inch board under the brake pedal of the car, so that the travel of the brake pedal is restricted to the range in which it would normally move when driving. When the brake system is operating normally, the distance the brake pedal can move is restricted by the pressure of the fluid in the lines and the pads pressing on the rotor. With the bleed screw open, the pedal could be pushed beyond that range, right to the floor. Should that occur, the pistons in the master cylinder will be pushed beyond their normal range of movement. This could rupture the piston seals within the master cylinder, which will require replacing the master cylinder.

Check the brake fluid level in the master cylinder reservoir. Because bleeding will evacuate fluid from the system, the level of fluid in the reservoir will drop during bleeding. It is important that the fluid level not drop below the level at which air could enter the brake lines. Be sure that the reservoir is full before beginning the bleed process and then monitor the fluid level throughout the process. There is usually a mark molded into the plastic of the reservoir indicating the "full" level.

Locate the "bleeder screw" on the top of the brake caliper. The bleeder screw is actually a small nut with a nipple on it, not a screw (Fixed caliper brakes usually have two bleeder screws, one on each side). It should have a small rubber cap on it to protect it from dirt, which you must remove. Be sure not to lose or damage that cap, because it must be reinstalled when bleeding is completed.

Always block the brake pedal before manually bleeding. If the pedal goes to the floor, it could damage the master cylinder. It should be depressed no further than its normal length of travel.

The bleeder kit includes a fitting or nozzle that fits onto the bleeder screw on the caliper.

Using a box end wrench, loosen the bleeder screw and then retighten it enough that it can be easily opened. Leaving the wrench on the screw, install the clear plastic hose onto the bleeder screw (either over the nipple or pressed onto it with fittings included with the bleeder kit). Using a clear hose is important, because the key to the bleed process is observing the fluid as it is pushed out of the caliper to see whether it contains any tiny air bubbles. The other end of the hose goes into a container. If you are using a container that is open at the top, rather than sealed, put enough brake fluid in the container to immerse the hose end in brake fluid to prevent sucking air back into the system.

Open the bleeder screw after you have your assistant depress the brake pedal. It should only be necessary to turn the bleeder screw about 1/3 to 1/2 of a turn to permit fluid to flow out. If you've replaced the caliper, fluid may not flow out at first because the caliper is empty.

Have your assistant tell you when the brake pedal is near the end of its normal travel and then close the bleeder screw.

When the pedal has returned to the top of its travel, check the fluid level in the master cylinder reservoir. Then repeat the process: open the bleed screw as your assistant gradually depresses the brake pedal. When the pedal nears the bottom of its normal travel, tighten the bleed screw while

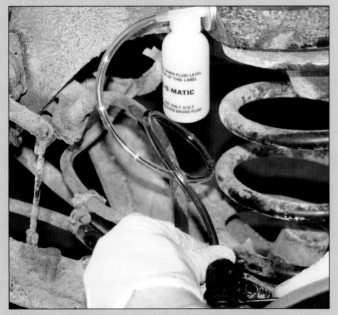

Watch the fluid escaping until there are no bubbles contained in the fluid. That's why it's useful to have a hose that is clear: you need to see the bubbles escaping to know whether you've done the job correctly.

the pedal is still depressed. Then allow the pedal to return to the top of its travel.

Repeat this process, periodically checking the fluid level in the master cylinder reservoir and adding fluid as necessary to keep it at the full level. As explained in this chapter, brake fluid absorbs water vapor, so use only new brake fluid from a previously opened container.

As it flows from the caliper during bleeding, watch the brake fluid for air bubbles. The objective is to keep bleeding until no air bubbles—not even tiny ones—are present in the fluid. When you think you have achieved that, double-check the fluid level in the master cylinder and then test the feel of the brake pedal. It should feel firm and hard. If it sinks gradually to the floor, there is still air in the line and you'll need to renew the bleed process. Pumping the brake pedal after initial bleeding can dislodge air bubbles in the system, which you can eliminate with further bleeding.

Keep bleeding until you do get that hard pedal. Then firmly tighten the bleeder screw and reinstall the rubber boot. Add brake fluid, as necessary, to the master cylinder reservoir.

Though it is time consuming, bleeding the entire system generally can be accomplished in the same manner as bleeding a single line, with the following qualifications:

When bleeding an entire brake system, there will be a bleeding sequence that must be followed. For a rear-wheel drive vehicle the order in which to bleed the calipers is usually: right rear, left rear, right front, and left front. For a front-wheel drive vehicle, it is usually: right rear, left front, left rear, and right front. But this is not invariably so, and the only way to be sure is to check the factory shop manual.

As indicated in the sidebar in this chapter, on some vehicles equipped with an anti-lock brake system (ABS), it may be impossible to fully replace the brake fluid without using a proprietary scan tool to activate the ABS control module, which retains brake fluid unless activated either by a scan tool or by a stop that activates the ABS brakes. If the ABS system is "integral" (master cylinder, ABS pump, and modulator are one unit) the system must be depressurized by pumping the brake pedal as many as fifty times before bleeding even a single caliper. On other vehicles with ABS, no special bleeding procedure is required. The factory shop manual will provide the required information.

If you decide to bleed the entire system and are looking for a less tedious way to do it, you may wish to invest in one of the vacuum bleeders that are available at consumer-friendly prices, such as the Mity-Vac (online at mityvac.com). The hand-pump version of the Mity-Vac costs about $40 and powered versions are about $150.

Brake Fluid

There are three categories of Brake Fluid: DOT-3, DOT-4, and DOT-5. Your vehicle will use either DOT-3 or DOT-4, which is a glycol ether-based fluid. Which one should be used will be stated in the owner's manual and on the cap of the master cylinder fluid reservoir. DOT-5 is a silicone based brake fluid that is not recommended for use in most vehicles and would cause lasting damage to the braking system.

There is much disparity of opinion over when brake fluid should be changed. Some automobile manufacturers have no recommended replacement interval. On the other hand, many professional mechanics believe it should be replaced every 60,000 miles.

The core issue is the water content of the brake fluid. As mentioned in the text, brake fluid is hygroscopic—meaning that it absorbs water—as part of the design of the product. Were water to be able to form into drops in the brake lines, it would vaporize under the heat of braking and cause loss of braking force in the hydraulic brake lines. But, the presence of water in the brake fluid lowers the fluid's boiling point, which is one of its most crucial specifications.

You can purchase test strips at auto parts stores or online that will allow you to test brake fluid for its moisture content. FASCAR is one manufacturer of these and claims that the strips test for other forms of brake fluid deterioration, as well. A package of 25 FASCAR strips costs about $25.

So, what about new fluid? Are they all the same?

No. Even within the DOT categories, there are differences in fluids. The Department of Transportation categories are minimum performance standards. So, the DOT-3 or DOT-4 classification merely assures that the fluid doesn't fall below the performance floor.

The two most important criteria for brake fluid are wet and dry boiling points, which are specified in a federal motor vehicle safety standard, number FMVSS 116. "Dry boiling point" is defined as 0% water in the fluid. "Wet boiling point" is defined as 3.7% water in the fluid. The DOT-3 minimum for wet boiling is 401 degrees F and the wet boiling point minimum is 248 degrees F. For DOT-4, it's 446 degrees F and 311 degrees F, respectively. FMVSS 116 also contains specifications dealing with the fluid's effect on rubber, its viscosity, chemical stability, resistance to oxidation, and color.

Of the two, wet boiling point is the most important for a street-driven vehicle. So-called "racing" brake fluids may have a higher dry boiling point, but the expectation is that the street vehicle will almost always have some amount of moisture in its fluid. So, when you look at bottles of brake fluid from the parts store shelf, it's the wet boiling point that you should be comparing.

It should not, incidentally, be automatically assumed that a DOT-4 fluid is better than a DOT-3 fluid merely because the minimum boiling points are higher for one than the other. First, one brand of DOT-3 may have a higher boiling point than another brand of DOT-4 fluid, just because the first brand makes a better quality fluid. Second, though DOT-4 fluid initially has a higher boiling point, the differences in its chemical composition from DOT-3 also result in a more rapid decrease in boiling point once it begins to absorb moisture. In short, DOT-3 lasts longer.

There is also a DOT-5.1 fluid, sometimes called DOT-4 Plus. This is not DOT-5. It is basically a newer version of DOT-4, but designed to meet the boiling point standards of DOT-5. So, DOT-5.1 has a dry boiling point of 509 degrees F and wet boiling point of 356 degrees F. Though it is compatible with both DOT-3 and DOT-4, it is vastly more expensive than either.

Synthetic brake grease, of the type used to lubricate slide pins and sliding portions of caliper bolts that double as sliders.

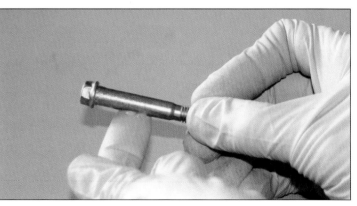

Lubricate the caliper mounting bolt by applying a thin coating only to the unthreaded portion of the bolt.

to anti-seize compounds and thread locking compounds, such as Loctite, because they have lubricating properties. Using anti-seize requires reducing torque values by 25%. Use of thread lockers requires reducing torque values by 10%. There is, however, no need to use either unless it is recommended in the factory manual.

Now reinstall the brake caliper. If it was completely removed, install the upper mounting bolt or pin first, tightening it finger tight. Then install the lower bolt, also finger tightening it. Slides are installed by tapping them into place.

To verify that everything is properly installed, take two of the lug nuts and tighten them against the rotor. They'll hold it in place against the hub so that you can turn the rotor by hand and listen for any noise. If you have open-ended lug nuts, put them on backwards, i.e., with the end that usually goes against the wheel facing outside; that way, the flat surface is against the rotor. If you hear any noise that's not coming from the friction surface of the new pads, track down the problem.

If the rotor turns quietly, use a torque wrench to finish tightening the caliper mounting bolts to the torque value specified in the factory manual. Do not put anti-seize compound or thread-locking compounds on these bolts, unless instructed to do so by the factory manual. Repeat the same steps on the other side of the car.

After completing both brakes, reinstall the wheels and tighten the lug nuts so that the wheels are secure. Leave the final tightening until the car has been lowered to the ground. When it has been lowered, finish tightening the lug nuts to the torque value specified in the factory manual using a criss-cross pattern.

NOTE: *Before* driving the car, be sure to pump the brakes a few times until you have a hard pedal. Pumping the brakes pushes the caliper pistons outward to the rotors. After that, recheck the fluid level in the master cylinder reservoir. A mark is molded into the reservoir side indicating the "full" level. Add fresh fluid as needed. Then gently test drive the vehicle.

When you're satisfied that everything is working properly, you may choose to "bed in" the brake pads. Manufacturers of high performance brake pads typically recommend specific brake bedding procedures for their products. Any brake pad, however, can benefit from being properly bedded in.

Basically, bedding in brakes is accomplished by making a series of three near-stops to get the brakes hot, but *not* bringing the car to a complete stop. Then, still without stopping, the brakes are allowed to cool as the car is driven and the process is repeated two more times, always without stopping. The idea is to transfer a microscopic layer of pad material to the rotor, which will increase the "adherent friction" of the brakes, i.e., the creation and almost simultaneous breaking of chemical bonds between the pads and the pad material on the rotor whenever the brakes are applied. The effect of adherent friction on brake performance is most pronounced in high-speed stops.

It is very important, should you choose to bed in the brake pads, that you not allow the car to come to a complete stop during the process. If the hot brake pad is allowed to rest against the hot brake rotor, the result will be a heavy transfer of pad material where the pad touches the rotor. That will rapidly burnish through use into a high spot on the rotor, which will lead to vibration and brake judder and can eventually create a hot spot that will warp the rotor.

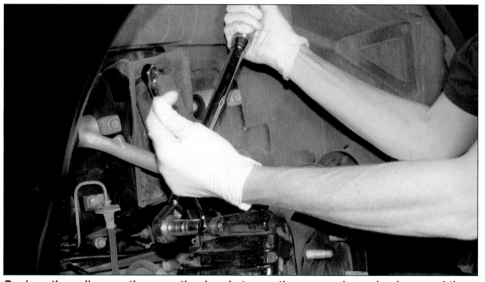

Replace the caliper on the mounting bracket once the new pads are in place, and then tighten the caliper mounting bolts to specification with a torque wrench.

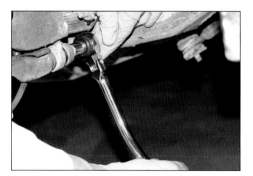

When the caliper is of a type that slides over the top mounting bolt and then swivels down, tighten the lower caliper bolt.

Complete the job with a torque wrench.

SELECTING AND MAINTAINING TIRES

Maintaining tires is easy: keep them properly inflated and rotate them at the appropriate intervals.

Selecting tires is more complex. Every tire is a compromise between competing capabilities. To select the best tire for you, it is necessary to prioritize. For example, the higher the dry pavement cornering power the tire can support, the less it will be able to evacuate water under the tread on a wet road at speed—and vice versa.

Selecting the best tires for the car (for you) requires determining the compromise you want to make between the various competing priorities. It depends on your preferences: dry vs. wet pavement performance; ride quality vs. precise handling; long life vs. cornering power, etc.

Of course, you might decide that you'll just select the safest tires. But, that's a meaningless standard. The safest possible tire on a dry road at 65 mph is not the safest tire on that same road when it's raining. The complexity in selecting tires is in selecting between design compromises to find the combination that will best suit the conditions in which you drive, and the way you drive.

Parts for this job

None, unless it's time for new tires.

Tools for this job

Tire pressure gauge
1/2-inch breaker bar and socket
   for lug nuts
Air compressor
   (optional, but convenient)

Time for this job

Checking air pressure in your tires shouldn't take much more than ten minutes. Rotating tires, once the car is on four jack stands, takes less than an hour.

Advance Planning

None, though this is a good job to integrate with something else that gets the vehicle off the ground, such as a changing the oil or doing a brake job.

Hazard Warning

Rotating tires requires lifting the vehicle and putting it on jack stands. As discussed in Chapter 2, always use jack stands and secondary supports.

Finish tightening the lug nuts after you have completed the job and lowered the car and then check them again. It might seem that this would be obvious. But it is remarkably easy, especially if you're rushing or someone's distracted you, to forget to finish tightening the lug nuts on one of the wheels. Always double-check.

Let's do it

Tire Inflation

A tire should be inflated to the *vehicle* manufacturer's recommended "cold" tire pressure. That pressure is specified in the owner's manual and on the vehicle "placard," a sticker affixed to the driver's door or door jamb. The placard also specifies the recommended tire size. Since 2003, the placard location has been specified by federal law. Before 2003. it also might be located on the underside of the trunk lid, on the rear door, inside the fuel filler door, or inside the glove box lid.

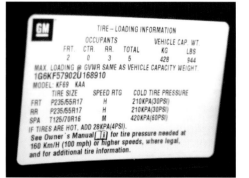

The vehicle "placard" gives the correct tire, size, type, and specifies the load rating, speed rating, and inflation pressure.

"Cold" means the temperature of the tire when it has not been driven *and* it is in the environment in which it will be driven. If, for some reason, it is necessary to check tire pressure in other circumstances, inflation pressure must be adjusted to compensate for temperature differences.

The basic rule is that tire pressure drops 1 psi for every 10 degrees F the ambient temperature drops, and increases 1 psi for every 10 degrees F rise in temperature.

So, if you live in Minnesota and that first cold front rolls in and ends the last warm autumn days, the tire pressure drops. If you set tire pressure in Minnesota and then drive to Florida, the tires will be overinflated when you get there. And if you set tire pressure in a heated garage, you need to add 1 psi for every 10 degrees F that the garage temperature exceeds outside temperature.

If you check the tire pressure in the afternoon, the warmest part of the day, add 2 psi to the recommended cold tire pressure. It is not possible to get an accurate tire pressure reading when a tire sitting in sunshine, because the black tires will absorb the sun's heat. Determine the difference between the pressure of the tires in sunlight and those on the opposite side of the car in the shade. The pressure of the tires in the sun must be set higher than those in the shade by that difference.

Tires also lose air over time: some of the air molecules sneak by the rubber molecules and escape from the tire. For that reason, tire pressure drops approximately 1 psi per month.

Of course, the internal and external frictions caused by driving heats tires, so driving also increases tire pressure. That, however, is expected and anticipated in the tire's design. A tire that is set at the correct pressure when "cold" will be at the correct pressure when hot.

A tire's sidewall may state the "maximum permissible inflation pressure." That is *not* a correct inflation pressure. That is a warning label: inflation when cold should never exceed that maximum pressure.

Keeping tires inflated to the correct pressure using a quality gauge is basic to both safety and tire life.

Check tire pressure with a gauge or, if the vehicle is equipped with one that gives specific "pounds per square inch" (psi) readings for each tire, with the "tire pressure monitoring system" (TPMS).

A tire pressure gauge should, of course, be accurate. But, beyond accuracy, it is very convenient for the gauge to have a valve allowing you to bleed air pressure through the gauge. That allows you to overfill the tire, hold the gauge in place, and then bleed air pressure down to the exact pressure setting. Gauges with this feature are more expensive than others, but well worth the extra cost.

Some tire pressure monitoring systems allow checking the specific psi for each tire. If your vehicle is equipped with one of these systems, it makes it easier to verify tire pressure regularly. But, many TPMS's are simply alerts: they warn you when a tire is "underinflated," as the federal government has defined that word.

Beginning with the 2008 model year, TPMS are required by federal law—a reaction to the Ford Explorer/Firestone tire roll-over accidents several years ago that resulted from underinflated tires on SUVs. Ironically, the TPMS mandated in response would not have prevented those deaths: a TPMS meeting federal standards need not alert until a tire is as much as 30% underinflated.

To put this in perspective: the outward appearance of a tire that is 30% underinflated is almost identical to that of a properly inflated tire. The sidewalls of an underinflated tire twist much more than those of a properly inflated tire

One of these tires is 10-psi low: is it this one?

Or this one? Yes, it was the other one. But, do you think you'd have noticed it just walking out to the car?

before transmitting steering inputs to the tread. An underinflated tire flexes more while rolling. All of that generates more heat and reduces cornering traction and evasive maneuverability. Underinflation also reduces the load capacity of the tire below its design specification.

An underinflated tire also "hydroplanes" (sometimes called "aquaplaning," this is when the tire literally climbs on top of a wedge of water that it is pushing in front of it) on wet pavement at lower speed. As it pushes water in front of it, the water's pressure on the underinflated tire pushes the center portion of the tread inward, away from contact with the pavement, reducing traction and lifting the tire from the pavement sooner than if it were evacuating water through the tread grooves.

Ralph Nader's Public Citizen group has joined with the Tire Industry Association, Goodyear, Firestone/Bridgestone,

Cooper Tire and others in a lawsuit against the National Highway Traffic Safety Administration seeking to void the current TPMS regulations, contending that they permit deadly underinflation. When Ralph Nader and the tire manufacturers agree, you should pay attention.

So, don't rely on a TPMS to warn you when tire pressure is too low, because it won't. If your TPMS does not allow you to read specific psi for each tire, check tire inflation pressures regularly with a gauge.

Tire Rotation

Rotating tires can, and should, be done on almost any car. Even cars with tires of different sizes on the front and the back should have the tires rotated. The only exception is a car with unidirectional tires of different sizes front and rear.

Rotating the tires isn't merely an economy measure to prolong tire life. It is a matter of safety, too. When all four tires wear evenly, the designed-in handling balance of the car is maintained, and continues to be maintained when a new set of tires is purchased. When one pair of tires wears prematurely and tires are replaced in pairs, handling balance is affected: one pair always has better grip than the other. Replacing only one tire upsets that balance even more, because it creates different tire circumferences and

levels of traction on the same axle. That's why, whenever possible, the spare should be included in the rotation pattern: it insures that you've always got at least four evenly worn tires.

There are two possible patterns for five tire rotation. One is to bring the rear tires to the front, but switch the sides of the car on which they are installed (i.e., RR to LF, LR to RF), move the front left tire to the left rear, the front right tire to the spare, and the spare to the right rear (LF to LR, RF to S, S to RR). The other pattern is to more the rear tires to the front on the same side, the right front to the left rear, the left front to the spare, and the spare to the right rear (LR to LF, RR to RF, LF to S, RF to LR, S to RR).

Using a five tire rotation is particularly important, when possible, on cars with all-wheel drive. These cars are more sensitive than rear wheel drive cars to variations in tire diameter. If the spare is not included in the rotation and it later becomes necessary to use it as a replacement tire, the difference in circumference can stress the drive axles on some all-wheel drive vehicles because they will pull unevenly. More information on this is in the next section.

When only a four tire rotation pattern is possible—the tires are of a different size front and back or the spare is a temporary use tire—the pattern to follow depends on the location of the drive axle.

On a front wheel drive car, the rear tires are moved to the front, on the same side, the front tires to the rear on opposite sides (LF to LR, RF to RR, LR to RF, RR to LF). On cars with rear wheel drive, four-wheel drive, or all-wheel drive, the tires should be rotated cross-wise, i.e., front to the opposite-side back, back to opposite-side front (RF to LR, LF to RR, LR to RF, RR to LF).

There are three special cases: directional tires and differently sized tires. If the tires on the front are a different size than the tires on the back, simply switch sides (LF to RF, RF to LF, LR to RR, RR to LR). If the tires are the same size, but are directional—that is, they are designed to be on only the specific side of the car, left or right, then switch front to back and back to front on the same side (LF to LR, RF to RR, LR to LF, RR to RF). If, however, the tires are both directional and are of different sizes front and back, rotation is impossible.

How often should you rotate the tires? The vehicle owner's manual probably specifies an interval. But, the recommendation of one major tire manufacturer (Goodyear) illustrates the general rules: rotate every 6,000 to 8,000 miles for front and rear drive vehicles, every 4,000 miles for vehicles with four- or all-wheel drive.

When you rotate tires, be sure to check and adjust tire pressures afterward.

Lug nuts should always be loosened before a car is lifted because it's easier: the wheel won't rotate when you try to loosen the lug nut.

Rotating tires requires adherence to the proper rotation pattern. Notice that these tires have a tread pattern that is not identical on each side, but can be faced either way. So these tires can be rotated from one side of the car to the other.

Because most cars weigh more at front than at back, and changing the location of the tire can affect its inflation pressure.

To rotate tires, position the vehicle where you will be doing the work, then loosen each of the lug nuts slightly with the breaker bar and socket or with a tire lug wrench. Then lift the car and put it on four jack stands (see Chapter 2). Remove and rotate the tires. Reinstall them and tighten the lug nuts until all have been firmly—but not finally—tightened. Lower the car to the ground, then complete tightening all of the lug nuts on each wheel in a criss-cross pattern (i.e., tightening one lug nut, then the one opposite it, etc., until all five are properly tightened).

Use a torque wrench to finish the tightening to the vehicle manufacturer's torque specification. Using a torque wrench is important, for two reasons: under tightening can lead to a loose wheel; over tightening can slightly distort the brake rotor, which causes pad material to transfer to the rotor, eventually creating hot spots in the rotor, a condition commonly called "warped" rotors (see Chapter 12).

When rotating the tires, also examine them for severely uneven wear, foreign objects in the tread, or damage. Uneven tire wear can be caused by driving style, overinflation, underinflation, improper balance, improper wheel alignment, or worn suspension components.

You may notice indentations on the sidewalls of the tires. That is not a sign of a defective tire. It is a result of the tire's construction: indentations occur where the radial sidewall plies overlap. These areas are actually stronger than the rest of the sidewall, so there is less flex under air pressure. On the other hand, an outward bulge in a sidewall is an indication that plies are separating. A tire with a sidewall bulge is dangerous and should be replaced immediately.

Replacing tires

Eventually, it becomes time to replace tires. Ideally, you replace all of them at the same time, as a set. That way, all tires have the same tread depth and

the vehicle's designed-in handling balance is preserved.

Should it become necessary to replace only two tires, you should purchase tires identical to the remaining tires. If that is not possible, the new tires should be of the same type and construction as the other tires (i.e., same number of plies of the same materials) and as closely matched as possible in tread pattern.

When replacing two tires, the new tires must *always* go on the rear axle, never the front. The tires with the least tread should always be on the front axle, so that they will be the first to lose adhesion on a slippery surface. If front tires lose grip, the loss of adhesion can be corrected by letting off the gas. If the rear tires loose grip first, it creates a nasty skid that may be made worse by decelerating.

The circumstances in which it is acceptable to replace only one tire are very limited. It is permissible when the car has been on a five tire rotation pattern: the new tire is held as the spare and the remaining tires are rotated on a four tire rotation pattern until they are replaced with new tires identical to the spare. A single tire can also be replaced when it was almost new and the replacement is otherwise identical, so that the tires' construction are the same and there is very little difference in circumference.

In other circumstances, both tires on the same axle should be replaced. Otherwise, you will have one tire with better traction than the other on the same axle, which will create unbalanced tire response, particularly on slippery surfaces, under emergency braking, and during evasive maneuvers.

With some all-wheel drive and four-wheel drive vehicles, it is necessary to replace *all four* tires if even one tire must be replaced. For the most part, this is a requirement only on those vehicles with "automatic" or "part-time" four-wheel or all-wheel drive systems that power the second axle through a viscous coupling when the first axle begins to slip, then disengages when wheel speeds equalize. In these systems, differences in tire circumference can keep the viscous coupling engaged at all times, eventually

overheating and destroying it. However, most full-time all-wheel drive systems, and those four-wheel drive systems that use a differential between front and rear axles, are able to tolerate the differences in tire diameter that result from replacing tires in axle pairs.

When remaining tread depth is 2/32 inch, a tire's "wear bars" (also called "tread wear indicators") appear. Wear bars extend the width of the tire and consist of a short section of tire where the tread isn't quite as deep as it is on most of the tire. So, these bars wear bald while there is still minimal tread on the rest of the tire.

A tire with visible wear bars must be replaced. However, you shouldn't wait that long.

As the tread of a tire is worn away, so is the tire's ability to evacuate water on wet pavement and provide traction in snow. At a tread depth of 4/32 inch, a tire's susceptibility to aquaplaning is much greater than it was when new. The tread grooves cannot evacuate water as rapidly, so water builds up in front of the tire at a lower speed, and the tire is forced onto the water. When tread is worn to 6/32 inch, traction in snow is significantly less than when the tire was new. In fact, winter tires designed for "severe snow service" often have a second set of wear bars at 6/32 inch of remaining tread.

The most accurate way to measure the tread depth is with a tire depth gauge, which costs less than $5 at any auto parts store. But, you can also use a penny and a quarter. If the tread is shallower than the distance between the edge of a penny and the top of Lincoln's head, it's 2/32 inch or less. If the tread is about as deep as the distance between the edge of a quarter and the top of Washington's head, it's about 4/32 inch. The distance between the bottom of the Lincoln Memorial on the back of a penny and the coin's bottom edge is about 6/32 inch.

Tires also can become too old to be safe, even though they still have adequate tread. Rubber retains flexibility through use, so a tire that has been in service for

If you can see the top of Lincoln's head, the tires must be replaced.

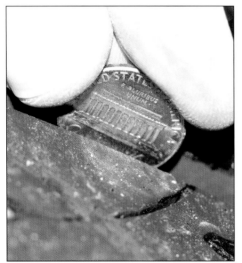

If you can see the bottom of the Lincoln Memorial, the tires are still good.

If you can see the top of Washington's head, the tires should be replaced, because their wet-weather performance has been seriously diminished by wear.

a long time and still has adequate tread isn't being used very often. Eventually, the tire begins to atrophy. Some European countries prohibit using tires more than 6 years old. All experts agree that tires ten years old should be removed from service.

Selecting the Correct Tires for You & Your Car:

You can judge a tire by its tread, its profile, the number of plies, and the material from which they're made. Together, these give a very good idea of the tire's performance capabilities.

Tire treads are made up of "blocks" of rubber separated by "grooves." The ratio of the surface covered by the grooves to the surface area covered by blocks is called the "void ratio." Basically, the wider the grooves, the better the tire will evacuate water from under the tread; the larger the rubber blocks, the better will be the tire's grip on dry pavement. A ring of rubber that is solid all the way around the tire's circumference, separated only by grooves to its sides without lateral

These are the various parts of a tire. Tire design tells you a lot about how a tire will perform.

grooves, is a "rib." One or more ribs may be at or near the center of the tread to provide straight-ahead tracking stability.

When the lateral grooves separating tread blocks are cut at an angle, these grooves are called "slits." The steeper the "slit angle," the better the tire will evacuate water. This also reduces tire noise and decreases tread wear. Making the grooves deeper is another way to improve wet pavement performance and decrease wear.

The part of the tire that curves between the tread and the sidewall is the "shoulder." This area comes in contact with the pavement during cornering. Slits in the tread may extend into the shoulder, there may be angular slits cut only into the shoulder, or both. Either way, these are called "sipes," and are designed to improve wet-road cornering capability.

Though many tires have symmetric tread patterns—the same on both sides of the tread—many tires use an asymmetric pattern. An asymmetric pattern is tailored to emphasize particular capabilities on each side of the tread. For example, an asymmetric pattern may have larger blocks on the outside half of the tread and smaller blocks with larger grooves on the inner side. The larger blocks improve dry-pavement traction, the smaller blocks with larger grooves evacuate water well, and the result is a tire with improved cornering grip without loss of wet-weather traction.

The tread pattern can be even more specialized: it can be unidirectional. Designing a tire to roll in a specific direction allows arranging all of the blocks and grooves to work optimally in that single direction, and also reduces rolling resistance. Reducing a tire's rolling resistance is important in low profile performance tires with large block patterns because rolling resistance hinders acceleration and reduces fuel economy.

Profile is also informative. A tire is part of the vehicle's suspension: it flexes when the car goes over a bump or begins to make a turn. Tires with lower profiles have less sidewall flex. That means quicker, more direct steering response.

Puncture Repairs

Not every tire calamity requires replacing the tire. Sometimes all you need is the proper finger in the dike: a puncture repair. But, as with all things, there is a right way and a wrong way, and as with all things associated with tires, the wrong way can be unsafe.

Repairs of punctures through the tread belt that do not exceed 1/4 inch are generally permitted by tire manufacturers without affecting the tire's speed rating or load capacity, provided that the repair is done properly.

A puncture is repaired "properly" if it accomplishes two things: a "plug" in the hole seals the interior of the tire from moisture (which is rather important, since most radials have steel belts which can rust); and a "patch" is applied to the innerliner of the tire, i.e., the part that retains the airtight seal inside the tire, which seals the air chamber of the tire. Both are required for a proper repair.

This means removing the tire from the wheel. The path through the tread must be completely filled to prevent moisture from reaching the steel used in the tread belts. This requires using special tools to ream any debris from the hole and shape it to the correct dimensions for the "stem" that will be cemented into the hole to fill it. The innerliner, which holds the air, must be buffed and a patch properly cemented to it to retain air without leaking

If you discover that you have a nail or other object in the tread, you should have the puncture repaired, even if the tire is presently holding air. The object creates a moisture path that can rust steel plies.

Tire manufacturers do not approve of puncture repair to a speed-rated tire if the puncture occurs in the sidewall or shoulder of the tire. These areas have fewer plies than the tread and, consequently, flex more, are weaker, and are more difficult to patch. Tire companies do not wish to assume any liability for a repair in these areas, should the tire be driven to its rated speed.

But, it also means a harsher ride because the tire is, in effect, a stiffer spring.

In conjunction with a tire's profile, it is useful to decode the sidewall to learn the tire's construction, load index, and speed rating. In very general terms, tires with higher speed ratings are made of more plies and with plies of stronger material than tires with lower speed ratings. That makes them stiffer, which gives better steering response, but poorer ride quality, than tires of a lower speed rating.

Steel is commonly used for tread plies because it provides puncture resistance and directional stability. Many steel belted radials are constructed with "cap plies." These are tread plies made of a different material, such as nylon, laid over the steel belts and extending beyond their sides. The edges of the steel belts may be covered by reinforcing material that extends part of the way up the shoulder. Because these stiffen the tread, they improve steering response. However, because they do not extend up the sidewall, they do not diminish ride quality and are not considered sidewall plies.

Taking all of this together, a tire that emphasizes dry-pavement traction and cornering will have a larger percentage of the tread devoted to blocks than a tire that is designed for "all-season" performance on wet pavement and snow. Wider, lower-profile tires emphasize cornering power and handling precision, at the expense of ride quality. But, carefully selecting design elements allows emphasizing seemingly contradictory elements in a single tire.

For example, many performance cars and sport sedans were originally equipped with speed-rated tires not suitable for snowy roads. But, unidirectional low-profile tires are available in "performance all-season" tread designs that are designated as "winter" M&S (mud and snow) tires, yet are speed-rated to 168 mph. This is accomplished by combining the elements of unidirectional tread, high slit angle, angled sipes, and multiple tread ply construction to create a tire that has a good void ratio and still develops high dry-road traction.

One available feature in new tires is "run-flat" capability, which allows driving on a deflated tire for about 50 miles at about 50 mph. These designs use very stiff sidewalls, strong enough to support some of the weight of the vehicle even when the tire is not inflated. For that reason, they are offered only in low profile sizes. Run-flat tires are generally more expensive than conventional tires and do require specialized equipment for mounting. But, they won't leave you stranded.

There are also specialized tires for "severe snow service." These have very deep and wide grooves with high, tall tread blocks. The rubber used is softer than in conventional tires, so these wear much more rapidly on dry pavement. Typically, these tires are speed-rated no higher than R, Q, or T. These are tires designed for deep snow, not for an urban winter environment where roads may be slick, but are generally plowed. On dry pavement, their tread design results in substantially less evasive capability and much longer stopping distances than all season tires. If you do install severe service tires, put them on all four wheels so that you do not seriously upset the handling balance of the vehicle on dry pavement— where these tires spend most of their time, even in the snowiest climates.

Alignment and Wheel Balancing

Though no tire is perfectly round, most problems attributed to tires are actually balance problems, and occasionally alignment issues.

To get the best performance from tires, the wheels must be properly aligned. There are three categories of alignment: "front-end alignment," "four-wheel alignment," and "thrust angle alignment." Though a front-end alignment is the least expensive, the best choice is either a four-wheel alignment for a vehicle with independent rear suspension or a thrust alignment for cars with solid rear axles. Either way, the objective is to get all four wheels pointing in the proper direction.

Alignment involves setting "camber," "caster," and "toe-in." Automobile manufacturers designate the appropriate range of settings for these variables, and exceeding those ranges normally increases tire wear and may adversely affect the vehicle's handling.

Camber is the extent to which the wheel, when viewed from directly in front, leans inward (negative camber) or outward (positive camber) at the top of the wheel. Increasing negative camber improves cornering power, but it also aggravates "bump steer," the tendency of the car to pull one way or the other when a wheel hits a bump and the other wheel momentarily has more grip. Excessive negative camber will also wear the inner edge of the tire prematurely because the tire sits at an angle to the pavement.

Caster is the extent to which the pivot axis of steered wheels either leans forward (negative) or backward (positive) at the top pivot point. If you visualize the front wheel and fork of a motorcycle, you'll get the idea: the forks slope backward, which is positive camber to an extreme (for a car) degree. Positive caster increases steering self-centering and tends to lean the wheel inward at the top in a corner, which improves the tires' cornering grip.

Toe-in is the extent to which the wheels point inward ("positive toe"). All cars are designed with some adjustment to toe, either inward (positive) or outward (negative), to compensate for the steering effect of the bushings in the suspension. Front-wheel drive vehicles, for example, tend to pull the front tires inward, so they are normally designed to have negative toe. Rear-wheel-drive vehicles push the front tires outward, so these vehicles normally are designed with positive toe.

Vehicles with independent rear suspension also have a recommended toe setting for the rear wheels. This is related to "thrust angle" on a car with a solid rear axle. Thrust angle is the extent to which the axle is not perpendicular to the imaginary centerline of the vehicle. On a solid axle car, this imparts a steering angle to the rear wheels that forces the car to "crab-track," where the body sits at a slight angle to the vehicle's direction of travel. Though an incorrect thrust angle requires relocating the rear axle on a solid axle vehicle, the equivalent problem on an independent rear suspension vehicle can be eliminated by a proper four-wheel alignment.

Very few roads are actually level. Most roads have a designed-in tilt toward the right to drain rain. So, the recommended caster and camber will be slightly different on each side of the vehicle to compensate. This is called "cross camber" and "cross caster." You may notice it when driving on a multiple lane road that is close to flat, because the vehicle will have a tendency to drift left. That is an indication of a correct alignment.

Tire balance is also important. There are two types of tire imbalance, "static" and "dynamic." Static imbalance causes the tire to bounce—it has a heavier spot that is accentuated by the centrifugal force of rotation. Dynamic imbalance is a side-to-side heavy spot. The tire shimmies as the heavy spot tries to twist the tire on its axis of rotation.

Modern tires and vehicles are more sensitive to wheel and tire imbalance than were vehicles of 20 or 30 years ago. Imbalances are felt more easily in lighter vehicles and in vehicles with stiffer suspensions. Lower profile tires and wider wheels are more susceptible to dynamic imbalance than narrower, taller tires. Ultimately, the job of properly balancing a tire has become more complex and the equipment needed to do the job has become more sophisticated as tire technology has advanced.

One of the keys to achieving a proper balance is "match mounting." Match mounting is simple in concept. Based on the premise that no wheel is perfectly round and that no tire is perfectly round, the concept of match mounting identifies the low spot on the wheel, then identifies the low spot on the tire, and mounts the tire on the wheel so that the low spots are directly opposite one another.

Even with match mounting, there may still be imbalances, static or dynamic, which must be offset by the placement of wheel weights. Many tire stores use "clip-on" weights that are placed on the wheel's rim, where the tire's bead sits. These are unattractive and can cause corrosion on the rim of an alloy wheel. A better solution is adhesive weights, which can be placed on the interior circumference of the wheel, sometimes in conjunction with clip on weights used on the interior rim of the wheel. However, if the wheel is not new and has, consequently, accumulated grease and road grime on the interior surfaces, this may not be practical unless the wheel is carefully cleaned first.